# Group Behavior

# PSYCHOLOGY INFORMATION GUIDE SERIES

Series Editors: Sydney Schultz, M.L.S., Consultant, Library and Publications Services, and Duane Schultz, Adjunct Professor of Psychology, American University, Washington, D.C.

---

The above series is part of the
# GALE INFORMATION GUIDE LIBRARY

The Library consists of a number of separate series of guides covering major areas in the social sciences, humanities, and current affairs.

General Editor: Paul Wasserman, Professor and former Dean, School of Library and Information Services, University of Maryland

Managing Editor: Denise Allard Adzigian, Gale Research Company

# Group Behavior

## A GUIDE TO INFORMATION SOURCES

*Volume 2 in the Psychology Information Guide Series*

**Gloria Behar Gottsegen**

*Professor and Chairperson*
*Department of Specialized Services in Education*
*Herbert H. Lehman College*
*City University of New York*
*Bronx*

*Research Assistant*
**Mary O'Neill Berry**

***Gale Research Company***
*Book Tower, Detroit, Michigan 48226*

**Library of Congress Cataloging in Publication Data**

Gottsegen, Gloria B
    Group behavior.

    (Psychology information guide series ; v. 2)
    (Gale information guide library)
    Includes indexes.
       1. Social groups—Bibliography. 2. Small groups—
Bibliography. 3. Social group work—Bibliography.
4. Group relations training—Bibliography. I. Title.
II. Series.
Z7164.07G67  [HM131]   016.30118   79-63744
ISBN 0-8103-1439-8

# VITA

Gloria Behar Gottsegen, professor and chairperson of the Department of Specialized Services in Education at Herbert H. Lehman College, City University of New York, received her Ph.D. degree from New York University in 1967. She is a past president of the Division of Humanistic Psychology, American Psychological Association; of the Division of School Psychology, New York State Psychological Association; and of the School Psychology Educators Council of New York State. She has coedited three volumes of PROFESSIONAL SCHOOL PSYCHOLOGY (New York: Grune and Stratton, 1960, 1963, 1969), and CONFRONTATION: ENCOUNTERS IN SELF AND INTERPERSONAL AWARENESS (New York: Macmillan, 1971). She is an associate editor of the journal, PSYCHOTHERAPY: THEORY, RESEARCH AND PRACTICE, coeditor of a section in the INTERNATIONAL ENCYCLOPEDIA OF PSYCHIATRY, PSYCHOLOGY, PSYCHOANALYSIS AND NEUROLOGY, and has authored or coauthored articles appearing in various journals.

# CONTENTS

Introduction . . . . . . . . . . . . . . . . . . . . . . . . . .   ix

Chapter 1 - Texts . . . . . . . . . . . . . . . . . . . . . . .   1
    A. General Group Texts . . . . . . . . . . . . . . . . . .   1
    B. Social-Psychological and Sociological Texts . . . . . . . . .   14
    C. Models and Methodologies . . . . . . . . . . . . . . . .   26

Chapter 2 - Group Problem Solving . . . . . . . . . . . . . . .   35

Chapter 3 - Interpersonal Interaction . . . . . . . . . . . . . .   41
    A. General Interpersonal Interaction . . . . . . . . . . . . .   41
    B. Roles . . . . . . . . . . . . . . . . . . . . . . . . . . .   50
    C. Group Cohesion and Group Conflict . . . . . . . . . . . .   52

Chapter 4 - Group Influences . . . . . . . . . . . . . . . . . .   59

Chapter 5 - Power in Groups . . . . . . . . . . . . . . . . . .   63
    A. Dynamics of Power . . . . . . . . . . . . . . . . . . .   63
    B. Leadership . . . . . . . . . . . . . . . . . . . . . . .   64
    C. Communication . . . . . . . . . . . . . . . . . . . . .   75

Chapter 6 - Group Therapy and T-Groups . . . . . . . . . . . .   79

Chapter 7 - Organizational Settings . . . . . . . . . . . . . . .   95

Chapter 8 - Educational Settings . . . . . . . . . . . . . . . .   105

Chapter 9 - Social Work Group Settings . . . . . . . . . . . . .   107

Chapter 10 - General Applied Settings . . . . . . . . . . . . . .   109

Chapter 11 - Bibliographical Reference Works . . . . . . . . . . .   117
    A. General Reference Works . . . . . . . . . . . . . . . .   117
    B. Group Behavior Sources . . . . . . . . . . . . . . . . .   129

Chapter 12 - Periodicals . . . . . . . . . . . . . . . . . . . .   135

# Contents

Chapter 13 – Organizations and Associations . . . . . . . . . . . . . .   169

Author Index . . . . . . . . . . . . . . . . . . . . . . . . . . . . . . .   183

Title Index . . . . . . . . . . . . . . . . . . . . . . . . . . . . . . . .   193

Subject Index . . . . . . . . . . . . . . . . . . . . . . . . . . . . . . .   203

# INTRODUCTION

At the onset, the area of GROUP BEHAVIOR would seem to be impossible to encompass. In one sense, anything that happens in the world, if it happens to or affects more than a single individual, could be termed an instance of group behavior. If one were to content oneself with such a definition, this book would run to many volumes. It is obvious that I have been selective. What follows is part explanation, part justification, for definitions, inclusions, and omissions.

The attempt has been made to identify those aspects of group behavior which capture the essentials of what goes on when people interact. This allows one to deal with the most basic group, the dyad, and to follow through the other forms of groups up the scale to nations and races. Because basic psychological and sociological principles help to account for some of what takes place, there is a somewhat unified account of group behavior from a social psychological perspective. This effort to adhere to basic principles leads to a natural demarcation of the field. Most psychological studies conducted on groups focus on the small group. Group research of this nature has grown into the field known as group dynamics and is the base upon which this work begins.

This is also the reason for including a section on basic social-psychological texts. Since much of the small-group field is somewhat specialized, it was felt that the student coming anew to this area would benefit from an acquaintance with more basic material. Furthermore, the texts included for the most part pay particular attention to small groups, often devoting a section to this topic.

Much of the applied work on small groups has occurred in clinical-therapeutic or industrial-organizational settings. Therefore, included are a number of such studies which were selected for their pertinence to the student of group behavior. Such inclusions either provide material which furthers the understanding of small group phenomena, or they rely for their purposes on the principles of small group theory implicitly, or they contain specific theoretical or experimental work on small groups.

# Introduction

Journals and periodicals in this area range over a wide spectrum of psychological and sociological topics. The same is true of source materials and associations because materials on group behavior are by their nature likely to appear in many disciplinary subfields. To limit entries to those which deal exclusively with small groups would be to overlook much valuable work which is closely related.

The section headings are self-explanatory. I have tried to balance theoretical and empirical entries as well as older classical works and developments over the last few years. The annotations are in all cases descriptive, not evaluative.

I would like to acknowledge gratefully the aid of Mary O'Neill Berry, my invaluable research assistant, without whose tireless efforts and dogged library activities much of this work would not have been accomplished. Thanks are also due to Barbara Zoldessy, who typed the manuscript with grace and intelligence.


Gloria Behar Gottsegen

# Chapter 1

## TEXTS

### A. GENERAL GROUP TEXTS

Altman, Irwin, and Terauds, Anita. MAJOR VARIABLES OF THE SMALL
GROUP FIELD. Arlington, Va.: Human Sciences Research, 1960. 730 p.

This report is a result of a program of research aimed at synthe-
sizing the knowledge accumulated in small group research. In
this volume, the authors review major variables of the field, including descriptions of variable subclasses, information on rates of
appearance, and outcomes of each variable's association with
other variables. A review of individual and group performance
effectiveness variables is also supplied. The variables are indexed and a bibliography of studies in the review sample is supplied.

Argyle, Michael. THE SCIENTIFIC STUDY OF SOCIAL BEHAVIOUR. London:
Methuen and Co.; New York: Philosophical Library, 1957. viii, 239 p.

The author presents the facts of social behavior, referring to previous research, and follows this with an examination of various
theories, given the available evidence. Dyads and small social
groups are discussed. The application of human relations findings
in industry and other social organizations is also examined. Twenty-
four pages of references accompany the text, and a number of
figures are presented, illustrating various theories of social behavior.

Bion, Wilfrid R. EXPERIENCES IN GROUPS AND OTHER PAPERS. London:
Tavistock Publications, 1961. 198 p.

The author uses a psychoanalytic approach to the study of groups,
and he himself is a member of the therapeutic groups whose encounters he describes. The book concludes with a "re-view"
chapter on group dynamics.

Bradford, Leland P., ed. GROUP DEVELOPMENT. Rev. ed. La Jolla, Calif.: University Associates, 1978. 234 p.

> This set of readings on group interaction and developmental phases covers group dynamics, group problems, roles, decision making, feedback and group self-evaluation, and development in group behavior in adult education. Three integrative analyses and a comprehensive annotated bibliography on small group behavior is included in this revised edition. Contributors include, Bales, Bradford, Benne, Festinger, Gibb, G. and R. Lippitt, and Thelen, among others.

Cabot, Hugh, and Kahl, Joseph A. HUMAN RELATIONS. CONCEPTS AND CASES IN CONCRETE SOCIAL SCIENCE. 2 vols. Cambridge, Mass.: Harvard University Press, 1953.

> Volume 1 of this set deals with concepts in human relations. A variety of excerpts from articles and books by other authors is included. Topics range from the clinical approach to social data and the responsibility of decision to group membership and value conflicts. Volume 2 is a collection of thirty-three case materials which can be used to test the ideas presented in volume 1. No set questions are included; the reader is encouraged to react spontaneously to the cases presented.

Calhoun, Donald W. PERSONS-IN-GROUPS: A HUMANISTIC SOCIAL PSYCHOLOGY. New York: Harper and Row, 1976. 484 p.

> The author presents a broad picture of what it means to be human and how this knowledge can be applied to resolving sociopsychological conflicts. Group experiences are examined from the group's and the individual's perspective. Case studies illustrate group experiences. Utopian communities and healing groups are analyzed as laboratories in the theory and application of social psychology. Each chapter includes annotated bibliographies. A glossary and an appendix of sociopsychological scales are supplied. An instructor's manual, prepared by Syd Skolsky and the author, includes a system of individualized student projects.

Cartwright, Dorwin, and Zander, Alvin, eds. GROUP DYNAMICS: RESEARCH AND THEORY. 3d ed. New York: Harper and Row, 1968. ix, 580 p.

> The field of group dynamics is located in its theoretical and social context, and a variety of issues are discussed in articles by the editors and other authors. Group membership, group pressures and standards, interpersonal power and influence, leadership, and motivational processes, and the structural properties of groups are examined. A chapter by the editors introduces each of the seven parts of the book. Only thirteen articles of the thirty-five reprinted in the original edition are included here. Each article is followed by its own list of references.

Cooper, Cary L., ed. THEORIES OF GROUP PROCESSES. New York: Wiley, 1975. x, 277 p.

> The editor writes the introductory chapter to this book on the history of human groups with particular attention to the divergence between the study of experimental and experiential group processes. In the rest of the book, the focus is on theory. Nine chapters are written by invited contributors, among them Chris Argyris, Martin Lakin, Robert Blake and Jane Mouton, and Robert Golembiewski and Mark McConkie. Topics such as leadership in experiential groups, a theory of experiential learning, and the concept of "trust" in group processes are explored. The volume is directed mainly at those engaged in practice or research with experiential groups.

Davis, Keith, and Scott, William G., eds. READINGS IN HUMAN RELATIONS. 2d ed. New York: McGraw-Hill, 1964. xi, 444 p.

> This is a selection of recent developments in the human relations field, intended as a supplementary volume in courses dealing with various aspects of the field. Articles have been gathered from a number of disciplines, and from both American and European authors and journals. Section titles include "Philosophy of Human Relations," "Motivation and Morals," "Communication," "Leadership," and "Human Relations Training and Development." References are contained within articles. Indexes of authors quoted and of periodicals and series quoted are supplied.

Diedrich, Richard C., and Dye, H. Allan, eds. GROUP PROCEDURES: PURPOSES, PROCESSES, AND OUTCOMES. SELECTED READINGS FOR THE COUNSELOR. Boston: Houghton Mifflin, 1972. xiv, 537 p.

> This book of readings is directed primarily at those taking introductory courses in group procedures such as counseling, dynamics, or therapy. The forty contributions are organized to represent the major areas in the field: purposes, processes, applications, outcomes, and ethical issues. The articles have been drawn from both professional and popular literature. Contributors include Herbert A. Thelen, Charles Seashore, Carl Rogers, Martin Lakin, and Max Rosenbaum. References accompany each article.

Dunnette, Marvin D., ed. HANDBOOK OF INDUSTRIAL AND ORGANIZATIONAL PSYCHOLOGY. Chicago: Rand McNally, 1976. 1,740 p.

> This volume presents thirty-seven chapters by forty-five scholars representing twenty-eight different academic and industrial organizations. The areas emphasized are strategies of research, research methodology, and theories of behavior.

Freud, Sigmund. GROUP PSYCHOLOGY AND THE ANALYSIS OF THE EGO. Translated and edited by James Strachey. New York: Norton, 1975. viii, 139 p.

> Originally published in 1921, and first translated the following year, this book continues trains of thought from parts of TOTEM AND TABOO (1912-13) and Freud's paper on narcissism (1914). It attempts to explain the psychology of groups by reference to changes in the psychology of the individual mind. It also further elaborates Freud's account of the anatomical structure of the mind.

Golembiewski, Robert T. THE SMALL GROUP. AN ANALYSIS OF RESEARCH CONCEPTS AND OPERATIONS. Chicago: University of Chicago Press, 1962. xii, 303 p.

> The author attempts to review previous research in small group analysis, and to evaluate its continuing utility. In doing so, he employs what he calls a "comparison-by-juxtaposition" approach to the available material, whereby he can evaluate the extent to which it converges toward a set of concepts and operations that will allow integration and synthesis of the field. No bibliography is given, but the book is amply endowed with footnotes.

Hare, A. Paul. HANDBOOK OF SMALL GROUP RESEARCH. 2d ed. New York: Free Press, 1976. xvi, 781 p.

> The author reviews the literature, providing a catalog of small group research and some ideas on how it may be organized. The three sections present essentially the same material, but approached in different ways. The process and structure of groups is discussed, followed by a section on variables which affect the group. Performance characteristics complete the overview. The appendix on statistical techniques which appeared in the first edition has been replaced by appendixes on the history of the field, on applications of the research, and on suggested laboratory experiments. Intended as a reference work, the book includes a bibliography of 6,037 entries.

Hare, A. Paul; Borgatta, Edgar F.; and Bales, Robert F., eds. SMALL GROUPS. STUDIES IN SOCIAL INTERACTION. Rev. ed. New York: Alfred A. Knopf, 1965. xvi, 706 p.

> The editors divide the book into three parts: theoretical and historical background of small group study, empirical studies from the perspective of the acting subject, and studies from the viewpoint of an observer of the group. The 1955 edition contains an annotated bibliography which is omitted here.

Harrison, Albert A.  INDIVIDUALS AND GROUPS:  UNDERSTANDING
SOCIAL BEHAVIOR.  Monterey, Calif.: Brooks/Cole, 1976.  xiii, 672 p.

This introductory text in social psychology does not assume any
prior knowledge of either sociology or psychology.  The author
pays special attention to the group, devoting six of the twelve
chapters in the book to group processes, including areas such as
interaction in the dyad, interaction in small groups, performance
in small groups, behavior in organizations, and intergroup relations.  A twenty-seven-page glossary and a forty-eight-page bibliography are supplied.

Hinton, Bernard L., and Reitz, H. Joseph, eds.  GROUPS AND ORGANIZA-
TIONS:  INTEGRATED READINGS IN THE ANALYSIS OF SOCIAL BEHAVIOR.
Belmont, Calif.: Wadsworth, 1971.  590 p.

This book of readings assembles materials extending from relations
between two people to relationships characteristic of large organizations.  It thus brings together the phenomena of groups and
organizations.  Beginning with a section on the parameters of
groups and organizations, the readings go on to deal with small
group formation and development, group structure, functioning,
and influence on individual behavior, intragroup and intergroup
processes, and organizational processes, structure, and dynamics.
A short introduction precedes each section.  References accompany each article.

Homans, George C.  THE HUMAN GROUP.  New York: Harcourt, Brace,
1950.  509 p.

The author studies five groups, using the recurrent elements and
processes of activity, interaction, sentiment, norms, "internal"
or "external" system.  The small group thus appears as a social
system which responds to its environment in a self-adjusting manner; its parts are mutually interdependent.  As such, it is considered the basis of the larger society, which must, for its survival, retain some of the aspects of the small group itself.

_____.  SOCIAL BEHAVIOR:  ITS ELEMENTARY FORMS.  Rev. ed.  New
York:  Harcourt Brace Jovanovich, 1974.  xi, 386 p.

The author's approach is to view social structure not as a purely
causative agent, but as a product of human behavior in groups.
If this is so, then the processes which result in social structure
must themselves be examined.  Homans does this by stating general propositions from which more specific empirical propositions
are derived, then presenting research data in support.

Hunt, William A., ed. HUMAN BEHAVIOR AND ITS CONTROL. Cambridge, Mass.: Schenkman, 1971. 157 p.

> This book consists of eight papers plus introductory remarks by the chairperson at a symposium held by the American Association for the Advancement of Science in December 1970. They are mainly action or problem oriented, and attention is paid to the importance of milieu in determining the individual's behavior. Topics include personality-environment interaction in large organizations, contractual approaches to the modification of behavior in encounter groups, and disordered interpersonal behavior. References accompany each article.

Huszar, George B. de. PRACTICAL APPLICATION OF DEMOCRACY. New York: Harper and Bros., 1945. xvi, 140 p.

> The author outlines the problems he tackles as disintegration and inaction. He suggests that social units, in the form of problem-centered groups, can build social structure, and so we attain integration and action. The application of this method is illustrated in a variety of fields. Finally, the author relates the significance of the method to the individual taking part in it, and discusses its effects on him or her. A selected bibliography is supplied.

Johnson, David W., and Johnson, Frank P. JOINING TOGETHER: GROUP THEORY AND GROUP SKILLS. Englewood Cliffs, N.J.: Prentice-Hall, 1975. 448 p.

> This book uses the experimental method to teach theoretical and empirical knowledge of group behavior. The reader learns how to apply that knowledge to the development of skills necessary for effective functioning in groups. Activities and exercises to train the reader as a group member are included. Topics discussed include leadership, decision making, communication, power, cohesion, and problem solving. References are supplied.

Klein, Josephine. THE STUDY OF GROUPS. London: Routledge and Kegan Paul, 1956. 200 p.

> The structure of small groups is studied by means of situations which Klein sets up to illustrate basic assumptions operating in the life of a group. Moving through the book, the situations and theories become more complex until finally the structure of the group has been explored in its entirety. An experimental study of relationships in small groups is included in the appendix.

_____. WORKING WITH GROUPS. THE SOCIAL PSYCHOLOGY OF DIS-CUSSION AND DECISION. 3d ed. London: Hutchinson, 1966. 240 p.

Events in the life of the group are classified according to cate-gories of interaction: information, views, proposals, agreement, and individual self-expression. The theory outlined in early chapters is then applied to practical situations. The final part of the book deals with training in order to improve interaction, and it involves the technique of role playing. Pertinent biblio-graphic information is presented throughout the book.

Knowles, Malcolm S., and Knowles, Hulda F. INTRODUCTION TO GROUP DYNAMICS. Rev. ed. New York: Association Press, 1972. viii, 95 p.

This basic introductory text explains the origins of the study of groups, the approaches used, the theories constructed to account for group behavior, and the application of findings. The authors provide bibliographies; though not exhaustive, they guide the reader in expanding on the outline provided by the book.

Lifton, Walter M. GROUPS: FACILITATING INDIVIDUAL GROWTH AND SOCIETAL CHANGE. New York: Wiley, 1972. xi, 356 p.

The author directs his book at all those who find themselves in group environments with a need to understand the problems of group processes. He reviews the various kinds of group theories underlying different group approaches and techniques of helping. Problems in group counseling are discussed, and a chapter is devoted to the specific problems of the group counselor. Each chapter is summarized and includes a list of suggested readings. A bibliography of recent publications on group procedures in guidance, compiled by David G. Zimpfer, is also supplied.

Luft, Joseph. GROUP PROCESSES: AN INTRODUCTION TO GROUP DYNAMICS. 2d ed. Palo Alto, Calif.: Mayfield, 1970. v, 122 p.

The author attempts to broadly cover the field of face-to-face group study. He discusses basic issues in group processes, labo-ratory methods, and the Johari Window model. He goes on to examine group processes in a variety of contexts: organizational behavior, clinical psychology, and the educational setting. Current trends are reviewed. A ten-page list of references is included.

McGinnies, Elliott. SOCIAL BEHAVIOR: A FUNCTIONAL ANALYSIS. Boston: Houghton Mifflin, 1970. xi, 459 p.

The author attempts to construct a parsimonious and unified the-ory of social behavior, which emerges as an updated variety of functional behaviorism. He deals with a broad range of topics in group behavior: social influence and conformity, social factors in perception and judgment, behavior in small groups, leadership, and persuasion. Each chapter is followed by a list of references.

Mills, Theodore M. THE SOCIOLOGY OF SMALL GROUPS. Englewood Cliffs, N.J.: Prentice-Hall, 1967. viii, 136 p.

This introductory text sets out to show the reader a variety of ways of thinking about groups from a sociological orientation. Laboratory studies are described from the point of view of their social context. Group processes are dealt with, and the group is viewed throughout as a dynamic system. Footnotes appear in the text, and a short set of selected references is included.

Mills, Theodore M., and Rosenberg, Stan, eds. READINGS ON THE SOCIOLOGY OF SMALL GROUPS. Englewood Cliffs, N.J.: Prentice-Hall, 1970. viii, 247 p.

The emphasis in these readings is theoretical. The collection presents the view that the small group is the interface between the individual and the larger society. It deals with a set of variables--social, personal, contextual, and cultural--that make up the "field of forces," which together cause observable processes. Some selections deal with the dynamic relations between these variables. The five parts treat the relevance of small groups, theoretical perspectives, observing and experimenting, the empirical study of structure and dynamics, and change and growth in groups. References accompany each article.

Napier, Rodney W., and Gershenfeld, Matti K. GROUPS: THEORY AND EXPERIENCE. Boston: Houghton Mifflin, 1973. xi, 311 p.

See also chapter 6, INSTRUCTOR'S MANUAL for this text by the same authors in "Group Therapy and T-Groups," (p. 88). The authors aim to provide experiences which will improve the reader's skills as a group member or facilitator and the understanding of group processes. The book deals with perception and communications, norms, pressures, goals, leadership, and problem solving. Each chapter has two parts: the first provides a conceptual framework for the particular topic, and the second contains applied training exercises related to that topic. The appendix concentrates on the practical skills a facilitator must acquire before intervening in groups. The reader is urged to consult this section before using the suggested skill exercises. References appear at the end of each chapter.

Northway, Mary L. A PRIMER OF SOCIOMETRY. Toronto: University of Toronto Press, 1952. vi, 48 p.

This basic text introduces the reader to the principles and applic-
cations of a technique for the study of social relations: sociometry. It deals with designing and administering a sociometric
test and treating the results, and gives information on reliability
and validity. Two appendixes present suggested problems for
research and suggestions for reporting a sociometric study.

Olmsted, Donald W. SOCIAL GROUPS, ROLES AND LEADERSHIP: AN
INTRODUCTION TO THE CONCEPTS. East Lansing: Michigan State University, 1961. vi, 55 p.

This monograph is directed toward social scientists and civic leaders concerned with applying group theory. It is composed of three
essays. The first deals with social groups and the problems involved in analyzing this concept. The second part emphasizes
the implications of social roles. The section on group leadership
reviews the literature, and suggests a more adequate approach to
the topic. Selected references are presented after each essay.

Olmsted, Michael S. THE SMALL GROUP. New York: Random House,
1959. 158 p.

The author aims at organizing and interpreting a body of research
and ideas, surveying findings and propositions in the study of
small groups. He presents some case studies in group behavior
and deals with the functions, culture, and social structure of the
group, the relation between the individual and the group, and
some thoughts on the sociology of small groups.

Penland, Patrick, and Fine, Sara. GROUP DYNAMICS AND INDIVIDUAL
DEVELOPMENT. New York: Marcel Dekker, 1974. xiv, 151 p.

This book is an interdisciplinary effort, combining the perspectives
of behavioral scientist and resource specialist. Its aim is to extend the group processes currently used in the fields of library,
media, and information science from decision making and discussion to individual self-development through communicative involve-
ment. There are sections on small group service, group topography and dynamics, roles, encounter simulations, program and
session development, and planning and evaluation. A bibliography is included.

Raven, Bertram H., and Rubin, Jeffrey Z. SOCIAL PSYCHOLOGY: PEOPLE
IN GROUPS. New York: Wiley, 1976. xx, 591 p.

This textbook in social psychology has been written around what
the authors consider its most basic concept: the interaction of
people in groups. They deal with the issues of people alone and
together, becoming aware of others and ourselves, liking and dis-
liking, friendship and aggression, and interdependence. Social
power and interpersonal influence are examined, as are group

9

structure, performance effectiveness, and leadership. The final
chapter looks at conflict, harmony, and tension between groups.
The appendix discusses research methods in social psychology. A
glossary of terms and a list of references are supplied.

Reeves, Elton T. THE DYNAMICS OF GROUP BEHAVIOR. New York:
American Management Association, 1970. 399 p.

The author presents a layman's introduction to group dynamics in
the interests of elucidating the way people work in groups. The
language used in the book reflects the author's aim at clarity.
Kinds and properties of groups are discussed; effects of group and
individual on each other, role conflict, and group effectiveness
are among other topics included. A glossary of terms is supplied.

Shaw, Marvin E. GROUP DYNAMICS: THE PSYCHOLOGY OF SMALL
GROUP BEHAVIOR. New York: McGraw-Hill, 1976. 464 p.

Various aspects of small group behavior are viewed as features of
social interaction. The processes involved are discussed a number
of times throughout the book as the group is described in a variety of settings. The author thus attempts to demonstrate the in-
terrelated nature of group processes. There are extensive references and a glossary of terms.

Sheperd, Clovis R. SMALL GROUPS: SOME SOCIOLOGICAL PERSPECTIVES.
Scranton, Pa.: Chandler, 1964. xi, 130 p.

This introductory text summarizes the social-psychological and
sociological literature on small groups, organized both within
pure and applied social science and according to the standpoint
of positivism and symbolic interactionism. An appendix describes
features of the successful group. Nine abstracts of pertinent literature appear at intervals through the later part of the book.
Each chapter contains a selected bibliography as well as detailed
footnotes.

Sherif, Muzafer. THE PSYCHOLOGY OF SOCIAL NORMS. New York:
Harper, 1936. xii, 209 p.

The author deals with the phenomenon of rules and standards
which governs the lives of individuals within society. The formation of norms is discussed, first as external to the individual, and
therefore themselves part of the stimulus situation, and later as
internalized factors determining the individual's behavior. The
importance of social values and their interaction with basic needs
are investigated.

Sherif, Muzafer, and Sherif, Carolyn [W.]. AN OUTLINE OF SOCIAL PSY-
CHOLOGY. Rev. ed. New York: Harper and Bros., 1956. xix, 792 p.

> The authors emphasize the importance of viewing behavior and
> experience as products of interaction between the individual and
> his or her setting. The importance of perception as a function of
> group membership is also pointed out. Group structures and norms
> are discussed, as well as reference groups and group prejudice.
> Group relations experiments, conducted under the authors' direc-
> tion since the first edition of the book, are included here. Ref-
> erences are included at the end of each chapter.

Sherif, Muzafer, and Wilson, M.O., eds. GROUP RELATIONS AT THE
CROSSROADS: THE UNIVERSITY OF OKLAHOMA LECTURES IN SOCIAL
PSYCHOLOGY. New York: Harper and Bros., 1953. viii, 379 p.

> These lectures were delivered at the Second Conference in Social
> Psychology held at the University of Oklahoma 10-14 April 1952.
> The collection includes contributions from Muzafer Sherif, Anne
> Anastasi, Gardner Murphy, and Leon Festinger, and covers topics
> in the group relations area such as communication, social percep-
> tion, reference groups, and leadership. Each article has a list
> of references, and there are general subject and author indexes.

Shibutani, Tamotsu. SOCIETY AND PERSONALITY: AN INTERACTIONIST
APPROACH TO SOCIAL PSYCHOLOGY. Englewood Cliffs, N.J.: Prentice-
Hall, 1961. x, 630 p.

> The author approaches the study of people by regarding them pri-
> marily as participants in groups. In doing so, he employs ele-
> ments of both pragmatism and psychoanalysis, and reduces all con-
> cepts to behavioristic terms. Group behavior is discussed from
> the viewpoints of structure, participation, role playing, communi-
> cation, status, and norms. Social control, motivation, interper-
> sonal relations, and socialization form the core sections; each
> chapter has its own summary, conclusion, and list of suggested
> references.

Slater, Philip E. MICROCOSM: STRUCTURAL, PSYCHOLOGICAL, AND
RELIGIOUS EVOLUTION IN GROUPS. New York: Wiley, 1966. xii,
276 p.

> The author discusses the orientation of a group to its formal leader,
> observing parallels with rituals and belief systems of larger scale,
> and the possible theoretical framework which could account for
> both. Member-leader phenomena are related to general group
> bond changes, and to religious and mythological evolutionary par-
> adigms. Appendix 1 details some aspects of the goals of a group

leader; appendix 2 sounds cautionary notes regarding some of the examples used in the rest of the book. A short bibliography and index are included.

Smelser, Neil J. THEORY OF COLLECTIVE BEHAVIOR. New York: Free Press, 1962. xi, 436 p.

The author develops his theory from the assumptions that classification and analysis of collective behavior can be carried out under the same conceptual framework as all social behavior, and that forms of collective behavior proceed from the simple to the complex. The basic components of social action are set out, focuses of structural strain are discussed, and a typology of beliefs is arranged which forms the basis for a typology of collective behavior. Each type is then analyzed in detail: the panic, the craze, the hostile outburst, the norm-oriented movement, and the value-oriented movement. A forty-page bibliography is included.

Smith, Peter B., ed. GROUP PROCESSES: SELECTED READINGS. Baltimore: Penguin Books, 1970. 454 p.

This collection of readings provides examples of research in the field of small group behavior carried out in the 1950s and 1960s. Descriptive and predictive models are dealt with. The contributions cover structural and interpersonal models, social roles, norms and behavior change, and intergroup relations. Each section has a short introduction. Each reading is followed by a list of references, and some further readings are listed at the end of the book.

Sprott, Walter J. HUMAN GROUPS. Baltimore: Penguin Books, 1958. 219 p.

The author deals with small groups using three specific examples of permanent small groups: the family, the village, and the neighborhood. He goes on to discuss experimental small groups and concludes with a chapter on applications. The references, though specific to each chapter, are grouped at the back.

Sudnow, David, ed. STUDIES IN SOCIAL INTERACTION. New York: Free Press, 1972. vii, 455 p.

This is a collection of original research papers on naturally occurring social interaction, written by sociologists and anthropologists. The research is mostly of a nonexperimental nature. Its aim is to develop concepts and methods for analyzing such empirical materials. Contributors include Harold Garfinkel, Harvey Sacks, Aaron V. Cicourel, and Matthew Speier. Page-by-page notes are supplied at the end of the book.

Tedeschi, James R., and Lindskold, Svenn. SOCIAL PSYCHOLOGY: INTER-
DEPENDENCE, INTERACTION, AND INFLUENCE. New York: Wiley,
1976. xiii, 705 p.

This text is intended for advanced undergraduate or graduate students. The chapters are treated under five interpretive headings:
orientations and methods, defining the social situation, interdependence and influence, positive and negative social interactions,
and the person in groups and society. Each has an integrative
preview and ends with a summary and set of suggested readings.
Outlines of the chapters are also provided.

Thibaut, John W., and Kelley, Harold H. THE SOCIAL PSYCHOLOGY OF
GROUPS. New York: Wiley, 1959. xiii, 313 p.

The authors begin with the study of the simplest interpersonal relationship, the dyad, then apply these concepts to larger groups.
The result is a functionalistic theory of interpersonal relations in
which the primary focus is on solutions to the problems which
arise as a result of interdependency.

Tiger, Lionel. MEN IN GROUPS. New York: Random House, 1969. xx,
254 p.

The author explores the relationship between biology and sociology in an attempt to discuss the hypothesis that the behavior of
men in groups partly reflects a biologically transmitted tendency.
This tendency is expressed in various cultural forms which contain
a common factor. The existence of this factor, the reasons for
its evolution, and its effect on individuals and societies are discussed. The male bond is examined in the contexts of politics,
war, work, play, initiations, and secret societies. A bibliography is included.

Znaniecki, Florian. SOCIAL ACTIONS. New York: Farrar and Rinehart,
1936. xix, 746 p.

The author originally intended his work as an outline of social
psychology, which expanded to become a descriptive and classi-
ficatory account of a variety of social actions. It covers the
origins, composition, and structure of social actions, cooperative and educational guidance, participative and purposive submission, intercollective opposition, aggression, altruism, hostility,
and the connection between social and nonsocial actions. An
eighty-five-page section of references is included, with many
comments and notes by the author.

## B. SOCIAL-PSYCHOLOGICAL AND SOCIOLOGICAL TEXTS

Baron, Robert A., and Liebert, Robert M., eds. HUMAN SOCIAL BEHAV-
IOR. A CONTEMPORARY VIEW OF EXPERIMENTAL RESEARCH. Homewood,
Ill.: Dorsey Press, 1971. xv, 559 p.

> This collection of readings deals with many social-psychological
> topics, several of which have relevance to group behavior, such
> as conformity, interpersonal attraction, decision making. There
> are eight sections following an introductory overview, each pre-
> ceded by an introduction. The sections combine text and read-
> ings; a list of references follows each section. There are also
> subject and author indexes.

Becker, Howard P., and Boskoff, Alvin, eds. MODERN SOCIOLOGICAL
THEORY IN CONTINUITY AND CHANGE. New York: Dryden Press, 1957.
xiii, 756 p.

> This symposium of sociology deals with substantive theory and its
> development to the mid-1950s. It includes sections on main
> strands in theory and methodology, specializations in modern
> sociology (including small groups, the sociology of knowledge,
> law, religion, and art), relationships between sociology and allied
> fields, and sociological research and theory in Britain, France,
> Germany, Italy, and Japan. Selected bibliographies follow each
> article, and bibliographies by the editors are supplied at the end
> of the volume.

Berelson, Bernard, ed. THE BEHAVIORAL SCIENCES TODAY. New York:
Basic Books, 1963. viii, 278 p.

> This collection of papers was originally broadcast as part of the
> Forum series of the Voice of America. Topics and contributors
> include "Institutional Organization of the Behavioral Sciences"
> by Ralph W. Tyler, "Methods of Research" by Samuel A. Stouffer,
> "Small Groups" by George C. Homans, and "The Mosaic of the
> Behavioral Sciences" by Robert K. Merton.

Berkowitz, Leonard, ed. ADVANCES IN EXPERIMENTAL SOCIAL PSYCHOL-
OGY. Vol. 1. New York: Academic Press, 1964. xi, 319 p.

> This is the first of ten volumes which seek to report up-to-date
> research findings and to attempt generalizations and interpretations
> of the material presented. Most of the work is experimental
> research, but some field research is included. Each volume
> covers a variety of topics (except volume 9, which is devoted to
> equity theory). Volume 1 deals with topics such as cultural in-
> fluence upon cognitive processes, coalition formation, communi-
> cation networks, and leadership effectiveness. Contributors

include Harry C. Triandis, Stanley Schacter, Marvin E. Shaw, Fred E. Fiedler, and William J. McGuire. References follow each article.

_____. ADVANCES IN EXPERIMENTAL SOCIAL PSYCHOLOGY. Vol. 2. New York: Academic Press, 1965. xi, 348 p.

This volume deals with some of the influence processes that are the concern of social psychology. Eight chapters cover topics such as group problem solving, the concept of aggressive drive, situational factors in conformity, social power, and inequity in social exchange. Contributors include the editor, Albert Bandura, Jonathan L. Freedman and David O. Sears, Edward E. Jones and Keith E. Davis, and John Schopler. References follow each article.

_____. ADVANCES IN EXPERIMENTAL SOCIAL PSYCHOLOGY. Vol. 3. New York: Academic Press, 1967. xi, 333 p.

Four of the six chapters in this volume were written by European sociologists, thus broadening the scope of the field and its on-going work. Topics covered include social performance, communication effects, attitude change, and persuasion. Contributors include Robert P. Abelson, Michael Argyle, Serge Moscovici, and Percy H. Tannenbaum. References follow each chapter.

_____. ADVANCES IN EXPERIMENTAL SOCIAL PSYCHOLOGY. Vol. 4. New York: Academic Press, 1969. xi, 386 p.

This volume presents seven articles dealing with cognitive dissonance theory, sociolinguistics, status congruence, attitudes and attraction, and empathy. Contributors include Elliot Aronson, Donn Byrne, Nico H. Frijda, Ezra Stotland, Harry S. Upshaw, and Susan M. Ervin-Tripp. References follow each article.

_____. ADVANCES IN EXPERIMENTAL SOCIAL PSYCHOLOGY. Vol. 5. New York: Academic Press, 1970. xii, 392 p.

The seven articles in this volume cover such topics as media violence and aggressive behavior, studies on leader influence and innovation, black and white relationships, theoretical aspects of fear communications, perceived freedom, experimental findings on families, and decision making. Contributors include Richard E. Goranson, Edwin P. Hollander, Irwin Katz, Howard Leventhal, Ivan Steiner, Nancy Walker, and Kenneth Dion. References follow each chapter.

_____. ADVANCES IN EXPERIMENTAL SOCIAL PSYCHOLOGY. Vol. 6. New York: Academic Press, 1972. xiii, 310 p.

Topics in this volume include self-perception theory, factors affecting altruism, interpersonal attitudes, the Prisoner's Dilemma Paradigm, and implicit personality theory. Contributors include Leonard Berkowitz, Daryl J. Bem, and Charlan Nemeth. References follow each chapter.

_____. ADVANCES IN EXPERIMENTAL SOCIAL PSYCHOLOGY. Vol. 7. New York: Academic Press, 1974. xi, 354 p.

This volume contains six papers covering topics such as integration theory applied to social attribution, physical attractiveness, conflicts and bargaining, and processes in delay of gratification. Contributors include Norman H. Anderson, Ellen Berscheid and Elaine Walster, and Walter Mischel. References follow each paper.

_____. ADVANCES IN EXPERIMENTAL SOCIAL PSYCHOLOGY. Vol. 8. New York: Academic Press, 1975. xii, 340 p.

This volume deals with topics such as group tasks, group interaction process, group performance effectiveness, objective self-awareness, reactance theory and the learned helplessness model, and the reluctance to transmit bad news. Contributors include Vernon Allen, Arie W. Kruglanski, Robert A. Wicklund, and Jack W. Brehm. References follow each article.

_____. ADVANCES IN EXPERIMENTAL SOCIAL PSYCHOLOGY. Vol. 10. New York: Academic Press, 1977. x, 341 p.

This volume presents, among others, articles on the catharsis of aggression, moral internalization, effects of violent and nonviolent movies on juvenile delinquents' behavior, normative influences on altruism, and four papers dealing with the ethogenic approach. Contributors include the editor, Rom Harre, Barry R. Schenkler, Lee Ross, and Shalom H. Schwartz. References follow each article.

Berkowitz, Leonard, and Walster, Elaine. EQUITY THEORY: TOWARD A GENERAL THEORY OF SOCIAL INTERACTION. ADVANCES IN EXPERIMENTAL SOCIAL PSYCHOLOGY. Vol. 9. New York: Academic Press, 1976. xvii, 263 p.

Equity theory is a current attempt to provide a general theory of social psychology. In this volume, the first article introduces equity theory and research by reviewing the literature already available. The next five articles offer speculations as to where the authors think equity theory should and will go in future years. The final chapter is a commentary on the preceding papers. Contributors include Elaine Walster, Gerald S. Leventhal, Melvin J. Lerner, L. Rowell Huesmann, and George C. Homans. Chapter 2 includes an annotated bibliography. General references are presented at the end of the book.

Brehm, Jack W. and Cohen, Arthur R. EXPLORATIONS IN COGNITIVE DISSONANCE. New York: Wiley, 1962. xiv, 334 p.

This is a summary of research into the theory of cognitive disso- nance. It describes the original theoretical statement, reviews the evidence bearing on the theory, and presents the research to date as well as a number of previously unpublished experiments which bear on derivations of the theory. These are described in their entirety. The relationship of dissonance theory to other psycho- logical models is discussed, and its application to social issues indicated. A list of references is included.

Chadwick-Jones, J.K. SOCIAL EXCHANGE THEORY: ITS STRUCTURE AND INFLUENCE IN SOCIAL PSYCHOLOGY. New York: Academic Press, 1976. vi, 431 p.

This book explores three major social exchange theories: those of Thibaut and Kelley, Homans, and Blau. In each case, the author conducts a theoretical analysis followed by a review of empirical studies designed to test the theory. The author also cites studies which appear relevant, even though they were not designed to test the theory directly. A wide range of published criticisms of the theories is also cited and, in some cases, ex- panded on. Recent developments in the theory are also present- ed. An extensive bibliography is included.

Collins, Barry E., and Ashmore, Richard D. SOCIAL PSYCHOLOGY: SOCIAL INFLUENCE, ATTITUDE CHANGE, GROUP PROCESSES, AND PREJUDICE. Reading, Mass.: Addison-Wesley, 1970. vii, 389 p.

This basic textbook deals with a small number of topics in depth. It is divided into four parts, as the title indicates. Group pro- ductivity and leadership are given the most attention among the group processes. Each section has a short introduction; each chapter is summarized. A bibliography is included.

Cooley, Charles H. HUMAN NATURE AND THE SOCIAL ORDER. New York: Scribner, 1902. Reprint. Introduction by Philip Rieff. Foreword by George Herbert Mead. New York: Schocken, 1964. xxxviii, 444 p.

Cooley's doctrine of society is here elaborated as a matter of social consciousness. The "other" is as immediate as the "self." This volume deals with the process of social communication as the stuff of which the self is made. After such basics as heredity and instinct, suggestion and choice, the author discusses the meaning and various phases of "I," and such topics as leadership and freedom. There is no bibliography.

_____. SOCIAL ORGANIZATION. A STUDY OF THE LARGER MIND. New York: Scribner, 1913. xvii, 436 p.

The author concentrates on the enlargement and diversification of social intercourse from a mental rather than a material point of view. The primary aspects of organization are discussed, including social and individual aspects of mind. Communication, its significance and growth, is dealt with, followed by a discussion of the democratic mind, social classes, institutions, and public will. The text is indexed but contains no bibliography.

_____. SOCIAL PROCESS. New York: Scribner, 1918. Reprint. Introduction by Roscoe C. Hinkle. Foreword by Herman R. Lantz. Carbondale: Southern Illinois University Press, 1966. xiv, 430 p.

This volume deals with the nature of society and social change and has relevance for the functionalistic approach to sociology. The organic view of the process of human life is discussed, followed by personal aspects of social process, degeneration, and social factors in biological survival. Chapters on group conflict, valuation, and intelligent process complete the book, which has no bibliography.

de Rivera, Joseph, comp. FIELD THEORY AS HUMAN SCIENCE: CONTRIBUTIONS OF LEWIN'S BERLIN GROUP. New York: Gardner Press, 1976. vii, 533 p.

This book comprises a series of studies by the original group that surrounded Kurt Lewin. Half of the volume is original Lewinian papers, published in English for the first time; the other half deals with the development of the work of Lewin's associates in the area of emotion and will. Part 1 is entitled "The Dynamics and Structure of Activity"; part 2 is "The Structure of Situations and Dynamics of Feeling."

Ekeh, Peter P. SOCIAL EXCHANGE THEORY. THE TWO TRADITIONS. Cambridge, Mass.: Harvard University Press, 1974. xv, 237 p.

The author examines the two major strands of social exchange theory in an effort to understand the continued existence of each. Besides these two, the theory of the British individualistic Homans and that of French collectivistic Levi-Strauss, Ekeh discusses the contributions of several other thinkers, such as Frazer, Mauss, and Malinowski, not usually credited with influential status in the debate. A ten-page list of references is included.

Festinger, Leon, and Katz, Daniel, eds. RESEARCH METHODS IN THE BEHAVIORAL SCIENCES. New York: Holt, Rinehart and Winston, 1953. xi, 660 p.

The editors have assembled a set of readings which amply illustrate the use of scientific methodology in the study of human
problems. Although most of the contributions are of a social-
psychological nature, the reader is assured that the approaches
and methods discussed will have more general application. The
readings are divided into four sections: research settings, sampling
procedures, data collection, and data analysis. A chapter on
the application of research findings closes the book.

Freedman, Jonathan L.; Carlsmith, J. Merrill; and Sears, David O., eds.
READINGS IN SOCIAL PSYCHOLOGY. Englewood Cliffs, N.J.: Prentice-
Hall, 1971. 573 p.

This is a general text on social psychology, composed of a set
of readings. Several of the eight sections deal explicitly with
group processes (structure, dynamics, leadership, conformity), and
other sections contain articles of interest to those concerned with
group behavior (person perception, interpersonal attraction, persuasion). Each reading is followed by a list of references.

Helson, Harry. ADAPTION-LEVEL THEORY: AN EXPERIMENTAL AND
SYSTEMATIC APPROACH TO BEHAVIOR. New York: Harper and Row, 1964.
xvii, 732 p.

This volume describes the concept of adaptation and its place in
the fields of sensory processes and psychophysical judgments. From
this starting point, experiments are conducted dealing with problems of perception, affectivity, learning, cognition, and interpersonal relations conceived as modes of adaption to focal, contextual, and residual stimuli. The emphasis is on empirically
verifiable aspects of behavior. The appendix supplies tables and
computations. A list of references is included.

Hiller, E.T. SOCIAL RELATIONS AND STRUCTURES: A STUDY IN PRIN-
CIPLES OF SOCIOLOGY. New York: Harper and Bros., 1947. xii, 692 p.

The author approaches the study of human relations from two perspectives, the personal and the collective. He observes that the
content of such relations is contained in the rights, duties, priv-
ileges, reciprocities, and obligations which refer to justice,
power, respect, prestige, and other factors. This book is an
attempt to provide a method for interpreting these data. One
section of the book deals with the organization of social relations: institutions, groups, and societies. Each chapter is followed by problems or exercises. Readings listed at the end of
each chapter are suggested for further study rather than as source
materials.

Hollander, Edwin P., and Hunt, Raymond G., eds. CURRENT PERSPECTIVES IN SOCIAL PSYCHOLOGY. 4th ed. New York: Oxford University Press, 1976. 590 p.

> This collection of fifty-three readings is divided into eight sections. The editors have tried to reflect the general trends in the areas under investigation. The topics of social learning, role, norms, attitudes, leadership, and group processes are among those included in the field of group behavior. A thirty-six page bibliography appears at the end.

Insko, Chester A., and Schopler, John. EXPERIMENTAL SOCIAL PSYCHOLOGY: TEXT WITH ILLUSTRATIVE READINGS. New York: Academic Press, 1972. xv, 561 p.

> This textbook concentrates on the field of experimental social psychology. It strives to offer an adequate grounding for the undergraduate by presenting original materials along with more explanatory textbook discussion. There are three major divisions: attitude and belief change, interpersonal processes, and small groups. Among the topics covered in the latter section are pre-interaction variables, group processes, structure, and intergroup relationships.

Jones, Edward E., and Gerard, Harold B. FOUNDATIONS OF SOCIAL PSYCHOLOGY. New York: Wiley, 1967. 739 p.

> The field of social psychology is explored from an experimental perspective. A considerable portion of the book deals with group processes, drawing largely on the model developed by John Thibaut and Harold Kelley (see p. 13). Each chapter is summarized, and a glossary of terms is supplied.

Kardiner, Abram. THE INDIVIDUAL AND HIS SOCIETY: THE PSYCHODYNAMICS OF PRIMITIVE SOCIAL ORGANIZATION. New York: Columbia University Press, 1939. xxvi, 503 p.

> This is a collaborative effort of psychology and social anthropology in coming to terms with and understanding more about some primitive cultures, in this case aboriginal. It involves the application of psychoanalytic concepts to a society at large, to first the Polynesian Marquesans, and then the Tanala of Madagascar. The third part of the book examines the theoretical issues involved in the derivation and application of psychosocial concepts, and the application of principles of psychopathology to sociological problems.

Krech, David; Crutchfield, Richard S.; and Ballachey, Egerton L. INDIVIDUAL IN SOCIETY: A TEXTBOOK OF SOCIAL PSYCHOLOGY. New York: McGraw-Hill, 1962. 564 p.

The authors have written an introduction to social psychology, using the interpersonal behavior event as the unit of analysis. The text is divided into four parts: basic psychological factors, social attitudes, the social and cultural habitat, and groups, organizations, and the individual. Topics in the last part include group structure, leadership, group change, and group effectiveness. Excerpts of previously published materials appear in boxes throughout the text. Sets of guides are supplied, preceding and summarizing more lengthy discussions; part summaries and chapter glossaries also appear.

Lewin, Kurt. A DYNAMIC THEORY OF PERSONALITY: SELECTED PAPERS. Translated by Donald K. Adams and Karl E. Zener. New York: McGraw-Hill, 1935. ix, 286 p.

This collection of readings was originally a set of separate articles; therefore, some duplication occurs. Titles include "On the Structure of the Mind" (chapter 2), "The Psychological Situations of Reward and Punishment" (chapter 4), "Substitute Activity and Substitute Value" (chapter 6), and "Survey of the Experimental Investigations" (chapter 8).

_____. FIELD THEORY IN SOCIAL SCIENCE: SELECTED THEORETICAL PAPERS. Edited by Dorwin Cartwright. New York: Harper and Row, 1951. xx, 346 p.

This work is included because Lewin is a founder of the study of group dynamics. Here he deals with some fundamental issues in the philosophy of science, describes his principles of understanding these issues, and applies these principles to a variety of fields, including group dynamics. His research is summarized in the last chapter. The appendix is a technical analysis of some of the author's concepts.

Lindzey, Gardner, and Aronson, Elliot, eds. THE HANDBOOK OF SOCIAL PSYCHOLOGY. 2d ed. Vol. 1: HISTORICAL INTRODUCTION/SYSTEMATIC POSITIONS. Reading, Mass.: Addison-Wesley, 1969. xv, 653 p.

The historical introduction in this volume is presented in an article by Gordon W. Allport. The remaining seven articles all deal with systematic positions. Included are stimulus-response theory, mathematical models, the Freudian position, cognitive theories, field theories, role theories, and organizations. Contributors include Seymour M. Berger and William W. Lambert, Seymour Rosenberg, Calvin S. Hall, Robert B. Zajonc, and Morton Deutsch. References accompany each article. In this, as in the other volumes of the HANDBOOK (see below), detailed author and subject indexes are provided.

_____. THE HANDBOOK OF SOCIAL PSYCHOLOGY. 2d ed. Vol. 2: RESEARCH METHODS. Reading, Mass.: Addison-Wesley, 1969. xv, 819 p.

Ten articles are presented, each dealing with a different aspect of methodology in social psychology. Included are topics such as data analysis, attitude measurement, systematic observational methods, interviewing, and content analysis. Contributors include the editors, Frederick Mosteller, Robert Abelson, Karl E. Weick, John W.M. Whiting, and D.O. Hebb. References follow each article.

_____. THE HANDBOOK OF SOCIAL PSYCHOLOGY. 2d ed. Vol. 3: THE INDIVIDUAL IN A SOCIAL CONTEXT. Reading, Mass.: Addison-Wesley, 1969. xiii, 978 p.

A variety of topics are encompassed by the ten articles in this volume ranging from social motivation, socialization, personality and social interaction, to the nature of attitudes and attitude change, person perception, psycholinguistics, and aesthetics. Contributors include Leonard Berkowitz, William J. McGuire, Henri Tajfel, Renato Taguiri, and D.E. Benlyne. Each article has its own list of references.

_____. THE HANDBOOK OF SOCIAL PSYCHOLOGY. 2d ed. Vol. 4: GROUP PSYCHOLOGY AND PHENOMENA OF INTERACTION. Reading, Mass.: Addison-Wesley, 1969. xvii, 694 p.

In this volume, the editors have assembled eight readings which treat specific areas in some detail. Topics include group problem solving, structure, leadership, and collective behavior. Contributors include Harold H. Kelley and John W. Thibaut, Barry E. Collins and Bertram H. Raven, Cecil A. Gibb, Alex Inkeles, and Stanley Milgram. Each article is followed by a list of references.

_____. THE HANDBOOK OF SOCIAL PSYCHOLOGY. 2d ed. Vol. 5: APPLIED SOCIAL PSYCHOLOGY. Reading, Mass.: Addison-Wesley, 1969. xiv, 1,036 p.

Nine articles in this volume deal with a variety of areas of applied social psychology. Topics include prejudice, mass media, industry, economics, politics, education, international relations, religion, and mental health. Contributors include John Harding, Harold Proshansky, Victor H. Vroom, David O. Sears, J.W. Getzels, and Amitai Etzioni. References accompany each article.

McGrath, Joseph E. SOCIAL PSYCHOLOGY: A BRIEF INTRODUCTION. Chicago: Holt, Rinehart and Winston, 1964. 166 p.

This basic textbook reviews the development of social psychology as a science, presenting an eclectic set of theories and showing their interrelationships. The largest of its five sections deals with the group. A short list of references is supplied.

Mead, George H. MIND, SELF, AND SOCIETY FROM THE STANDPOINT OF A SOCIAL BEHAVIORIST. Chicago: University of Chicago Press, 1934. xxxv, 401 p.

The author regards individuals as agents of influence, both of others, and, in role-playing fashion, of themselves. The group can thus affect persons by being presented to them in their own experience, whereby they assume the group's attitudes.

Merton, Robert K. SOCIAL THEORY AND SOCIAL STRUCTURE. Enl. ed. New York: Free Press, 1968. xxiii, 702 p.

This work covers a wide expanse of the sociological field, dealing with theoretical sociology and its relationship to empirical research, the problem of anomie, bureaucratic structure and personality, the sociology of knowledge, and the sociology of science. Over 150 pages are devoted to reference group behavior, and there is also a chapter on interpersonal influence. References appear in footnotes throughout the text.

Mills, Judson, ed. EXPERIMENTAL SOCIAL PSYCHOLOGY. New York: Macmillan, 1969. ix, 466 p.

The editor intends this as a text for advanced courses in experimental social psychology. Sections cover the topics of interpersonal attraction, hostility, and perception; attitude change; group pressure and conformity; interdependence in groups; and the experimental method. The contributors are actively engaged in research and present the then-current state of knowledge in their respective specialties. References are listed at the end of each section.

Moreno, Jacob L., ed. THE SOCIOMETRY READER. Glencoe, Ill.: Free Press, 1960. xxiv, 773 p.

This collection is divided into four main sections. The first part deals with the concepts of "tele," social atom, networks, role, and integration. Part 2 describes sociometric measurement, statistical methods and models, and the concepts of reliability and validity. Major areas of exploration covered in part 3 are: childhood and early adolescence; high school and college level; community, industry, and the armed forces; and perceptual sociometry. Part 4 is concerned with the history of sociometry. References are supplied with each article, and the appendix describes global developments in the field for the decade 1950-60.

Parsons, Talcott; Bales, Robert F.; and Shils, Edward A. WORKING PAPERS IN THE THEORY OF ACTION. New York: Free Press, 1953. 269 p.

This is a set of five working papers, or working drafts, which are, for the most part, not empirically tested or developed into logically integrated wholes. The areas covered include the superego and the theory of social systems, the equilibrium problem in small groups, and phase movement in relation to motivation, symbol formation, and role structure. No bibliography is supplied; the reader is referred to some background materials in the preface.

Proshansky, Harold, and Seidenberg, Bernard, eds. BASIC STUDIES IN SOCIAL PSYCHOLOGY. New York: Holt, Rinehart and Winston, 1965. xvii, 743 p.

This book of readings is intended for undergraduate use in general social psychology courses. The readings proceed from more basic to more complex psychological processes. There is a general introduction as well as more specific introductions to each section. Topics in group behavior include interpersonal influence, norms and roles, leadership, and group structure and process. Each reading is followed by a list of references.

Rohrer, John H., and Sherif, Muzafer. SOCIAL PSYCHOLOGY AT THE CROSSROADS. New York: Harper, 1950. viii, 437 p.

This is a collection of papers presented at a University of Oklahoma conference dealing with a variety of social-psychological topics. It includes a section on group structures and individual roles, and articles on roles, multiple group membership, and intergroup relations. References follow each article.

Rose, Arnold M., ed. HUMAN BEHAVIOR AND SOCIAL PROCESSES. AN INTERACTIONIST APPROACH. Boston: Houghton Mifflin, 1962. xv, 680 p.

The author and his collaborators have assembled a body of material on the theory of symbolic interaction and show its usefulness for research in a variety of areas. Each article is separately referenced, and subject and author indexes are provided.

Sahakian, William S., ed. SOCIAL PSYCHOLOGY: EXPERIMENTATION, THEORY, RESEARCH. Scranton, Pa.: Intext Educational Publishers, 1972. 632 p.

This text attempts to embrace the field of social psychology systematically, emphasizing the most influential and recent contributors. Three of the twelve sections deal directly with group
behavior. Some readings are followed by bibliographies; others
are footnoted throughout. A dual table of contents is supplied,
one describing the chronological design of the text, the other
grouping the readings according to a systems and theories approach.

Secord, Paul F., and Backman, Carl W. SOCIAL PSYCHOLOGY. New
York: McGraw-Hill, 1974. xvii, 647 p.

One author is a sociologist, the other a psychologist. The text
is thus an integrated viewpoint, organized by topic into seventeen chapters divided into four sections: social influence processes, group structure and process, the individual and the social
system, and socialization.

Shaw, Marvin E., and Costanzo, Philip R. THEORIES OF SOCIAL PSYCHOL-
OGY. New York: McGraw-Hill, 1970. ix, 414 p.

In this book, theories are considered within the broader framework
of their orientation. Each section reviews a general orientation
and then considers theories which adopt that general approach.
Orientations include reinforcement, field-theoretical, cognitive,
and psychoanalytic. There is also a section on transorientational
approaches, that is, those that draw on one or more traditional
orientations, or represent unique orientations. The final part of
the book compares and contrasts the theories in the preceding
chapters. A list of references and a glossary of terms are included.

Sherif, Muzafer, and Sherif, Carolyn W. SOCIAL PSYCHOLOGY. 3d ed.
New York: Harper and Row, 1969. 616 p.

This major revision of AN OUTLINE OF SOCIAL PSYCHOLOGY
(see p. 11) treats varied topics in terms of verified psychological principles, with applications clarified by illustrations. Recent research methods and findings are included, both field and
laboratory. Problems of inconsistency and change are handled
along with the achievement of social-psychological stability.
An interdisciplinary approach is used. Chapter outlines are supplied, and the reference list is extensive. An instructor's manual is also provided. The text is intended for undergraduate,
graduate, or seminar courses.

Stouffer, Samuel A. SOCIAL RESEARCH TO TEST IDEAS: SELECTED WRITINGS
OF SAMUEL A. STOUFFER. New York: Free Press, 1962. xxxi, 314 p.

This collection of selected writings describes the author's efforts
to test empirically ideas about human relationships.  The work
described makes and tests propositions of a sociological or social-
psychological nature, and also attempts to improve the tools required for such testing.  Part 1 is mainly substantive, dealing
with topics such as relative deprivation, role conflict, and the
relationship between attitudes and behavior.  Part 2 is mainly
methodological, and includes articles on case studies, correlation
analysis and the H-Scale.  A bibliography of Stouffer's work is
provided.

Watson, Goodwin, and Johnson, David [W.].  SOCIAL PSYCHOLOGY: ISSUES
AND INSIGHTS.  2d ed.  Philadelphia: Lippincott, 1972.  xii, 499 p.

The authors emphasize the application of social psychology to
social problems and include methodological data to enable the
reader to evaluate critically the material presented.  Social
interaction, dyads, group membership, and productivity are included, along with a section on intergroup conflict.  Each section is summarized, and there is a thirty-five-page bibliography.

Wrightsman, Lawrence S., Jr.  SOCIAL PSYCHOLOGY IN THE SEVENTIES.
Monterey, Calif.: Brooks/Cole, 1972.  xx, 698 p.

The text is organized around the two themes: assumptions about
human nature and the complexity of human social behavior.  The
author and his collaborators aim at being comprehensive, reviewing the past as well as looking to the future.  Interpersonal and
group processes comprise one section.  Each chapter is summarized and followed by a list of suggested readings.  An eleven-
page glossary and a forty-nine-page list of references are supplied.

Zajonc, Robert B.  SOCIAL PSYCHOLOGY: AN EXPERIMENTAL APPROACH.
Belmont, Calif.: Wadsworth, 1966.  viii, 120 p.

This book was written as an introductory text on social psychology for beginning students in general psychology courses.  The
author does not claim to be fully representative of current research trends, but rather tries to emphasize some of the unsolved
problems of social psychology.  The first section deals with
behavioral dependence or social behavior, the second section explores social interaction, and the third examines group processes.
In each case, the main problems and findings are presented,
along with discussion of some typical experiments.  A list of
references is provided.

## C. MODELS AND METHODOLOGIES

Arrow, Kenneth J.; Karlin, Samuel; and Suppes, Patrick, ed.  MATHEMATI-
CAL METHODS IN THE SOCIAL SCIENCES, 1959.  PROCEEDINGS OF THE

FIRST STANFORD SYMPOSIUM. Stanford, Calif.: Stanford University Press, 1960. viii, 365 p.

> This collection of papers illustrates some research in which mathematical methods are employed to deal with problems in management and social sciences. The book is divided into three sections: economics, management, and psychology. In the psychology section, one paper is on utility theory, two on theory of measurement and testing, six on mathematical learning theory, and one on stochastic models of learning.

Bales, Robert F. INTERACTION PROCESS ANALYSIS: A METHOD FOR THE STUDY OF SMALL GROUPS. Reading, Mass.: Addison-Wesley, 1950. xi, 203 p.

> The author describes the development of a twelve-category system for interaction observation. The theoretical nature of social interaction is explored. Some data are presented on cumulative norms for the system.

Bartos, Otomar J. SIMPLE MODELS OF GROUP BEHAVIOR. New York: Columbia University Press, 1967. xii, 345 p.

> This book attempts to present some of the uses of mathematical models in the social sciences, along with the mathematical theory requisite for comprehending them. Although discussion of mathematical theory is kept to a minimum, the level of material presented is far from elementary. The reader is exhorted to do the exercises presented following most of the chapters. Matrix algebra and Markov chains are discussed, in the early part of the book, with the application of Markov chain models to social stratification and conflict resolution. Game-theoretical models comprise the latter part of the book, which concludes with a section on problems of model construction. A bibliography is supplied.

Ben-Zeev, Saul, et al. METHODS FOR STUDYING WORK AND EMOTIONALITY IN GROUP OPERATION. Chicago: Human Dynamics Laboratory, University of Chicago, 1954. 208 p.

> This monograph describes methods for measuring group-relevant aspects of personality and a system of recording, analyzing, unitizing, and interpreting sequences of group interaction. Some of the methods are a work-emotionality field graph and a self-perceptual Q-sort. The authors discuss in detail the development, field use, and interpretation of the instruments.

Berger, Joseph, et al. TYPES OF FORMALIZATION IN SMALL-GROUP RESEARCH. Boston: Houghton Mifflin, 1962. x, 159 p.

This technical work examines a number of models in small-group research in order to make explicit the logical structure of their assertions. This involves their translation into formal language, which can be quantitative (calculus) or nonquantitative (symbolic logic). An annotated bibliography is included.

Criswell, Joan H.; Solomon, Herbert; and Suppes, Patrick, eds. MATHE-MATICAL METHODS IN SMALL GROUP PROCESSES. Stanford, Calif.: Stanford University Press, 1962. viii, 361 p.

This is an edited version of the twenty-two papers presented at the Symposium on Mathematical Methods in Small Group Processes held at Stanford University, 20-23 June 1961. The introduction summarizes the topics covered. References appear at the end of each paper. No subject or author index is included.

Delbecq, Andre L.; Van De Ven, Andrew H.; and Gustafson, David H. GROUP TECHNIQUES FOR PROGRAM PLANNING: A GUIDE TO NOMINAL GROUPS AND DELPHI PROCESSES. Glenview, Ill.: Scott, Foresman, 1975. xv, 174 p.

This book deals with two highly structured approaches to the management of complex group decision making: the nominal group technique and the Delphi technique. The first involves a structured group meeting, which includes a clear sequence of problem-solving and decision-making steps. The Delphi process is a survey technique for decision making among isolated, anonymous respondents.

Elwell, Elizabeth A., and Malik, Leela G. A NEW PERSPECTIVE. New Delhi, India: R and K Publishing House, 1974. x, 139 p.

The authors present a new perspective of leadership, and develop this perspective as an analytical theoretical system. This new way of viewing leadership is as an adaptive action system made up of a particular variety of functions which can be represented as a set. This model of leadership involves a reordering of present knowledge of leadership. The authors describe the generation of the model and discuss its syntax and semantics. A bibliography is included.

Flament, Claude. APPLICATIONS OF GRAPH THEORY TO GROUP STRUC-TURE. Translated by Maurice Pinard, Raymond Breton, and Fernand Fontaine. Englewood Cliffs, N.J.: Prentice-Hall, 1963. 142 p.

The author demonstrates the potential of the theory of graphs for application to the behavioral sciences. The first part of the book is devoted to the theory of graphs, the second part to communica-

tion networks, and the third to balancing processes. The text
employs considerable mathematical notation and maintains a technical approach. A bibliography is included.

Hemphill, John K. GROUP DIMENSIONS. A MANUAL FOR THEIR MEA-
SUREMENT. Research Monograph no. R-87. Columbus: Bureau of Business
Research, Ohio State University, 1956. xi, 66 p.

This methodological work describes the development of an instrument for measuring thirteen dimensions of a group. It includes a
copy of the questionnaire, a scoring key with directions for its
use, and a profile chart. The scale was originally developed for
the Ohio State Leadership Studies.

Jahoda, Marie; Deutsch, Morton; and Cook, Stuart W. RESEARCH METHODS
IN SOCIAL RELATIONS WITH ESPECIAL REFERENCE TO PREJUDICE. New
York: Dryden Press, 1951. x, 757 p.

The authors attempt to provide a step-by-step account of methods
involved at each stage of the research process. The focus is on
the area of prejudice, and most of the illustrative material is
from this field. Part 1, "Basic Processes," deals with the major
steps of a scientific investigation of social relations. Part 2,
"Selected Techniques," deals with some specific methodological
problems in greater detail. Unlike part 1, part 2 is written by
a group of collaborators and so constitutes a volume of readings.
The bibliography and indexes are included in both parts.

McGrath, Joseph E., and Altman, Irwin. SMALL GROUP RESEARCH. A SYN-
THESIS AND CRITIQUE OF THE FIELD. New York: Holt, Rinehart and
Winston, 1966. ix, 601 p.

The authors' purpose is threefold: first, to summarize the extent
of knowledge in the small group area; second, to broaden the
perspective on the area through interpreting and integrating empirical findings; and third, to present a case study in the classification of social science knowledge. They describe the system
they use and its application to nearly 250 annotated entries.
There is a bibliography of 2,699 entries.

MacKenzie, Kenneth D. A THEORY OF GROUP STRUCTURES. Vol. 1:
BASIC THEORY; Vol. 2: EMPIRICAL TESTS. New York: Gordon and
Breach Science Publishers, 1976.

A mathematical approach is taken to the aggregation of individuals into groups. The author develops a theory of group structures which deals with the issues of how and why structures form
and change. Volume 1 provides definitions, assumptions, methodology, theory, and results. Volume 2 describes empirical tests

of the theory as presented in volume 1, demonstrating how to reason with and use the theory. The volumes are intended for joint use; cross-referencing between them is extensive. References are listed separately in each volume.

Mayer, Thomas F. MATHEMATICAL MODELS OF GROUP STRUCTURE. Bobbs-Merrill Studies in Sociology. Indianapolis: Bobbs-Merrill, 1975. 81 p.

The author points out the relevance of group structure as an element in understanding the dynamics of change and of the group as causal agent. He chooses mathematical representation of group structure as a concise formulation of the problem under investigation. The issues of structural solidarity, structural equilibrium, and structural hierarchy receive attention. In the interest of clarity, mathematical proofs are omitted; however, concepts of matrix algebra, abstract algebra, and integral calculus are employed. References and suggested further readings are supplied.

Miller, James G., ed. EXPERIMENTS IN SOCIAL PROCESS. A SYMPOSIUM ON SOCIAL PSYCHOLOGY. New York: McGraw-Hill, 1950. ix, 205 p.

This is a collection of social-psychological research which has application possibilities in problem areas. The focus is on methodology. Among the topics covered are effective leadership, committee operation, and group behavior. Laboratory experiments, survey research, and field experiments are among the techniques discussed.

Ofshe, S. Lynne, and Ofshe, Richard. UTILITY AND CHOICE IN SOCIAL INTERACTION. Englewood Cliffs, N.J.: Prentice-Hall, 1970. ix, 202 p.

The aim of the authors is to develop and test a predictive, utility-based model of social decision making. They examine the coalition game, in which the individual must choose between other individuals and his choice has repercussions on the outcome for everyone. Two appendixes present the data and the method of estimating alpha ratios from more than minimal data. References are supplied.

Rapoport, Anatol, and Chammah, Albert M. In collaboration with Carol J. Orwant. PRISONER'S DILEMMA: A STUDY IN CONFLICT AND COOPERATION. Ann Arbor: University of Michigan Press, 1965. xii, 258 p.

This book illustrates the application of mathematical models to the investigation of human behavior. A theory can then be constructed from the statistical regularities observed in the data. The authors describe the two-choice situation known as "Prisoner's Dilemma," a game which has no satisfactory solution. Markov chain models, equilibrium models, and classical dynamic models are discussed. Appendixes supply further technical and statistical information on the data, and there is a glossary of symbols.

Rashevsky, N. MATHEMATICAL THEORY OF HUMAN RELATIONS. AN APPROACH TO A MATHEMATICAL BIOLOGY OF SOCIAL PHENOMENA. Bloomington, Ind.: Principia Press, 1947. xiv, 202 p.

> The author presents an outline of a system of mathematical sociology. The structure of a society and the behavior of its members can be mathematically described in terms of integral equations. The book shows how social groups are formed within a society, and how their interaction determines the behavior of society as a whole. Mathematical relations are also derived, which govern physical conflict between social groups.

Riley, Matilda W., et al. SOCIOLOGICAL STUDIES IN SCALE ANALYSIS: APPLICATIONS THEORY PROCEDURES. New Brunswick, N.J.: Rutgers University Press, 1954. xii, 433 p.

> This book is directed toward researchers, primarily sociologists, using qualitative data. It describes how one kind of tool, the Guttman scale, has been adapted to be applied to a variety of theoretical problems. The contributors demonstrate how the cumulative scale may be used to order not only individuals but also groups on the objects of group action, by means of a continuum. One section of the book is devoted to the structuring of roles and deals with dyadic relationships.

Schutz, William C. THE INTERPERSONAL UNDERWORLD. Palo Alto, Calif.: Science and Behavior Books, 1966. xi, 242 p. Originally published as FIRO: A THREE-DIMENSIONAL THEORY OF INTERPERSONAL BEHAVIOR. New York: Holt, Rinehart and Winston, 1958.

> The author's objective is three-fold: theoretical--to describe a theory of interpersonal behavior consistent with the psychodynamic theory of personality; empirical--to present data from fifteen experiments which provide empirical cases for this theory; and methodological--to illustrate the application of the techniques of philosophy of science and of logic to the problems of behavioral science. FIRO is the name of the theory: Fundamental Interpersonal Relations Orientation. The basic tenet is that our basic orientations toward others help explain our own behavior as well as our interactions with others and theirs with us.

Shubik, Martin, ed. GAME THEORY AND RELATED APPROACHES TO SOCIAL BEHAVIOR: SELECTIONS. New York: Wiley, 1964. xi, 390 p.

> This book of readings illustrates the use of formal models in the study of behavior. The first group of articles broadly covers game theory and indicates its relevance to social analysis. The

next group deals with political choice, power, and voting. Another section addresses applications of game theory to bargaining, threats, and negotiations. A final group of articles discusses gaming. A bibliography is provided.

Solomon, Herbert, ed. MATHEMATICAL THINKING IN THE MEASUREMENT OF BEHAVIOR. SMALL GROUPS, UTILITY, FACTOR ANALYSIS. Glencoe, Ill.: Free Press, 1960. 314 p.

This book demonstrates some of the uses of mathematics in the social sciences in resolving substantive problems. It presents three papers on the mathematical study of small groups, a survey of Bernoullian utility theory, and a survey of mathematical models in factor analysis. Each paper is followed by a bibliography.

Suppes, Patrick, and Atkinson, Richard C. MARKOV LEARNING MODELS FOR MULTIPERSON INTERACTIONS. Stanford, Calif.: Stanford University Press, 1960. xii, 296 p.

The authors apply a mathematical theory of behavior to small-group experiments which resemble game situations. Among these are zero-sum, two-person situations; nonzero-sum, two-person situations; three-person, simple majority situations; and studies of communication, utility functions, monetary payoffs, and noncontingent reinforcement schedules. The authors recommend a prior knowledge of discrete probability theory; occasionally, knowledge of differential calculus is assumed. Their theoretical analysis of data is, for the most part, detailed. A bibliography is supplied.

Thomas, Dorothy S., and associates. SOME NEW TECHNIQUES FOR STUDYING SOCIAL BEHAVIOR. New York: Bureau of Publications, Teachers College, Columbia University, 1929. x, 203 p.

This book comprises a set of studies focusing on children. The purpose is to describe the development of a method for recording and analyzing the social and emotional responses of the child. It includes a reading on a method of studying spontaneous group formation, and a preliminary report on a study of a preschool gang. Each reading contains technical material pertinent to the study described.

Willner, Dorothy, ed. DECISIONS, VALUES, AND GROUPS. New York: Pergamon Press, 1960. xxix, 348 p.

This volume arose from the First Interdisciplinary Conference in the Behavioral Science Division held at the University of New Mexico in 1957. Its purpose is to indicate areas where interdisciplinary research can be of value, and to examine techniques for such research. Separate sections deal with various topics:

mathematical models in decision processes, conceptualizations and designs for research in values and evaluative processes, theoretical contributions to small group research, psychodynamic patterns of behavior, and special military problems. References are supplied with each article.

# Chapter 2

# GROUP PROBLEM SOLVING

Alker, Hayward R., Jr.; Deutsch, Karl W.; and Stoetzel, Antoine H., eds.
MATHEMATICAL APPROACHES TO POLITICS. San Francisco: Jossey-Bass,
1973. viii, 475 p.

Politics as a discipline is understood here as the science of the
ways decisions are made by people acting within functionally or
territorially defined networks and constellations of organizations.
Systematic analysis is seen as crucial to the discipline, one expression of which is the formal language of mathematical logic
or statistics. There are four sections to the book: statistical
models and data analysis, rational choice theories, structural
theories, and simulation models. References appear with each
article.

Avis, Warren E. SHARED PARTICIPATION: FINDING GROUP SOLUTIONS
TO PERSONAL, CORPORATE AND COMMUNITY PROBLEMS. Garden City,
N.Y.: Doubleday, 1973. ix, 180 p.

The author describes the problem-solving technique known as
"shared participation." This involves considering all solutions
and information contributed by group members on a particular
problem. These are discussed and a voluntary consensus is reach-
ed on a solution. Instructions for the process and a working example are supplied in the appendix.

Collins, Barry E., and Guetzkow, Harold. A SOCIAL PSYCHOLOGY OF
GROUP PROCESSES FOR DECISION-MAKING. New York: Wiley, 1964.
254 p.

The book comprises a blend of empiricism and theory, and draws
heavily on the rigorous empirical work of other writers, presenting sufficient detail that the reader can examine the abstractions
and generalizations made by the authors. Chapter 1 contains an
overview of the rest of the book and a short discussion of some
elementary technical concepts used throughout the book.

Davis, James H. GROUP PERFORMANCE. Reading, Mass.: Addison-Wesley, 1969. 115 p.

> Performance is examined by comparing and contrasting individual and group efforts. Variables affecting group performance are explored. These include the size, composition, cohesion, and structure of the group.

Elliott, Harrison S. THE PROCESS OF GROUP THINKING. New York: Association Press, 1928. x, 229 p.

> The author discusses the ways in which democratic participation may be attained in group discussion and decision making. Group thinking is the suggested methodology; its procedure is outlined and the place of emotion is explored. Appendixes on legislative bodies and on conducting conferences on a group-thinking basis are supplied.

Gouran, Dennis S. DISCUSSION: THE PROCESS OF GROUP DECISION-MAKING. New York: Harper and Row, 1974. ix, 199 p.

> The author explores the dynamics of decision-making discussion, approaching the topic from an interdisciplinary standpoint. The cognitive aspects as well as the social-emotional factors are dealt with. Each chapter is summarized, followed by a set of exercises and a list of references. The book includes an analysis of a sample discussion.

Hall, Darl M. DYNAMICS OF GROUP ACTION. 3d ed. Danville, Ill.: Interstate Printers and Publishers, 1964. 243 p.

> The theory and practice of problem solving form the main focus of this book. The author also devotes space to the philosophies and goals of groups, to communications systems, and to group growth and the development of maturity. To enable the reader to begin at any number of points in the book and not feel lost, the author has added page references indicating forward and backward connections and has cross-indexed ideas marked with asterisks. The appendixes present a number of issues for groups to tackle for their own improvement.

Maier, Norman R.F. PROBLEM SOLVING AND CREATIVITY IN INDIVID-UALS AND GROUPS. Monterey, Calif: Brooks/Cole, 1970. xii, 493 p.

> The book is a collection of studies on individual and group problem solving, which were carried out in the author's laboratory over several years. Most have been published before. There are eight parts, each preceded by an introduction. The first four parts focus on individual problem solving and the possibility of a unique factor in creativity. The last four parts emphasize

group problem solving, including a section on the role of the leader in this process. A final section discusses applications.

_____. PROBLEM-SOLVING DISCUSSIONS AND CONFERENCES: LEADER-SHIP METHODS AND SKILLS. New York: McGraw-Hill, 1963. vii, 261 p.

The author's concern is with improving the effectiveness of a leader in group problem solving and decision making. He outlines the principles of group behavior and how they can be used to reduce sources of frustration in a group meeting and to use group resources effectively for cooperative problem solving. The book concludes with a set of nine problem-solving principles.

Niemi, Richard G., and Weisberg, Herbert F., ed. PROBABILITY MODELS OF COLLECTIVE DECISION MAKING. Columbus, Ohio: Charles E. Merrill, 1972. x, 414 p.

This is a collection of sixteen original papers on probability models of collective decision making. The editors' introduction creates a framework for the articles, and their conclusion contains a critique of probability modeling. The readings are divided into four parts: constitutional design, coalition formation, the paradox of voting, and spatial modeling of competition. The complexity of mathematics used varies from one paper to another. A bibliography is supplied.

Perlman, Helen H[arris]. SOCIAL CASEWORK: A PROBLEM-SOLVING PRO-CESS. Chicago: University of Chicago Press, 1957. xv, 268 p.

The author views the common elements in the diverse field of casework as the operations of the process of problem solving. In turn, problem solving in casework is explored in relation to problem solving in general. The first part of the book defines the casework situation. Then the initial phase of casework is viewed as a cross section in which the dynamic components of casework can be seen in interaction. Two samples of case material are supplied by way of illustration. A bibliography is also included.

Siegel, Sidney, and Fouraker, Lawrence E. BARGAINING AND GROUP DECISION MAKING: EXPERIMENTS IN BILATERAL MONOPOLY. New York: McGraw-Hill, 1960. x, 132 p.

This is an example of some interdisciplinary work in psychology and economics. The paradigm used is the bilateral monopoly situation, which involves bargaining between two rivals who must reach agreement if either is to function. Thus, the process of small-group decision making is studied, because the process of bargaining is a process of reconciling individual and group interests.

The authors suggest ways of generalizing this model to conflicts involving more than two parties. Appendixes supply tables used in the experimental sessions. References are included.

Smith, William S. GROUP PROBLEM-SOLVING THROUGH DISCUSSION: A PROCESS ESSENTIAL TO DEMOCRACY. Rev. ed. Indianapolis: Bobbs-Merrill, 1965. vi, 205 p.

The author discusses theory related to problem-solving discussion and leadership in this process. In so doing, he hopes that participants in discussion may acquire the fundamental principles of democracy. The overall aim is to achieve a system of problem solving which will be of use to groups and individuals in overcoming obstacles in a practical fashion. Appendixes supply a bibliography, glossary of terms, roles in discussion, criteria for democratic procedures, and a suggested course plan for one quarter.

Steiner, Ivan D. GROUP PROCESS AND PRODUCTIVITY. New York: Academic Press, 1972. viii, 204 p.

The author examines a limited number of phenomena in the area of group process and productivity, and describes a small but consistent network of interrelationships. Potential and actual productivity are treated as dependent variables, and attention is focused on the factors that influence them. Task performance is the central issue--what groups can and do accomplish when situations call for a joint product. Unitary and divisible tasks are considered; effects of group size and composition are examined. Motivation and group cohesion are explored, and there is a discussion of system and process in relation to groups. A list of references is supplied.

Vroom, Victor H., and Yetton, Philip W. LEADERSHIP AND DECISION-MAKING. Pittsburgh: University of Pittsburgh Press, 1973. xiii, 233 p.

The authors deal with the problem of how much a leader should involve subordinates in the decision-making process. This issue of leadership style is tackled from two sides: how it should be solved, and how, in practice, it is solved by managers. The authors show the need for situation-specific variables to be included in a theory of decision making, and proceeed to do that in their program of research described here.

Wrightsman, Lawrence S., Jr.; O'Connor, John; and Baker, Norma J., eds. COOPERATION AND COMPETITION: READINGS ON MIXED-MOTIVE GAMES. Monterey, Calif:: Brooks/Cole, 1972. viii, 348 p.

This set of readings deals with the problem of conflicting motives. More specifically, the editors review the effects of various factors on cooperation. These include the effects of payoffs to the participants, the influence of a participant's attitudes and personality, the effects of the strategy of the other participant, and the possibilities for communication. Each section has an introduction, some research reports, and a summary of recent studies on the topic. A glossary and a separate bibliography of over one thousand items are included.

# Chapter 3

# INTERPERSONAL INTERACTION

## A. GENERAL INTERPERSONAL INTERACTION

Altman, Irwin, and Taylor, Dalmas.  SOCIAL PENETRATION:  THE DEVEL-
OPMENT OF INTERPERSONAL RELATIONSHIPS.  New York:  Holt, Rinehart
and Winston, 1973.  ix, 212 p.

> The authors develop a set of ideas on the growth of interpersonal
> relationships from an interdisciplinary perspective.  This book
> describes the results of their investigations for a broad spectrum
> of readers.  It describes properties of the social penetration pro-
> cess, and discusses extensions of the basic framework, including
> both individual differences and conflict in social penetration.
> A bibliography is supplied.

Argyle, Michael.  THE PSYCHOLOGY OF INTERPERSONAL BEHAVIOR.
Baltimore:  Penguin Books, 1967.  223 p.

> The author spans the field of the psychological study of behavior
> among people.  He deals with the social techniques people use
> in social settings and the styles they adopt when using them.
> Interpersonal perception and the determinants of friendship are
> also discussed, and attention is paid to the relations between
> interpersonal behavior and the group and culture in which peo-
> ple live.  Applications of the topic are dealt with in the study
> of mental disorder and in professional social skills.  A section on
> methods of teaching social skills is included.  References and a
> list of works for further reading are provided.

_____.  SOCIAL INTERACTION.  New York:  Atherton Press, 1969.  504 p.

> This textbook in social psychology deals with the field of social
> behavior in two ways.  First, it presents an analysis of social
> behavior in terms of the basic elements of interaction:  the ver-
> bal and nonverbal aspects of speech, bodily contact, gestures,

orientation, proximity, eye movements, and facial expression.
Second, it relates social interaction to its biological roots and
to the culture in which it occurs. A wide range of fields is
drawn on. The list of references spans fifty pages.

_____, ed. SOCIAL ENCOUNTERS: READINGS IN SOCIAL INTERACTION.
Chicago: Aldine-Atherton, 1973. 416 p.

This is a collection of readings on studies which illustrate new
research strategies in the field of social behavior. As such, it
is a companion volume to the author's SOCIAL INTERACTION
(see above). The main ideas in the approach described here are
the study of the detailed processes of social interaction at the
level of the elements of interaction, and the relation of social
behavior to its cultural setting and biological basis. Among the
topics covered are two-person interaction, interaction in groups
and organizations, and training in social skills. Each section
has a short introduction. References accompany each article,
and a list of further readings is supplied.

Bennis, Warren G., et al., eds. INTERPERSONAL DYNAMICS. ESSAYS
AND READINGS ON HUMAN INTERACTION. 3d ed. Homewood, Ill.:
Dorsey Press, 1973. xiv, 608 p.

This book of readings focuses on human interactions. As such, it
involves groups to some degree, though the analysis of group behavior is not its primary objective. Rather, the readings concentrate on the individual's emotional expressions, self-confirmation,
and personal change. The book closes with a section on the
improvement of interpersonal relationships. The editors seek to
bridge those works which focus on experimental studies and on
more general social psychology. Each section is preceded by an
editor's introduction.

Berscheid, Ellen, and Walster, Elaine H. INTERPERSONAL ATTRACTION.
Reading, Mass.: Addison-Wesley, 1969. xii, 129 p.

The authors discuss why people like the people they like, or the
determinants of interpersonal attraction. They look at the person
who is attracted and investigate the rewards which the attractive
other person provides, which may be the key to his or her attractiveness. These include reduction of anxiety, stress, loneliness,
or insecurity; propinquity; reciprocity of liking; or similarity.
References are included.

Crosbie, Paul V., ed. INTERACTION IN SMALL GROUPS. New York:
Macmillan, 1975. xii, 572 p.

This collection of thirty-three readings focuses on the motivational or social-psychological theories of group behavior, especially
exchange theory and balance theory. Also included are research

articles employing laboratory, field, and survey techniques. The three major divisions in the book--group formation, emergent group structures, and mediating group processes--are subdivided so that a wide range of topics is covered, including affiliation motives; sociometric, leadership, and communication structures; interpersonal power; conformity; and deviance. Each division is introduced by the editor. All articles have a list of references, and a bibliography is supplied.

Davis, Murray S. INTIMATE RELATIONS. New York: Free Press, 1973. xxv, 332 p.

The author deals with interpersonal relations between intimates, meaning friends, lovers, spouses, and siblings. Discussion is limited to those relations where the interacting individuals are relatively equal in power and status. Relationships are also, for the most part, two-person. Notes to the chapters and references are presented at the end of the book.

Duck, Steve W., ed. THEORY AND PRACTICE IN INTERPERSONAL AT-TRACTION. New York: Academic Press, 1977. 448 p.

The editor has assembled this set of readings to provide informa-tion on the topics covered as well as some insight into the meth-odology required. The first section deals with the major theories in the field, the second section describes empirical studies, and the third section puts interpersonal attraction in the context of other theories and discusses how these could account for attrac-tion processes.

Filley, Alan C. INTERPERSONAL CONFLICT RESOLUTION. Glenview, Ill.: Scott, Foresman, 1975. 180 p.

The author looks at win-lose and win-win strategies for conflict resolution. He demonstrates how conflict situations can be re-cast as decision-making and problem-solving situations of bene-fit to the parties involved. Leadership roles, the development of problem-solving attitudes, and personal styles of conflict resolu-tion are discussed. Exercises for practice are included.

Gergen, Kenneth J. THE PSYCHOLOGY OF BEHAVIOR EXCHANGE. Reading, Mass.: Addison-Wesley, 1969. xi, 109 p.

The author develops a theory of human interaction. The orienta-tion is that of behavior exchange, a tradition which draws heavi-ly on the results of experimental studies. Special attention is paid to interpersonal bargaining and to norms and roles. No bibliography is supplied, but a list of references follows each chapter.

Gibb, Jack R.; Platts, Grace N; and Miller, Lorraine F. DYNAMICS OF
PARTICIPATIVE GROUPS. Boulder: University of Colorado, 1951. vi, 81 p.

This manual, intended for circulation only to students of group
dynamics at the University of Colorado, is set up as a study
guide or handbook for groups seeking improvement. The authors
see it as having several uses: a reference book, a source of
discussion topics, and a combined laboratory manual and textbook.
It deals with principles of participative action as well as applications of these principles. A selected, classified bibliography
is supplied.

Goffman, Erving. THE PRESENTATION OF SELF IN EVERYDAY LIFE.
Garden City, N.Y.: Doubleday, 1959. xii, 259 p.

Various subtle features of social situations are analyzed, and the
text becomes a qualitive guide for such analysis. The author
makes the point that everyday life necessitates the playing of a
variety of roles on the part of any individual. He uses the
framework of theatrical performance to describe the processes involved.

_____. STRATEGIC INTERACTION. Philadelphia: University of Pennsylvania
Press, 1969. x, 145 p.

The author has written two essays on the analysis of behavior.
"Expression Games: An Analysis of Doubts at Play" examines
situations where a person must interpret the intentions and thoughts
of another when his or her observable behavior may not be a
reliable index. The other essay, "Strategic Interaction," concentrates on the more general problem of interpreting behavior
in situations that involve mutual independence. The author seeks
to demonstrate the limited analytical significance of communication in strategic interaction and thus to prepare the reader to
locate its limited place in the study of face-to-face conduct.

Heider, Fritz. THE PSYCHOLOGY OF INTERPERSONAL RELATIONS. New
York: Wiley, 1958. ix, 322 p.

The author uses a few basic elements to analyze complex interpersonal relations. The focus of attention is on the person rather
than the group; but because the person must in large part spend
time interacting, the elements of a group are present. Heider
seeks to construct a language to adequately represent a great
number of interpersonal relations. In so doing, underlying concepts must be identified, the patterns of which will suggest further relations, which demand further concepts, and so on. An
appendix presents a notation for representing interpersonal relations. A bibliography is included.

Hovland, Carl I.; Janis, Irving L; and Kelley, Harold H. COMMUNICA-
TION AND PERSUASION. PSYCHOLOGICAL STUDIES OF OPINION
CHANGE. New Haven, Conn.: Yale University Press, 1953. xii, 315 p.

    The research described in this book deals with four factors of
opinion change: the communicator, the stimuli transmitted (or
content of communication), the audience (considered both as a
group and as individuals), and their responses (both overtly expressed as well as retained over time if change occurs). Each
chapter is accompanied by references, and the book contains
seventeen figures and eighteen tables.

Kidder, Louise H., and Stewart, V. Mary. THE PSYCHOLOGY OF INTER-
GROUP RELATIONS: CONFLICT AND CONSCIOUSNESS. New York:
McGraw-Hill, 1975. xv, 128 p.

    The authors approach the field of prejudice from a practical per-
spective. Most of the material refers to North American black-
white and male-female relations; however, some material from
other lands and cultures is also included. There are five chapters, each stating a thesis at the beginning and elaborating it
by means of illustrative work. Questions left unanswered by
current research are aired, and the implications of the work for
society are discussed. A bibliography is included.

Kiesler, Charles A. THE PSYCHOLOGY OF COMMITMENT: EXPERIMENTS
LINKING BEHAVIOR TO BELIEF. New York: Academic Press, 1971. xii,
190 p.

    This is a research monograph describing a series of experiments
carried out by the author and several collaborators. One aspect
of commitment is studied, namely behavioral commitment, mostly
of the social kind. Discussion includes attitudes and behavior,
commitment and dissonance, forewarning, and self-attribution.
There is a section on commitment to future interaction with others
which deals with the effect of groups on commitment. The final
section deals with implications and related issues. References
are supplied.

Laing, Ronald D.; Phillipson, Herbert; and Lee, A. Russell. INTERPERSONAL
PERCEPTION. New York: Springer; London: Tavistock, 1966. vii, 179 p.

    The focus of the book is on dyadic encounters and the perceptions,
actions, and experiences that occur therein. Most of the discussion centers around husband-wife relations, but the principles are
applicable to wider settings. The authors present a theory and
develop a method for investigating dyads. The book is divided
into three parts: theory, method, and the questionnaire used
(the Interpersonal Perception Method, or IPM). A sample IPM
chart of a notional dyad is included.

Lippitt, Ronald; Watson, Jeanne; and Westley, Bruce. THE DYNAMICS OF PLANNED CHANGE. A COMPARATIVE STUDY OF PRINCIPLES AND TECHNIQUES. New York: Harcourt, Brace, 1958. viii, 312 p.

The concept of planned change is the focus of this book. The principles and techniques of change are described, and the areas of change potential in individual, group, and community settings are explored. The authors attempt a formulation of a general theory of change which may be applicable to planned change in a variety of settings. Attention is paid also to the training of change agents. A bibliography is included, divided into sections corresponding to the settings in which change agents work: individual, small group, organization, and community.

Mills, Theodore M. GROUP STRUCTURE AND THE NEWCOMER. AN EXPERIMENTAL STUDY OF GROUP EXPANSION. Oslo: Oslo University Press, 1957. 32 p.

The author and a team of collaborators conducted an experimental investigation of the relation between the newcomer and the group. Specifically, they tested the set of factors associated with the structure of the group. Using two role players interacting with a naive subject, they explored the newcomer's relationship with the subject, in particular, the extent to which each of the three members accepted and felt accepted by the others (i.e., the phenomenon of integration).

Parsons, Talcott; and Bales, Robert F.; with James Olds et al. FAMILY, SOCIALIZATION, AND INTERACTION PROCESS. Glencoe, Ill.: Free Press, 1955. xvii, 422 p.

The authors attempt to understand the functioning of the family and its place as part of the structure of modern society. To do this, facets of the family are explored from the standpoints of various disciplines; small-group theory is one of these. Two appendixes accompany the text: one on biological analogies to the social-psychological field, the other on analyzing equilibrium systems.

Schacter, Stanley. THE PSYCHOLOGY OF AFFILIATION: EXPERIMENTAL STUDIES OF THE SOURCES OF GREGARIOUSNESS. Stanford, Calif.: Stanford University Press, 1959. 141 p.

The author investigates the conditions which influence the human tendency to affiliate, for example, the effects excited by states of emotion and anxiety. Further data on the effects of birth order on affiliation are described. The effects of group membership on emotional states and the social determinants of emotional states are also discussed.

Scheidlinger, Saul. PSYCHOANALYSIS AND GROUP BEHAVIOR: A STUDY IN FREUDIAN GROUP PSYCHOLOGY. New York: W.W. Norton, 1952. 245 p.

The author takes a psychoanalytic view of the group using Freudian concepts to understand formation of an interaction in the group. These include identification, object-ties, and growth-promotion. The leader is seen as symbolic of the parent, and this conceptualization is evaluated with respect to education, social group work, and group psychotherapy. A bibliography is included.

Schmitt, Raymond L. THE REFERENCE OTHER ORIENTATION: AN EXTENSION OF THE REFERENCE GROUP CONCEPT. Carbondale: Southern Illinois University Press, 1972. xviii, 238 p.

The author conducts an intensive examination of the reference group literature. He emphasizes the importance of a set of reference group cognate concepts, otherwise known as a reference other orientation, which has emerged from this body of theory. Although maintaining a largely theoretical focus, the book has some implications for applied areas. A bibliography is included.

Sherif, Muzafer, and Cantril, Hadley. THE PSYCHOLOGY OF EGO-INVOLVEMENTS. New York: Wiley, 1947. viii, 525 p.

The development of ego-involvement and component ego attitudes depends on identification with membership and reference groups. Deprivation of various kinds, coupled with lack of social identification results in gangs which provide the missing security within their own set of status relationships and norms. Two chapters are devoted to the re-formation of the ego in adolescence.

Sherif, Muzafer, and Hovland, Carl I. SOCIAL JUDGEMENT. ASSIMILATION AND CONTRAST EFFECTS IN COMMUNICATION AND ATTITUDE CHANGE. New Haven, Conn.: Yale University Press, 1961. xii, 218 p.

The authors divide their work into two parts. The first deals with studies of judgment, wherein findings from psychophysical experiments are related to processes in social judgment. Part 2 focuses on studies of attitudes and communication effects. The findings are summarized, and applications and further research are suggested.

Sherif, Muzafer, and Sherif, Carolyn W. REFERENCE GROUPS: EXPLORATION INTO CONFORMITY AND DEVIATION OF ADOLESCENTS. New York: Harper and Row, 1964. xiv, 370 p.

This book is about group processes in a specific setting. The groups are composed of adolescents in present-day city life. The authors provide their research methodology as well as a body of

case material on their subjects. The result is a combination of
group dynamics and the applied area of youth problems and intergroup conflict. An appendix details the instructions to observers
of groups used in the study. A reference list is supplied.

Stock, Dorothy, and Thelen, Herbert A. EMOTIONAL DYNAMICS AND
GROUP CULTURE. EXPERIMENTAL STUDIES OF INDIVIDUAL AND GROUP
BEHAVIOR. New York: New York University Press for the National Training
Laboratories, 1958. xviii, 296 p.

The research program described considers the group as a system
whose properties depend upon its members and their network of
interaction, and views emotional factors as focal points of study.
The theory of group operation thus developed incorporates many of
Wilfrid R. Bion's basic ideas. Research is reported throughout the
book, and the theory is modified as findings indicate. Several
appendixes are included.

Stogdill, Ralph M. INDIVIDUAL BEHAVIOR AND GROUP ACHIEVEMENT.
A THEORY. THE EXPERIMENTAL EVIDENCE. New York: Oxford University Press, 1959. xi, 352 p.

The author sets out to develop a theory of organization achievement. Two assumptions are involved: that a group's structure
and activities can be described in terms of the behaviors of its
interacting members, and that input behaviors of group members
are transformed into forms of value represented by aspects of group
achievement. The author tests his theory by reference to experimental literature. The core chapters--interaction and group structure, performance and group operations, expectation and group
purpose, group structure and operations, and group achievement--
all have sections on research in their respective areas. A list of
794 references is supplied.

Tagiuri, Renato, and Petrullo, Luigi, eds. PERSON PERCEPTION AND INTER-
PERSONAL BEHAVIOR. Stanford, Calif.: Stanford University Press, 1958.
xx, 390 p.

This is a collection of twenty-three papers from the 1957 Harvard
Symposium on Person Perception. Contributors include Solomon
Asch, Lee Cronback, Fritz Heider, and Theodore Newcomb.
Topics range from phenomenal causality and Ojibwa metaphysics
of being to problem solving and group effectiveness. Each paper
is followed by a list of references.

Tedeschi, James T., ed. THE SOCIAL INFLUENCE PROCESSES. Chicago:
Aldine-Atherton, 1972. x, 432 p.

This book of readings examines the processes involved in social
influence from a variety of standpoints. The effects of an individ-

ual's perception of the situation, personality factors, the role of cognitive complexity, and attraction are some of the aspects considered. The tactical use of social power and the source of influence are also dealt with. Finally the editor and two of his colleagues attempt a general theory of social influence process as they affect the target individual. Each reading includes a list of references and a general index is provided.

Tedeschi, James T.; Schlenker, Barry R.; and Bonoma, Thomas V. CONFLICT, POWER AND GAMES: THE EXPERIMENTAL STUDY OF INTERPERSONAL RELATIONS. Chicago: Aldine-Atherton, 1973. x, 270 p.

The authors present a wide-ranging review and integrative model for the linear analysis of social influence. The organizing concept in the book is the Subjective Expected Utility (SEU) theory, which is represented by a flow diagram. Theoretical accounts of social interaction in laboratory game situations are discussed. The models illustrated are linear and additive.

Triandis, Harry C. INTERPERSONAL BEHAVIOR. Monterey, Calif.: Brooks/ Cole, 1977. xiii, 329 p.

The author presents a summary of the literature in the field of interpersonal behavior, and a theoretical framework for use in the study of this field. His major predictor variable is the behavioral intention, which is a function of social, affective, and cognitive determinants. The model is applied to the literature. Techniques of changing interpersonal behaviors and applications to specific settings are discussed. Twenty-seven pages of references are included.

Zaleznik, Abraham, and Moment, David. THE DYNAMICS OF INTERPERSONAL BEHAVIOR. New York: Wiley, 1964. ix, 520 p.

This book deals with the structure and dynamics of groups in work situations. It involves theory, case studies, and experimental problems. Part 1 examines group and interpersonal processes; part 2 looks at interpersonal dynamics; part 3 discusses organizational aspects of group behavior; and part 4 is concerned with a research index comprising field and experimental studies, research summaries and theories, and survey research.

Zander, Alvin, and Medow, Herman. GROUP ASPIRATIONS AND GROUP COPING BEHAVIOR. Ann Arbor: Research Center for Group Dynamics, Institute for Social Research, University of Michigan, 1964. vi, 174 p.

The authors describe a series of laboratory experiments on group goals. Groups of high school boys were instructed to choose

goals and allowed to change the goals several times if they so
wished. A number of other variables were explored in different
studies, for example, social influences on group aspirations, and
observers' expectations or members' test anxiety and competence
as determinants of group aspirations. A list of references follows
each study.

# B. ROLES

Biddle, Bruce J.; Twyman, J. Paschal; and Rankin, Earl F., Jr. THE CON-
CEPT OF ROLE CONFLICT. Arts and Science Studies, Social Studies Series
no. 11. Stillwater: Oklahoma State University of Agriculture and Applied
Science, n.d.

> The authors provide an annotated bibliography on role conflict and
> examine the logical relationships among definitions of role conflict,
> suggesting some further definitions. They also describe a general
> set of constructs applicable to role conflict as well as to the
> broader area of role theory. Section 1 of the paper sets out the
> conceptual system, section 2 presents the findings relating to role
> conflict, and section 3 is the annotated bibliography of fifty-two
> entries.

Gross, Neal; Mason, Ward S.; and McEachern, Alexander W. EXPLORATIONS
IN ROLE ANALYSIS: STUDIES OF THE SCHOOL SUPERINTENDENCY ROLE.
New York: Wiley, 1958. xiv, 379 p.

> This book analyzes the problems of consensus on role definition,
> role-conflict resolution, and conformity to expectations. The
> authors report a group of empirical studies set up to explore these
> issues. The appendix presents tabulated data and examples of the
> scales and original instruments used in the studies. Each chapter
> is followed by a list of notes and references.

Haas, J. Eugene. ROLE CONCEPTION AND GROUP CONSENSUS: A
STUDY OF DISHARMONY IN HOSPITAL WORK GROUPS. Columbus: Bureau
of Business Research, Ohio State University, 1964. xiv, 138 p.

> This study employs the concept of social role in the activity of
> the group. It involved 198 persons on ten hospital stations in two
> hospitals. The findings indicate that low role consensus in per-
> manent groups is directly related to annoyance and disharmony.
> Instruments used include the Role Performance Rating Chart and
> the Role Conception Inventory, copies of which are supplied in
> appendixes. A short bibliography is included.

Lumpkin, Katherine D. THE FAMILY: A STUDY OF MEMBER ROLES. Chapel
Hill: University of North Carolina Press, 1933. xix, 184 p.

This book applies some basic sociological principles of family relationships and organization to a group of families who were subjects of an intensive case study. Part 1 explores theoretically the
social process in family life: the roles of family members, inter-
role relationships, and the family social situation. Part 2 focuses
on member roles in the case study: family role patterns, member
role conflicts, and the process of role adjustment. Tables are
contained in the appendix.

Moment, David, and Zaleznik, Abraham. ROLE DEVELOPMENT AND INTER-
PERSONAL COMPETENCE: AN EXPERIMENTAL STUDY OF ROLE PERFOR-
MANCES IN PROBLEM-SOLVING GROUPS. Cambridge, Mass.: Harvard
University Press, 1963. xvi, 346 p.

This book presents a description of the results from a series of
experimental studies designed to explore the performances of individuals in problem-solving groups and the relation between individual development and motivation and performance in the group.
The authors focus on development and its relation to work styles
in interactions with other people. The implications of applying
developmental theory to education for executive responsibility are
discussed. A series of appendixes present the technical data relating to the study. A short bibliography is included.

Perlman, Helen [Harris]. PERSONA: SOCIAL ROLE AND PERSONALITY.
Chicago: University of Chicago Press, 1968. 245 p.

The author deals with the importance of roles as fundamental to
the way persons present themselves to the world. She concentrates on vital roles which involve not only a person in those
roles but also at least one other person. The importance of roles
in work, in marriage, and in parenthood is stressed for the adult
personality. Role problems such as ambiguity and identity concerns are discussed. Notes and references are presented for each
chapter.

Preiss, Jack J., and Ehrlich, Howard J. AN EXAMINATION OF ROLE
THEORY: THE CASE OF THE STATE POLICE. Lincoln: University of
Nebraska Press, 1966. xi, 286 p.

The authors present a series of interlocking studies on a state
police department whose administration wanted information about
the structure and operation of its organization. Their intention
was to delimit the boundaries of role analysis, exploring from a
role theoretical perspective, the processes of role acquisition, role
expectations, and role performance. Appendixes provide examples
of the technical material used. A bibliography is included.

Rommetveit, Ragnar.  SOCIAL NORMS AND ROLES:  EXPLORATIONS IN
THE PSYCHOLOGY OF ENDURING SOCIAL PRESSURES WITH EMPIRICAL
CONTRIBUTIONS FROM INQUIRIES INTO RELIGIOUS ATTITUDES AND SEX
ROLES OF ADOLESCENTS FROM SOME DISTRICTS IN WESTERN NORWAY.
Translated by Elizabeth Rokkan.  Oslo:  Akademisk Forlag; Minneapolis:  Uni-
versity of Minnesota Press, 1955.  xi, 167 p.

> The book is divided into two parts.  Part 1 comprises a theoreti-
> cal study of the psychology of enduring social pressure.  Part 2
> describes empirical work carried out on the basis of the theoreti-
> cal framework developed in part 1.  A set of appendixes presents
> the instruments used in the study, both in the original Norwegian
> version and in their English translation, along with the scoring
> procedures.

Zander, Alvin; Cohen, Arthur R.; and Stotland, Ezra; in collaboration with
Bernard Humovitch and Otto Riedl.  ROLE RELATIONS IN THE MENTAL
HEALTH PROFESSIONS.  Ann Arbor: University of Michigan, 1957.  vii,
211 p.

> This is a report of a study carried out at the Research Center for
> Group Dynamics of the Institute for Social Research on intergroup
> attitudes and behavior among the members of three professional
> groups:  psychiatrists, psychiatric social workers, and clinical
> psychologists.  The conditions which seem to determine these feel-
> ings are examined.  The methods used to obtain the data are in-
> cluded in the text and elaborated in the appendix in three sec-
> tions:  the sample, the interview, and tables of data.

## C.  GROUP COHESION AND GROUP CONFLICT

Benne, Kenneth D; Bradford, Leland P.; and Lippitt, Ronald.  GROUP
DYNAMICS AND SOCIAL ACTION.  New York: Anti-Defamation League of
B'nai B'rith, 1950.  61 p.

> The authors aim to facilitate problem solving in groups and organi-
> zations, noting that society is increasingly group centered.  Through
> a description of the activities of a "society for democracy" they
> show how a group can function so that democracy is increased, not
> discouraged.  Through this device, techniques are presented which
> can be applied to a variety of other groups.  The book ends with
> a set of dos and don'ts for social action in order that the planned
> solution of action problems might be achieved.

Billig, Michael.  SOCIAL PSYCHOLOGY AND INTERGROUP RELATIONS.
New York: Academic Press in cooperation with the EUROPEAN JOURNAL OF
EXPERIMENTAL SOCIAL PSYCHOLOGY, 1976.  x, 428 p.

This volume takes a critical stance on many traditional approaches to the study of intergroup behavior. Billig emphasizes the political dimension which he considers a fundamental aspect of the field. Experimental studies of conflict are examined, and an attempt is made to integrate findings from other disciplines. Topics include Freud's group psychology, post-Freudian group psychology, gaming and rational conflict, group ideology, and the context of intergroup relations. References are supplied.

Blau, Peter M. EXCHANGE AND POWER IN SOCIAL LIFE. New York: Wiley, 1964. 352 p.

The author's starting point is that any theory of social structure requires first that the processes involved in interpersonal relations be understood. He moves through the processes of structure, cohesion, exchange, power, and change, culminating in a discussion of social forces. A chapter-by-chapter synopsis of the book appears at the beginning.

Chase, Stuart, in collaboration with Marian Tyler Chase. ROADS TO AGREE-MENT. SUCCESSFUL METHODS IN THE SCIENCE OF HUMAN RELATIONS. New York: Harper and Bros., 1951. xiii, 250 p.

The author probes the area of conflict and discourses on both the art and science of agreement. In exploring various potential tension-producing areas, he suggests five factors which may defuse discord and promote agreement. Training clinics and laboratories are included, as are role playing and the place of semantics in producing agreement. A short bibliography is supplied.

Cook, Lloyd A., ed. TOWARD BETTER HUMAN RELATIONS. Detroit: Wayne State University Press, 1952. 121 p.

This set of five lectures was originally presented as the first annual Leo M. Franklin Lectures in Human Relations. The contributors represent various disciplines, and the topics include functional democracy in human relations, intergroup relations, and the group dynamic approach to achieving change in people. References are contained within the articles.

Coser, Lewis A. THE FUNCTIONS OF SOCIAL CONFLICT. New York: Free Press, 1956. 188 p.

The author defines social conflict as a struggle over values and claims to power, status, and scarce resources. In this struggle, the opponents aim to injure, neutralize, or eliminate their rivals. The focus of the book is on the functions of social conflict, by which Coser means the consequences of such conflict that result in increased adjustment or adaptation of certain groups or social

relationships. In so doing, he seeks to effect a balance in the
study of social conflict, too often regarded with respect to its
negative aspects. Chapter-by-chapter notes and references are
included.

Dean, John P.; and Rosen, Alex; with the assistance of Robert B. Johnson.
A MANUAL OF INTERGROUP RELATIONS. Chicago: University of Chicago
Press, 1963. xxv, 193 p.

The authors--one a sociologist, one a social worker--seek to make
available to intergroup practitioners some of the outcomes of research in intergroup relations. The focus is on the interracial
field, and problems of communication, desegregation, and integration in an organizational setting are discussed. The authors
then broaden the area of application to the community at large.
A selected bibliography of thirty annotated entries is included.

Deutsch, Morton. THE RESOLUTION OF CONFLICT; CONSTRUCTIVE AND
DESTRUCTIVE PROCESSES. New Haven, Conn.: Yale University Press, 1973.
xi, 420 p.

The author presents a summary of his own thought and work in the
field of conflict resolution. The book is divided into three parts.
The first part is a set of seven theoretical essays dealing with such
topics as cooperative and competitive processes, group formation,
and intergroup conflict. The second part consists of five research
papers, which include experimental studies of trust and suspicion,
the effects of threat, and strategies of inducing cooperation. The
third part is a concluding essay on factors influencing the resolution of conflict. A bibliography is included.

Gardner, Eric F., and Thompson, George G. SOCIAL RELATIONS AND
MORALE IN SMALL GROUPS. New York: Appleton-Century-Crofts, 1956.
ix, 312 p.

The authors develop a number of instruments for measuring social
relations. Specifically, they measure each person's estimate of
how well other group members can satisfy several of his or her
psychological needs. The social relations indexes are shown to be
predictors of the group-effectiveness component of morale, and of
fraternity subjects' membership and leadership in other organized
groups. A short bibliography is included.

Greco, Marshall C. GROUP LIFE: THE NATURE AND TREATMENT OF ITS
SPECIFIC CONFLICTS. New York: Philosophical Library, 1950. xvi, 357 p.

The author takes a social organismic approach to the study of psychopathology. His understanding of such a problem is that its
roots lie in forces related to the whole of life (group life), rather

than to individual, internal workings of the mind. The emphasis is ahistorical: it is the current significance of one's life-forces that is at issue. The neurotic symptom is a way of reconciling the group elements that dominate the person and are in conflict. Thus the neurotic must be seen in terms of motives that are an incident of this current group life. A bibliography is supplied, along with a list of publications of staff members in the Research Center for Group Dynamics, University of Michigan, compiled by Ronald Lippitt.

Israel, Joachim. SELF-EVALUATION AND REJECTION IN GROUPS: THREE EXPERIMENTAL STUDIES AND A CONCEPTUAL OUTLINE. Uppsala, Sweden: Almqvist and Wiksell, 1956. 250 p.

The author develops part of a theory of small group functioning by concentrating on the processes of evaluation and rejection in groups. Cohesiveness, social reality, self-evaluation in groups, and rejection of deviants are discussed. Experimental studies are described: one concerns the rejection of deviants under threat, another focuses on the differential rejection of superior and inferior group members, and the final one deals with conflict between self-evaluation and the evaluation of self by the groups.

Lewin, Kurt. RESOLVING SOCIAL CONFLICTS: SELECTED PAPERS ON GROUP DYNAMICS. New York: Harper, 1948. xviii, 230 p.

The author begins with the problem of democratic reeducation. To achieve and maintain democracy, special attention must be paid to leadership, values, and the structure of the group. Some specific group conflicts and their solutions are described. The book concludes with a section on group prejudice and tension.

Libo, Lester M. MEASURING GROUP COHESIVENESS. Ann Arbor: Survey Research Center, Institute for Social Research, University of Michigan, 1953. ix, 111 p.

This book deals mainly with the concept of attraction-to-group. Libo discusses the concept and methods for both its measurement and its experimental manipulation. The development and investigation of two measures are presented: a behavioral measure involving locomotion, and a projective technique. Miscellaneous exploratory studies are discussed in the appendix. A list of references is supplied.

Mikalachki, Alexander. GROUP COHESION RECONSIDERED: A STUDY OF BLUE COLLAR WORK GROUPS. London: School of Business Administration, University of Western Ontario, Canada, 1969. xiii, 122 p.

This book describes a study of group cohesion in an industrial setting. The author attempts to denote what it is, what conditions facilitate its development, and what its effects are on variables such as absenteeism, level of productivity, and tension. There is a section on the four types of cohesive groups. Appendixes provide information on the methodology of the study with examples of the instruments used. A list of references is supplied.

Nye, Robert D. CONFLICT AMONG HUMANS. New York: Springer, 1973. xv, 203 p.

The author explores some of the factors which make for conflict among individuals and groups of individuals, and also ways of reducing or preventing conflict. Prejudice, conformity and obedience, and aggressiveness are discussed in relation to their part in producing conflict and in relation to methods for defusing conflict situations. A list of references is supplied.

Seashore, Stanley E. GROUP COHESIVENESS IN THE INDUSTRIAL WORK GROUP. Ann Arbor: Survey Research Center, Institute for Social Research, University of Michigan, 1954. vi, 107 p.

This study of group cohesiveness describes the background and theoretical orientation of the investigation, and explores cohesiveness in relation to other variables: anxiety (especially concerning work), productivity standards, and the conditions which may facilitate cohesiveness. The latter factor includes member similarity, occupational prestige, and opportunity for interaction. A bibliography is supplied.

Sherif, Muzafer. IN COMMON PREDICAMENT: SOCIAL PSYCHOLOGY OF INTERGROUP CONFLICT AND COOPERATION. Boston: Houghton Mifflin, 1966. xv, 192 p.

Sherif works toward a social psychology of international relations through an examination of the roots of aggression and an experimental study of intergroup conflict. Measures for the reduction of intergroup conflict are explored, and their implications on a wider social basis are discussed. A reference list is included.

Sherif, Muzafer, and Sherif, Carolyn W. GROUPS IN HARMONY AND TENSION. New York: Harper, 1953. xiii, 316 p.

Intergroup tensions are experimentally induced. The authors' purpose is to develop methods of judging a variety of phenomena in an experimental group setting. Included are learning, judgmental, motivational, and perceptual processes. Illustrations accompany the text.

Stogdill, Ralph M.  TEAM ACHIEVEMENT UNDER HIGH MOTIVATION.
Research Monograph 113.  Columbus:  Bureau of Business Research, Ohio State
University, 1963.  xvi, 92 p.

> The author and his colleagues tested the hypothesis that, given
> conditions of high motivational inputs, three aspects of organiza-
> tion achievement--morale, integration, and productivity--may be
> positively correlated.  Ratings were made of six football games on
> four variables: coordination, structure, pressure, and spirit.  The
> results support the hypothesis.  Examples of the rating scales and
> record forms are included.

Watson, Goodwin, ed.  CIVILIAN MORALE.  THE YEARBOOKS OF THE
SOCIETY FOR THE PSYCHOLOGICAL STUDY OF SOCIAL ISSUES.  Vol. 2.
New York:  Reynal and Hitchcock, 1942.  xii, 463 p.

> This collection of readings is designed to present the then-avail-
> able research on morale.  It is divided into five parts:  theory of
> morale, how morale develops, the state of American morale, morale
> in industry, and recommendations.  Contributors include the editor,
> Gordon W. Allport, Kurt Lewin, Ronald Lippitt, Theodore New-
> comb, Otto Klineberg, and Gardner Murphy.  The bibliography is
> alphabetized and numbered separately for each chapter.

Williams, Robin M., Jr.  THE REDUCTION OF INTERGROUP TENSIONS: A
SURVEY OF RESEARCH ON PROBLEMS OF ETHNIC, RACIAL, AND RELIGIOUS
GROUP RELATIONS.  New York:  Social Science Research Council, 1947.
xi, 153 p.

> In this report for the publishers, the author surveys the techniques
> used by action agencies which seek to resolve conflict and reduce
> hostility in interracial and intercultural group relations in the
> United States.  He analyzes the assumptions underlying these pro-
> grams and suggests research to test them.  Major theorems and
> working hypotheses are presented which have relevance for the
> social conflict problem.  A series of research projects is proposed
> and some designs outlined as suggestions for research planning.
> The appendix includes relevant research methods and techniques.
> A bibliography is also provided.

# Chapter 4

# GROUP INFLUENCES

Adorno, T.W.; Frenkel-Brunswik, Else; Levinson, Daniel J.; and Sanford, R. Nevitt. THE AUTHORITARIAN PERSONALITY. 2d ed. New York: W.W. Norton, 1969. xxxiii, 990 p.

The authors undertake a study of prejudice and its personality correlates. They develop a number of measures, relating to ideological trends, and their instruments are revised and elaborated with further investigation. Ethnocentrism, anti-Semitism and antidemocratism are measured, and interviews and projective techniques provide data on personality types. Applications of the research are discussed, and many tables and figures are provided. The authors cite 121 references.

Asch, Solomon E. SOCIAL PSYCHOLOGY. New York: Prentice-Hall, 1952. 646 p.

The psychological study of man is viewed as necessarily involving social behavior. The author discusses basic organization in psychological events and human interaction, which leads him to group theory. Considerable attention is given to group effects on judgments and attitudes. References appear at the end of each chapter.

Berg, Irwin A., and Bass, Bernard M., eds. CONFORMITY AND DEVIATION. New York: Harper and Bros., 1961. viii, 449 p.

This is a collection of hitherto unpublished papers which were presented at a symposium on conformity and deviation held at Louisana State University in March 1960. Social psychological aspects and clinical-experimental studies are presented. Contributors include Solomon Asch, Robert Blake and Jane Mouton, Donald Campbell, Milton Rokeach, Muzafer Sherif, and David Wechsler. Each article has a list of references.

Cohen, Bernard P., and Lee, Hans. CONFLICT, CONFORMITY, AND SOCIAL STATUS. Vol. 7. New York: Elsevier, 1975. xii, 203 p.

> The authors provide a history and case study of the development of a new paradigm for Asch-like conformity situations. Further, they describe new results regarding the process of resolving a conflict between a social stimulus and a visual stimulus. This information helps provide a method for studying this kind of conflict, and broadens our ideas about the processes of the dynamics of conformity. The model used by the authors is a revised Markov chain model.

Freedman, Jonathan L., and Doob, Anthony N. DEVIANCY: THE PSYCHOLOGY OF BEING DIFFERENT. New York: Academic Press, 1968. viii, 158 p.

> This is a report of an empirical study of deviancy. The authors produced feelings of deviancy by experimental manipulation, without specifying the precise nature of the deviancy. The behavior of those who are made to feel deviant is compared with those who are not. The phenomena of aggression, conformity, attitude change, and compliance are discussed in the context of the study. Each chapter is summarized. A short list of references is supplied.

Kiesler, Charles A., and Kiesler, Sara B. CONFORMITY. Reading, Mass.: Addison-Wesley, 1969. 114 p.

> This book is about the problem of social influence. The authors review the meaning of conformity as well as some relevant research. A distinction is made between compliance and private acceptance. Interpersonal and cognitive variables are considered in relation to private acceptance. The text is intended for beginning students of social psychology. Each section is summarized and a list of references is supplied.

Mehrabian, Albert. TACTICS OF SOCIAL INFLUENCE. Englewood Cliffs, N.J.: Prentice-Hall, 1970. viii, 152 p.

> This is a primer of behavior modification and a manual for applying its principles in the form of concrete actions. In discussing the methods of behavior modification, the author cites some principles and then demonstrates their application to various situations in which one desires change in one's own or another's behavior. Examples range from simple situations such as improving one's working habits to complex problems such as the management of large groups of persons or the ways in which people communicate their feelings and influence one another. A list of references is included.

White, Ralph K., and Lippitt, Ronald. AUTOCRACY AND DEMOCRACY: AN EXPERIMENTAL INQUIRY. New York: Harper and Bros., 1960. x, 330 p.

> The authors describe two experiments in which one of the authors acted as leader of a group of eleven-year-old children. In one group he was a democratic leader, in the other an autocratic one. Part 1 of the book deals with the actual experiments and the observed behaviors of the participants. Part 2 presents an interpretation of the findings. Part 3 describes some individuals in the groups and their backgrounds, and notes how their behavior illuminates the question of personality variables in the promotion of democracy. Part 4 discusses the implications of the findings. A bibliography is included.

Witt, Robert E. GROUP INFLUENCE ON CONSUMER BRAND CHOICE. Studies in Marketing no. 13. Austin: Bureau of Business Research, University of Texas, 1970. xi, 79 p.

> This study has two purposes: to investigate the influence of small informal social groups on the brand choices of group members, and to examine the relationship of reference theory to the consumer-purchase process. This enables the findings to be evaluated and also suggests areas of potentially fruitful research. The study is described in detail, and the appendixes supply examples of instruments used and some additional data. A bibliography is provided.

Zander, Alvin. MOTIVES AND GOALS IN GROUPS. New York: Academic Press, 1971. xiv, 212 p.

> This book summarizes the results of a series of studies on group aspirations and members' motives. The focus is on the plans or actions of members on behalf of the entire group. Interaction among members is secondary; the group and its needs are primary. The early studies in the series were designed to be most relevant to an educational setting. For these, the subjects were volunteer high school students and, in some cases, teachers. Each chapter closes with a summary, and the book concludes with an overview of all the findings. A list of references is supplied.

# Chapter 5
# POWER IN GROUPS

## A. DYNAMICS OF POWER

Bennis, Warren G., et al., eds. THE PLANNING OF CHANGE. 3d ed. New York: Holt, Rinehart and Winston, 1976. ix, 517 p.

The editors present a collection of readings dealing with discussions and evaluations of change technologies. An important aspect of their purpose is to provide material aid in the education and development of persons who can function as agents of planned change. Diagnostics of planned change are discussed, along with interventions for planned change. A final section deals with values and goals. Each reading includes references.

Cartwright, Dorwin, ed. STUDIES IN SOCIAL POWER. Ann Arbor: University of Michigan, 1959. ix, 225 p.

Throughout this collection, power is considered as the ability of one person or group to influence or control some feature of another person or group. Power is treated in some articles as an independent variable; its threatening potential and people's response to this are examined. The establishment of power and the determinants of power in natural groups are also dealt with. An effort is made to develop a theoretical framework for power. Each article is followed by a list of references.

Coyle, Grace L. SOCIAL PROCESS IN ORGANIZED GROUPS. New York: R.R. Smith, 1930. xvi, 245 p.

The author examines the processes by which an organized group acts. Topics include group formation, leadership, social functions, and communication. The conditions of group morale are also explored. The kinds of groups may vary; it is the pattern of relationships common to them that forms the subject matter under investigation. A selected bibliography is supplied.

Gamson, William A. POWER AND DISCONTENT. Homewood, Ill.: Dorsey Press, 1968. xi, 208 p.

The author approaches the issue of power from two perspectives which are both concerned with the same relationship but which ask different questions about it: the influence perspective and the social control perspective. Trust relationships, influence processes, the management of discontent, and the implications for social change and its study are all explored. A bibliography is included.

Kornhauser, Arthur W. PROBLEMS OF POWER IN AMERICAN DEMOCRACY. Detroit: Wayne State University Press, 1957. ix, 239 p.

This book of lectures focuses on the part played by conflicting interests and inequalities of power among individuals and organizations. It deals with analyses of the power structure, the effects of unbalanced distribution of influence and authority, and the compatibility of existing American power relations with full realization of democratic human relations. Discussion sections follow each of the five presentations. References are listed by chapter.

Lang, Kurt, and Lang, Gladys E. COLLECTIVE DYNAMICS. New York: Thomas Y. Crowell, 1961. xii, 563 p.

This volume focuses on certain dynamic aspects of social and institutional change. The processes whereby the thoughts and actions of persons are transformed in collectivities is discussed. Among the topics dealt with are crowd behavior, mass conversion, contagion, leadership, conformity, and social movements. The bibliography appears chapter by chapter.

## B. LEADERSHIP

Argyris, Chris. INCREASING LEADERSHIP EFFECTIVENESS. New York: Wiley-Interscience, 1976. xvi, 286 p.

This book deals with the theory of double loop learning (learning to change underlying assumptions and values), and the relation of such learning to a theory of effective leadership. The author examines how to change individuals' theories of action through an experiment which is described in the book. Part 1 presents the theoretical framework and the setting used to introduce the learning environment to potential subjects. Part 2 describes the learning seminars and the model of double loop learning. Part 3 deals with methodological issues. A short bibliography is included.

Bass, Bernard M. LEADERSHIP, PSYCHOLOGY, AND ORGANIZATIONAL
BEHAVIOR. New York: Harper and Bros., 1960. xiii, 548 p.

> This social psychology text discusses the interaction process and
> attempts to develop a theory based on both empirical evidence
> and reason, mostly drawing on the fields of sociology and psychol-
> ogy. Bass acknowledges the influence of works on leadership by
> political philosophers. Topics covered include ability to lead,
> coercive and permissive leadership, and status and esteem in re-
> lation to leadership. A bibliography of 1,155 entries is supplied.

Beal, George M.; Bohlen, Joe M.; and Raudabaugh, J. Neil. LEADERSHIP
AND DYNAMIC GROUP ACTION. Ames: Iowa State University Press, 1962.
365 p.

> The authors direct their book at the layman who wishes to be-
> come a more effective group member. The general processes of
> group interaction are discussed (dynamics, goals, techniques, and
> productivity), and group techniques to facilitate action toward
> goals are presented in the context of specific potentials, the
> nature of the desired goal, and the characteristics of the group.
> The importance of effective groups for the continuation of democ-
> racy is stressed. A chapter-by-chapter list of suggested readings
> is supplied.

Bellows, Roger. CREATIVE LEADERSHIP. Englewood Cliffs, N.J.: Prentice-
Hall, 1959. xiv, 338 p.

> The author's theory of leadership is eclectic. His emphasis is on
> a conception of leadership as a function of the group through the
> participation and expression of its members. The conditions of
> leadership are seen as dynamic and evolving. The focus is on
> the empirical in the discussion of planned adaptation and growth
> in leadership. The author stresses the creative aspect; leadership
> of this quality involves providing the conditions for achieving
> mutual goals and understanding. Tension and conflict are exam-
> ined, and leadership methods discussed. A bibliography is sup-
> plied.

Bogardus, Emory S. LEADERS AND LEADERSHIP. New York: Appleton-
Century, 1934. viii, 325 p.

> The author examines the phenomenon of leadership on the basis
> of biographies and other life records of leaders. From his re-
> search, he develops theories of the origins of leadership (heredity,
> social stimuli, and personality traits) and the principles of lead-
> ership. A set of appendixes gives lists of leaders and their
> achievements, a selected bibliography, and a rating scale.

Browne, Clarence G., and Cohn, Thomas S., eds. THE STUDY OF LEADER-
SHIP. Danville, Ill.: Interstate Printers and Publishers, 1958. 487 p.

> This is a collection of previously published material dealing with
> a number of aspects of leadership. No one theory pervades; in-
> stead, a sampling of many viewpoints is presented. The four
> parts of the book cover topics such as the measurement of leader-
> ship, the criteria of leadership, the dynamic aspects of leader
> behavior, perception, personality, and approaches to leadership
> training. Each contains a list of references.

Busch, Henry M. LEADERSHIP IN GROUP WORK. New York: Association
Press, 1938. vi, 305 p.

> The author directs his book at group workers, both professional
> and volunteer. He discusses social and educational factors af-
> fecting group work and devotes attention to leadership, including
> a chapter on educational leadership. The book closes with a
> commentary on the forms and uses of group records. Each chapter
> is summarized and has a list of references.

Campbell, Donald T. LEADERSHIP AND ITS EFFECTS UPON THE GROUP.
Ohio Studies in Personnel, Monograph no. R-83. Columbus: Bureau of Business Research, Ohio State University, 1956. xi, 92 p.

> The author constructs a definition of leadership in terms of its
> effects on the group. He examines measures of group morale and
> effectiveness, as well as leader behavior, authority and responsi-
> bility, leadership effectiveness ratings, and sociometric measures
> of personal interaction.

Coyle, Grace L., ed. STUDIES IN GROUP BEHAVIOR. New York: Association Press, 1937. x, 258 p.

> This is a collection of five case studies set up as part of a pro-
> gram of a social settlement in an American city. The author
> hopes to add to available information on group leadership, and
> intends the book both for group workers and for social scientists
> of more academic bent. An appendix provides a copy of the
> record form used in the study.

Dubin, Robert, et al. LEADERSHIP AND PRODUCTIVITY. SOME FACTS OF
INDUSTRIAL LIFE. San Francisco: Chandler, 1965. ix, 138 p.

> This is a book of four parts, each written by a different author
> and all dealing with the issue of the influence leaders can have
> on their followers and associates in increasing their productivity.
> Empirical knowledge is combined with sociological theory in this
> examination. Each analysis is made in the context of formal or-
> ganization theory. The importance of technology and of organi-
> zational variables is emphasized. References are contained with-
> in each section.

Fiedler, Fred E. A THEORY OF LEADERSHIP EFFECTIVENESS. New York: McGraw-Hill, 1967. 310 p.

> The author presents the results of his research over a fifteen-year period in the area of classifying groups and group tasks. A theory of leadership is developed, based on some of these data, and leadership problems are discussed. He highlights some implications for the selection and training of leaders in the interest of maximizing the effectiveness not only of the leaders themselves, but also of the groups and organizations in which they exist.

Fiedler, Fred E., and Chemers, Martin M. LEADERSHIP AND EFFECTIVE MANAGEMENT. Glenview, Ill.: Scott, Foresman, 1974. 166 p.

> This is largely a condensation of work already reported. It is addressed to students of management and to the practicing manager. Concepts and research on leadership are reviewed. The nature of the contingency model is discussed and empirical support for it is presented. The book concludes with chapters on the implications of the model for leader selections, promotion, rotation, and training.

Fiedler, Fred E.; and Chemers, Martin M.; with Linda Mahar. IMPROVING LEADERSHIP EFFECTIVENESS: THE LEADER MATCH CONCEPT. New York: Wiley, 1976. 230 p.

> This is a self-instructional manual designed to help the reader become a more effective leader. The manual is divided into four parts: identifying your leadership style, tools for diagnosing and classifying leadership situations, how to match your leadership style with your situation and how to change your leadership situation, and how to provide subordinate leaders with situations in which they can perform most effectively. The appendix supplies a copy of each of the scales necessary for applying the concepts of Leader Match.

Fleishman, Edwin A., and Hunt, James G., eds. CURRENT DEVELOPMENTS IN THE STUDY OF LEADERSHIP. Carbondale: Southern Illinois University Press, 1974. xx, 317 p.

> This is a collection of papers presented at a symposium held in 1971 at Southern Illinois University. The focus is chiefly on the history and research from the Ohio State leadership studies, and on work arising from Fiedler's model. Debate centers around whether there is one best style of leadership; no explicit verdict emerges.

Freeman, Graydon L., and Taylor E. HOW TO PICK LEADERS. A SCIENTIFIC APPROACH TO EXECUTIVE SELECTION. New York: Funk and Wagnalls in association with MODERN INDUSTRY MAGAZINE, 1950. vii, 226 p.

The authors attempt to discover from research work the common elements of the leadership pattern, and to show how that pattern can be used to improve the search for executive talent and render selection practices scientific. Included are chapters on recruiting and screening, aptitude testing, proficiency, and personality. The final chapter deals with career management for selectees.

Gordon, Thomas. GROUP-CENTERED LEADERSHIP. A WAY OF RELEASING THE CREATIVE POWER OF GROUPS. Boston: Houghton Mifflin, 1955. xii, 366 p.

The author describes one kind of leadership, in which the aim of the leader is to draw out the creative resources of the group members. The theoretical foundations of this kind of leadership are discussed and then it is put into practice in an experimental case study. A further case study in an industrial setting is described. The book is addressed to anyone responsible for the functioning and development of groups.

Gouldner, Alvin W., ed. STUDIES IN LEADERSHIP. New York: Harper, 1950. xvi, 736 p.

This is an anthology of analyses of leadership made by social scientists. It is divided into five sections, dealing with types of leaders, leadership and its group settings, authoritarian and democratic leaders, ethics and techniques of leadership, and affirmations and resolutions. Each section is prefaced by commentary by the editor, in which he describes frameworks for the articles and offers brief summaries.

Grace, Alonzo G., comp. and ed. LEADERSHIP IN AMERICAN EDUCATION. Chicago: University of Chicago Press, 1950. vi, 137 p.

This book constitutes the proceedings of the Cooperative Conference for Administrative Officers of Public and Private Schools held in 1950. The theme is the enhancement of the dynamic leadership required in an educational system which operates under a democratic government. Status correlates of leadership, lay leadership in education, personality as a factor in leadership, the role of state boards in education, and governmental responsibility for educational leadership are among the topics covered. Each paper contains a list of references. A panel discussion is presented along with a set of reports of commissions.

Guetzkow, Harold., ed. GROUPS, LEADERSHIP AND MEN: RESEARCH IN HUMAN RELATIONS. Pittsburgh: Carnegie Press, 1951. ix, 293 p.

This collection is the outgrowth of a conference funded by the
Human Relations and Morale Branch of the Office of Naval Research. The research reported is at various levels of completion.
The book is divided into three parts: research on group behavior,
research on leadership, and research on individual behaviors. The
appendix includes guides for preparing research proposals along
with explanations of some technical terms.

Haiman, Franklin S. GROUP LEADERSHIP AND DEMOCRATIC ACTION.
Boston: Houghton Mifflin, 1951. vii, 309 p.

The author attempts to describe both the philosophical-scientific
background and the practical techniques of group leadership.
Attitudes and skills of democratic leadership are discussed, as are
leadership training and overcoming resistance to change. Appendixes supply a leader rating scale, transcripts of group discussions
in which leadership is shared, case studies of leadership problems,
and a bibliography.

Halpin, Andrew W. THE LEADERSHIP BEHAVIOR OF SCHOOL SUPERINTEN-
DENTS. THE PERCEPTIONS AND EXPECTATIONS OF BOARD MEMBERS,
STAFF MEMBERS, AND SUPERINTENDENTS. Columbus: College of Educa-
tion, Ohio State University, 1956. x, 109 p.

This monograph summarizes several studies on leader behavior.
Procedures and concepts developed in these studies were then
adapted to study the leadership role of the school superintendent.
The procedure and findings of the study are described. Appendixes supply the technical materials used in the study. Tables
and figures are included, and there is a list of references.

Harnqvist, Kjell. ADJUSTMENT: LEADERSHIP AND GROUP RELATIONS IN
A MILITARY TRAINING SITUATION. Translated by W.J. Hilton-Brown.
Uppsala, Sweden: Almqvist and Wiksells, 1956. 214 p.

Some units of the Swedish Navy were the subjects for a study on
adjustment, leadership, and group relations. The focus is the
effects of changes in leadership and group relations, which resulted from a reorganization of the training units, on the con-
scripts' adjustment. The main hypotheses and the concepts and
methods involved in the study are discussed, and a series of op-
erational hypotheses is advanced and tested. Samples of the
questionnaires used are supplied in the appendixes. A list of
references is also presented.

Hollander, Edwin P. LEADERS, GROUPS, AND INFLUENCE. New York:
Oxford University Press, 1964. xiv, 256 p.

The author develops the theme that leadership is one aspect of a
broader influence process which feeds into others such as inter-

personal attraction, attitude change, and conformity. Part 1 introduces this theme. In part 2 four research papers deal with leadership and interaction in formal structures. Sociometric methods of assessment are described in part 3, notably the peer-nomination technique. Part 4 examines emergent leadership and its relation to status and conformity. Each section is preceded by a brief introduction. A bibliography is supplied.

Jennings, Eugene E. AN ANATOMY OF LEADERSHIP: PRINCES, HEROES, AND SUPERMEN. New York: Harper and Bros., 1960. xvi, 256 p.

The author discusses types of leaders and their place in society. He distinguishes three basic kinds. Their definition and history are described, and each type is related to modern organizational life. The conclusion is that present-day society has no real leaders to speak of because the large organization, so prevalent today, tends to inhibit leadership ability.

Jennings, Helen H. LEADERSHIP AND ISOLATION. 2d ed. New York: Longmans, Green, 1950. xvii, 349 p.

The author uses the sociometric approach to account for the choice process operating in groups. The study involves not only social structures but also personality dynamics. Investigation of the emotional demand of group members leads to the study of leadership and followership. The book includes twenty-two tables, a glossary of terms, and a bibliography.

Jones, Arthur J. THE EDUCATION OF YOUTH FOR LEADERSHIP. New York: McGraw-Hill, 1938. xix, 246 p.

Jones discusses the principles of leadership, its meaning and function, the characteristics of leaders, and the fundamentals of a leadership program. He presents material on leadership in several countries. He emphasizes the responsibility of schools for the selection and training of potential leaders and presents a program for leadership. References appear at the end of each section.

Laird, Donald A., and Laird, Eleanor C. THE NEW PSYCHOLOGY OF LEADERSHIP: BASED ON RESEARCHES IN GROUP DYNAMICS AND HUMAN RELATIONS. New York: McGraw-Hill, 1956. 226 p.

The authors demonstrate how the application of research in group dynamics can improve the personal leadership of executives, supervisors, personnel directors, and foremen. Aspects of management relations included are the six major functions of the successful leader, styles of leadership, ways to set goals, and the development of cooperative teams. A bibliography is included.

Lassey, William R., ed. LEADERSHIP AND SOCIAL CHANGE. Iowa City, Iowa: University Associates, 1971. 356 p.

> The editor has assembled a set of readings on leadership concepts and research, which constitute an overview of concepts about leadership behavior, its consequences, and the application of those concepts to leadership situations. The work presents a viewpoint on democratic or participative leadership strategies. Research is drawn from a variety of fields, with the emphasis on applied research results. There are five parts, each with an introduction: basic concepts, leadership and communication, organizational change and leadership, community change and leadership, and the study of leadership in small groups and organizations.

Liff, Zanvel, ed. LEADER IN THE GROUP. IN HONOR OF ALEXANDER WOLF, M.D., FOR HIS THIRTY-FIVE YEARS OF OUTSTANDING TEACHING, SUPERVISION, WRITING, AND CLINICAL PRACTICE. New York: Aronson, 1975. xvi, 329 p.

> This is a collection of articles by group therapists who approach their groups from a psychoanalytic perspective. They focus on the leadership philosophies and practices of Alexander Wolf and Emanuel K. Schwartz, and consider models and theories of leadership, differentiating between effective and ineffective leaders. They aim to extend the notions of psychoanalytically oriented leadership to the issues of prevention and education, and to the general problems of contemporary society.

McClelland, David C. THE ACHIEVING SOCIETY. Princeton, N.J.: Van Nostrand, 1961. 512 p.

> This trade book explores how the need for achievement promotes successful "entrepreneurship" in theory and in the laboratory. Topics covered include the achievement motive, achieving societies in the modern world and in the past, entrepreneurial behavior and characteristics, sources of need achievement and accelerating economic growth. A ten-page bibliography is included.

Maccoby, Michael. THE GAMES-MAN: THE NEW CORPORATE LEADERS. New York: Simon and Schuster, 1973. 234 p.

> The author sets out to develop a new framework for humanizing technology. He discusses the ways in which businessmen or leaders can optimize profit and growth by reinforcing people to fit their respective work roles. The author also provides an appendix which includes an interpretive questionnaire concerning the description of work and intellectual and psychological factors related to work. Social implications of work, personal values and factors operating outside the work situation are also discussed.

Petrullo, Luigi, and Bass, Bernard M., eds. LEADERSHIP AND INTERPER-
SONAL BEHAVIOR. New York: Holt, Rinehart and Winston, 1961.
xxxiv, 382 p.

> The editors have assembled a collection of readings which are
> organized into three major divisions concerning leadership and
> interpersonal behavior: theories, small group phenomena, and
> large organization phenomena. The theories presented have var-
> ied bases, including sociometry, homeostasis, decision theory,
> and ego psychology; the small groups include the work group,
> the laboratory task unit, and the family; the large organization
> section deals with leadership appropriate to organizational set-
> tings. Each reading has a list of references.

Pigors, Paul J.W. LEADERSHIP OR DOMINATION. Cambridge, Mass.:
Riverside Press, 1935. xiii, 354 p.

> The author discusses these two aspects of behavior--leadership and
> domination--either of which would be manifested by a leader.
> The meanings, origins, and techniques of leadership and domina-
> tion are discussed, and there is a section on the function of
> authority. The specific functions are initiation, administration,
> and interpretation. A chapter-by-chapter bibliography is sup-
> plied.

Rice, A. Kenneth. LEARNING FOR LEADERSHIP. INTERPERSONAL AND
INTERGROUP RELATIONS. London: Tavistock, 1965. xii, 200 p.

> This is a description of a series of residential training conferences
> in human relations. The primary task of the conferences is to
> provide opportunities to learn about leadership. The concepts
> and assumptions behind the conference design are discussed, fol-
> lowed by the resulting conference culture and structure. Con-
> ference events are described in some detail. Residential and
> nonresidential conferences are contrasted, issues involved in train-
> ing staff are examined, and a program of research work is sug-
> gested. A list of references is provided.

Ross, Murray G., and Hendry, Charles E. NEW UNDERSTANDING OF
LEADERSHIP. A SURVEY AND APPLICATION OF RESEARCH. New York:
Association Press, 1957. 158 p.

> The authors review leadership theory and present an account of
> research findings and their implications. Topics include leader
> activities, leader qualities, and group influence on the leader.
> A suggested program for leadership development is outlined.

Seeman, Melvin. SOCIAL STATUS AND LEADERSHIP; THE CASE OF THE
SCHOOL EXECUTIVE. Columbus: Bureau of Educational Research and Service, Ohio State University, 1960. xi, 156 p.

This study concerns the influences of community and culture on
leadership style.  The focus is on the status and role conceptions
of the members of the organization, that is, conceptions of
events which lie outside the organization proper.  Seeman discusses leadership ideology, role conflict and ambivalence in leadership, status factors in leader behavior, and leader effectiveness.
The final chapter presents some emerging theses on leadership.
Appendixes describe methodological problems, study design, and
the measuring instruments.  A bibliography is included.

Shartle, Carroll L.  EXECUTIVE PERFORMANCE AND LEADERSHIP.  Englewood Cliffs, N.J.:  Prentice-Hall, 1956.  xiii, 302 p.

This book is based in part on the outcome of an extensive leadership study program at Ohio State University.  Examples from research and observation are presented, and practical interpretations of research results are provided.  Types of organizations
are compared, showing how the purpose and climate of an organization affects administrative performance.

Stogdill, Ralph M.  HANDBOOK OF LEADERSHIP:  A SURVEY OF THEORY
AND RESEARCH.  New York: Free Press, 1974.  viii, 613 p.

The author has assembled four decades of research literature on
leadership.  Problems are discussed in chronological sequence.
Leadership is considered in terms of the person or the environment and as a feature of role differentiation or social interaction.
A bibliography of 151 pages is included.

_____.  LEADERSHIP AND STRUCTURES OF PERSONAL INTERACTION.
Research Monograph No. 84.  Columbus:  Bureau of Business Research, Ohio
State University, 1957.  90 p.

Two brief studies are described, one a sociometric study of personal interaction in organizations of varying sizes, and the other
a study of responsibility–authority relationships between superiors
and subordinates in large and small organizations.  The relationships between these measures and measures including leader behavior and status are discussed.

Stogdill, Ralph M., and Coons, Alvin E., eds.  LEADER BEHAVIOR: ITS
DESCRIPTION AND MEASUREMENT.  Research Monograph no. 88.  Columbus:
Bureau of Business Research, Ohio State University, 1957.  xiv, 168 p.

This is a collection of papers by the staff of the Ohio State
leadership studies.  They describe the development, analysis, and
application of a set of items designed to measure leader behavior.
Data are presented on the relationship between leader behavior
and attitude climate, effectiveness measures, and group descriptions.  A copy of the questionnaire and its instructions is supplied.

Stogdill, Ralph M.; Scott, Ellis L.; and Jaynes, William E. LEADERSHIP: A STUDY OF ROLE EXPECTATIONS AND PERFORMANCE. Columbus: Ohio State University Research Foundation, 1953. xiii, 252 p.

This report deals with the problem of discrepancies in work-role expectations and work performance among officers and civilians in a naval air development command. Categories were developed for several variables: description, reference, and discrepancy. The appendix presents samples of the forms used in the collection of data. A list of references is supplied.

_____. LEADERSHIP AND ROLE EXPECTATIONS. Research Monograph no. 86. Columbus: Bureau of Business Research, Ohio State University, 1956. xv, 168 p.

In a large research organization employees were asked to describe what they do and what they ought to do in their particular jobs. Areas explored include leader behavior, authority, responsibility, and work performance. Subordinates also described the "does" and "ought to do" behaviors of each subject. Relationships and discrepancies between performance and expectations were analyzed.

Stogdill, Ralph M., and Shartle, Carroll L. METHODS IN THE STUDY OF ADMINISTRATIVE LEADERSHIP. Research Monograph no. 80. Columbus: Bureau of Business Research, Ohio State University, 1955. xv, 77 p.

Leadership is treated as a relationship between members of a group--the interactions, behavior, perceptions, and status of some members vis-a-vis others. By collecting data on all group members, leadership can be studied in terms of organizational structure and function. The authors regard the methods they develop as suitable only for research purposes. Instructions for administration and scoring are included.

Tead, Ordway. THE ART OF LEADERSHIP. New York: McGraw-Hill, 1935. xi, 308 p.

The author directs his book at those who must influence or have authority over others, and at organizations concerned with enhancing leadership ability in their executives. He deals with topics such as leadership qualities, the leader as executive and teacher, the ways in which leaders wield influence, and problems of women leaders. The book closes with some comments on the training of leaders. Footnotes to chapters are presented.

Verba, Sidney. SMALL GROUPS AND POLITICAL BEHAVIOR. A STUDY OF LEADERSHIP. Princeton, N.J.: Princeton University Press, 1961. 273 p.

Small group analysis is applied to political behavior on the basis that the study of small groups is essential to any thorough political analysis. Experimental studies are considered in relation to

the political process. A short bibliography, including some unpublished material, is supplied.

Vroom, Victor H., and Yetton, Philip W. LEADERSHIP AND DECISION-
MAKING. Pittsburgh: University of Pittsburgh Press, 1973. xiii, 233 p.

The problem of leadership style is the focus of this book. The
authors discuss the extent to which managers should involve subordinates in making decisions. There are two perspectives: how
the problem should be solved, and how the problem is solved in
practice by managers. The issue of how leaders should choose
the extent of participation in decision making by subordinates
results in the development of a model that helps in making the
choice. The authors review empirical research in discussing how
practicing managers do make their choices. A technology for
leadership development is described, and the normative model is
revised.

Wittenberg, Rudolph M. THE ART OF GROUP DISCIPLINE. A MENTAL
HYGIENE APPROACH TO LEADERSHIP. New York: Association Press, 1951.
xi, 124 p.

Discipline is defined as a process of change that takes place
through the group of which the individual is a member. The focus
is on groups of young people in various settings. The author
discusses discipline in the individual, the community, the leader,
and the group. Some suggestions are made for the promotion of
the process that results in inner discipline. A digest of studies
on aspects of group and individual behavior is included.

Zaleznik, Abraham. HUMAN DILEMMAS OF LEADERSHIP. New York:
Harper and Row, 1966. xii, 235 p.

The author presents a psychological study of leadership, using the
principles of psychoanalysis to approach the problems encountered
by individuals who must exercise authority in organizations.
Among the topics included are conflicts in work, authority and
self-esteem, human dilemmas of leadership, the dynamics of
subordinacy, group formations in industry, and the management of
power in interpersonal relations.

# C. COMMUNICATION

Barnes, Douglas, and Todd, Frankie. COMMUNICATION AND LEARNING
IN SMALL GROUPS. London and Boston: Routledge and Kegan Paul, 1977.
152 p.

The authors describe a study in which they recorded thirteen-year-
old children talking in small, teacherless groups about school

learning tasks. In the analysis of these recordings, the authors
discuss the cognitive and social abilities displayed by the children.
They then describe ways to set up and study group work in schools,
and deal with the role of children's questions and the problems
involved in attributing meaning to conversations.

Berelson, Bernard. CONTENT ANALYSIS IN COMMUNICATION RESEARCH.
Glencoe, III.: Free Press, 1952. 220 p.

The author summarizes the field of content analysis to 1950 and
describes its uses in the social sciences and the humanities. Some
technical chapters deal with the units of content analysis, the
categories, and matters of procedure such as sampling. The
author's conclusions are illustrated by reference to the literature.
A bibliography is included, mostly on the uses of content analysis, but with additional material on technical, qualitative, and
general titles.

Brown, Charles T., and Keller, Paul W. MONOLOGUE TO DIALOGUE:
AN EXPLORATION OF INTERPERSONAL COMMUNICATION. Englewood
Cliffs, N.J.: Prentice-Hall, 1973. xv, 223 p.

This book explores two aspects of communication: speaking and
listening. The overt features of communication are discussed, as
is meaning, which the authors regard as translation not only of
the spoken word, but of all nonverbal cues also. The role of
emotion in communication, and the role of speech in arousing
emotion are examined. Other concerns include the influence of
expectation on listening; the role of discrimination, judgment,
and power in communicative processes; and the contrasts between
monologue and dialogue. Exercises for the student to learn by
are included at the end of each chapter, along with a statement
of objectives.

Cathcart, Robert S., and Samovar, Larry A., eds. SMALL GROUP COM-
MUNICATION: A READER. Dubuque, Iowa: William C. Brown, 1974.
415 p.

This collection of forty-three readings, grouped in four sections,
covers definitions, group operations, communication, and leadership. Each section has an introductory essay written by the
editors, which presents background information and an overview
of the readings. A short bibliography is given at the end of each
chapter.

Christie, Lee S.; Luce, R. Duncan; and Macy, Josiah, Jr. COMMUNICA-
TION AND LEARNING IN TASK-ORIENTED GROUPS. Technical Report
no. 231. Cambridge: Research Laboratory of Electronics, M.I.T., 1952. iv,
251 p.

Task-oriented groups are defined in electromechanical control
terms as involving inputs and outputs, nodes, transfer functions,
and feedback systems. Individual and group decision latency
are discussed, and noise in the coding-decoding of messages is
examined. Questionnaire attitudinal data are presented, and
their correlations with network properties are demonstrated. Appendixes supply technical data and information on the experiments.
A bibliography is included.

DuBois, Rachel D., and Li, New-Soong. THE ART OF GROUP CONVERSA-
TION: A NEW BREAKTHROUGH IN SOCIAL COMMUNICATION. New
York: Association Press, 1963. 160 p.

The authors describe the techniques of group conversation as a
means for establishing rapport in a group. They contrast it with
group discussion, and deal with some of the barriers to good
communication. There is a chapter on how to be the leader of
a group conversation. Another chapter to foster intergroup
understanding, and others for the benefit of intragroup relationships. Notes accompany each chapter. A bibliography for
leaders is included.

Haney, William V. COMMUNICATION: PATTERNS AND INCIDENTS.
Homewood, Ill.: Richard D. Irwin, 1960. 321 p.

Communication is conceptualized as a serial process. Phases involved are encoding, sending, medium, receiving, and decoding.
The author emphasizes the encoding and decoding phases; it is
in these phases that the root of miscommunication is frequently
found. Examples are given and an extensive bibliography is
supplied.

Katz, Elihu, and Lazarsfeld, Paul F. PERSONAL INFLUENCE; THE PART
PLAYED BY PEOPLE IN THE FLOW OF MASS COMMUNICATION. Glencoe,
Ill.: Free Press, 1955. xx, 400 p.

The authors divide their book into two parts. The first part deals
with the role of people in the study of mass media effects and
discusses intervening variables in mass communications and the
opinion leader idea. A section is devoted to norms and networks and the role of the group in the process of persuasion.
The second part reports a field study of the flow of everyday
influence in a midwestern community. Appendixes contain technical information related to the study. A bibliography is also
supplied.

Lebra, William P., ed. TRANSCULTURAL RESEARCH IN MENTAL HEALTH.
MENTAL HEALTH RESEARCH IN ASIA AND THE PACIFIC. Vol. 2. Honolulu:
University Press of Hawaii, 1972. xi, 440 p.

This set of papers was presented at a conference on social change
and cultural factors held at the East-West Center, University of
Hawaii, in 1969. The topics range from problems of development
and cultural patterns in communication to family dynamics, religious factors in mental health, and epistemic problems. The
latter section includes a chapter on group perceptions and group
relations. Most readings include references. A general index
is supplied.

Wilmot, William W. DYADIC COMMUNICATION: A TRANSACTIONAL
PERSPECTIVE. Reading, Mass.: Addison-Wesley, 1975. xv, 196 p.

In this book the author uses a transactional approach to deal with
the simplest context in which to observe the elements operating
in interpersonal communication relationships: the dyad. Part 1
discusses dyadic elements: the nature of dyadic transactions, perception of the self, and perception of the other. Part 2 presents
an analysis of dyadic communication from a relationship point of
view. Each chapter is summarized. The appendix lists categories of interpersonal response. A list of references is supplied.

# Chapter 6

# GROUP THERAPY AND T-GROUPS

Appley, Dee G., and Winder, Alvin E.  T-GROUPS AND THERAPY GROUPS
IN A CHANGING SOCIETY.  San Francisco: Jossey-Bass, 1973. xx, 209 p.

> The two kinds of groups are contrasted with respect to the pur-
> poses, theoretical frameworks, and practical applications of each.
> A historical overview of the encounter group movement is in-
> cluded.  Only one kind of group therapy, the psychoanalytic
> model, is considered as representing group therapy in general.

Bach, George R.  INTENSIVE GROUP PSYCHOTHERAPY.  New York: Ronald
Press, 1954.  xi, 446 p.

> This book deals with the theory and practice of intensive group
> psychotherapy.  The author directs his writing primarily to those
> in therapeutic settings, but acknowledges the value of the book
> for social psychologists because of the insights into group dynam-
> ics it provides.  Part 1 deals with clinical technique; part 2
> examines the nature of the therapeutic process that occurs in
> group therapy participation; and part 3 explores the group dynam-
> ic factors that influence the therapeutic process in the individ-
> ual participant.  A bibliography is included.

Back, Kurt W.  BEYOND WORDS.  THE STORY OF SENSITIVITY TRAINING
AND THE ENCOUNTER MOVEMENT.  New York:  Russell Sage Foundation,
1972.  Reprint.  Baltimore: Penguin Books, 1973.  xxi, 226 p.

> The author describes the origins and history of that movement
> known variously as T-groups, encounter groups, sensitivity train-
> ing, and human potential development.  The social setting and
> scientific base of the movement are discussed, and a section is
> devoted to practices and applications.  The author assesses its
> impact and speculates on its implications.  The possible negative
> aspects of the movement are also discussed.  A general bibliog-
> raphy is supplied, as well as an appendix of reports of research
> evaluating sensitivity training for 1945-70.

# Group Therapy and T-Groups

Batchelder, Richard L., and Hardy, James M. USING SENSITIVITY TRAIN-
ING AND THE LABORATORY METHOD. AN ORGANIZATIONAL CASE
STUDY IN THE DEVELOPMENT OF HUMAN RESOURCES. New York:
Association Press, 1968. 128 p.

> The purpose of the project reported here was to develop guide-
> lines which would increase the positive outcomes of sensitivity
> training used in the context of the YMCA. The authors describe
> the research and summarize the major findings. Application of
> the findings is described in the chapters on designing a laboratory
> and on the responsible use of this method. A glossary of terms
> and a bibliography are included.

Berger, M.L., and Berger, P.J., eds. GROUP TRAINING TECHNIQUES:
CASES, APPLICATIONS AND RESEARCH. New York: Halsted Press, 1973.
xvi, 191 p.

> This collection of papers includes a description of T-group pro-
> cesses and some evaluation research on learning experiences in
> groups. The subject of effective trainers is dealt with, and a
> new learning approach is described.

Berne, Eric [L.]. PRINCIPLES OF GROUP TREATMENT. New York: Grove
Press, 1966. xviii, 379 p.

> This is a systematic account of the use of transactional analysis
> in groups. The author surveys some important aspects of prac-
> tice, describes procedures for establishing a group therapy (or
> group "treatment") program, and compares some common methods
> of group therapy. Part 2 of the book deals with transactional
> analysis: its theoretical basis, its principles and techniques, its
> relationship to other kinds of group treatment, and the handling
> of some common games which take place in group treatment. A
> glossary of terms is supplied.

Blank, Leonard; Gottsegen, Gloria B[ehar].; and Gottsegen, Monroe G., eds.
CONFRONTATION: ENCOUNTERS IN SELF AND INTERPERSONAL AWARE-
NESS. New York: Macmillan, 1971. xi, 516 p.

> This book deals with the phenomenon of confrontation, the event
> which occurs when group processes generate an encounter with
> self and others. The contributors have written articles which
> stress the implications for encounter experience on interpersonal
> and intrapersonal behavior and for a variety of populations. En-
> counter experiences are related to existential and humanistic
> theory and practice. Case illustrations are plentiful and focus
> on the individual rather than the mechanics. Each chapter is
> followed by a bibliography.

Blumberg, Arthur, and Golembiewski, Robert T. LEARNING AND CHANGE IN GROUPS. Baltimore: Penguin Books, 1976. 208 p.

This is a humanistic description of the field of encounter groups and T-groups. The authors deal with basic concepts about learning in groups and varieties of group experiences. They discuss typical events in groups as well as leadership styles and roles. Issues and problems are presented, and research on group process and outcome is described. There is a list of references.

Bradford, Leland P.; Gibb, Jack R.; and Benne, Kenneth D. T-GROUP THEORY AND LABORATORY METHOD: INNOVATION IN RE-EDUCATION. New York: Wiley, 1964. 498 p.

This book of readings describes the development of the T-group as an educational medium and message. Many of the readings are written by experienced T-group trainers and provide a variety of viewpoints on the method. They demonstrate the ways in which group processes can be applied and cover a number of laboratory studies.

Burton, Arthur, ed. ENCOUNTER. THE THEORY AND PRACTICE OF ENCOUNTER GROUPS. San Francisco: Jossey-Bass, 1969. xiv, 207 p.

The contributors attempt, in thirteen readings, to present a theoretical adjunct to the practice of encounter groups while also explicating a methodology. The editor required each author to describe his operations in encounter groups and the theoretical constructs behind them. The picture is one of responsibility for growth being returned to the person, who is also made aware of his or her responsibility for social action.

Cooper, Cary L., and Mangham, I.L., eds. T-GROUPS: A SURVEY OF RESEARCH. New York: Wiley-Interscience, 1971. xvii, 283 p.

This book sets out basic and applied research in the T-group field. The format consists of an introductory overview to each section, summarizing the empirical work in that area, and a complete research article or two. The development of the group, the processes involved, and group effectiveness are discussed. Lists of references appear after each introductory article, and a further list of recent publications is supplied.

Driver, Helen I., ed. COUNSELING AND LEARNING THROUGH SMALL-GROUP DISCUSSION. Madison, Wis.: Monona, 1958. 464 p.

The first section of this book, written by the editor, comprises a complete volume in itself. It focuses on the multiple counseling method which uses small-group discussion as the learning medium for group members, resulting in their personal growth while receiving individual counseling from the group leader. An appendix summarizes fifteen projects of this kind. Section 2 presents thirty-nine articles by professional group leaders in a variety of fields. The focus is on small-group discussion as an aid in counseling, training, and treatment. A selected bibliography of 599 entries completes the book.

Durkin, Helen E. THE GROUP IN DEPTH. New York: International Universities Press, 1964. xii, 378 p.

The author divides her work into two major parts. The first part deals with group psychology under the following subheadings: group dynamic group psychology, convergence between group dynamics and psychoanalytic group psychology, and relationship between two ideologies. The second part describes three basic approaches to group psychotherapy: analytic group psychotherapy, existential group psychotherapy, and group dynamic psychotherapy. The author works toward a possible blend of group therapy and group dynamics which can be applied to an increasing range of groups. A bibliography is supplied.

Egan, Gerard. ENCOUNTER: GROUP PROCESSES FOR INTERPERSONAL GROWTH. Monterey, Calif.: Brooks/Cole, 1970. xvi, 424 p.

This book is about those groups in which the participants come together in order to grow in interpersonal effectiveness through the group experience. The author focuses on the kinds of group and individual actions which are most likely to make the group experience successful from the standpoint of interpersonal growth. There are discussions on group goals, the laboratory method, leadership, self-disclosure, and supportive behavior. A list of references is supplied.

_____. FACE TO FACE. THE SMALL-GROUP EXPERIENCE AND INTERPERSONAL GROWTH. Monterey, Calif.: Brooks/Cole, 1973. viii, 162 p.

In this book, the author presents a relatively nontechnical description and illustration of the theory underlying the small group as a means of human relations training. He attempts to clarify the kinds of behavior which facilitate growth in a face-to-face group. Readers are referred to the author's 1970 and 1971 publications (see above and below) for more detailed information. This volume contains an encounter group checklist to enable the reader to assess his or her own participation in the group and the quality of the group interaction.

_____, ed. ENCOUNTER GROUPS: BASIC READINGS. Monterey, Calif.: Brooks/Cole, 1971. xii, 351 p.

This collection of readings is designed to supplement the editor's text, ENCOUNTER: GROUP PROCESSES FOR INTERPERSONAL GROWTH (see above), and follows its general pattern. The editor's introduction and comments accompany each article. Topics covered include goals, leadership, and interactions such as communication processes, self–disclosure, support, and confrontation. References follow each article.

Fields, Sidney J. THE PERSON CIRCLE: A FIRST BOOK ON GROUP PSYCHOTHERAPY AND THE SMALL GROUP FIELD. Hicksville, N.Y.: Exposition Press, 1976. xvii, 183 p.

This is a kind of beginner's manual in group therapy, in particular that type of therapy derived from the psychoanalytic school. Most of the advice on tactics and strategies in group treatment is the product of clinical experience rather than research evidence.

Gazda, George M., ed. BASIC APPROACHES TO GROUP PSYCHOTHERAPY AND GROUP COUNSELING. 2d ed. Springfield, Ill.: Charles C Thomas, 1975. 560 p.

This collection of articles by twenty contributors constitutes a guide to basic theories in the related areas of group psychotherapy and group counseling. Included is a synopsis of the effectiveness of basic small group practices. Analytic and existential approaches are described, and group therapy with children is included. One chapter deals with points of ethical procedure for group practitioners.

Glass, Sheldon D. THE PRACTICAL HANDBOOK OF GROUP COUNSELING. Baltimore: B.C.S. Publishing Co., 1969. viii, 200 p.

This book presents the practical techniques of group counseling in the school setting. The skills necessary for knowing how, when, and where to use group counseling are emphasized. Theory is discussed only when practical and applicable. The author offers a model for resolving and/or enhancing the problems and successes involved in group work. Groups composed of children, adolescents, and parents are described. A glossary, footnotes, and bibliography are supplied.

Glasser, Paul; Sarri, Rosemary; and Vinter, Robert, eds. INDIVIDUAL CHANGE THROUGH SMALL GROUPS. New York: Free Press, 1974. xii, 515 p.

This book is aimed at practitioners in the helping professions. It sets out to supply them with methods of inducing desired changes in individuals through their participation in small groups. The first section describes the basic approach; the second section deals

with the activities of the professional from the beginning to the
end of the intervention process; next, the professional's activities
in the client's environment outside the group are described; and
lastly, the extension and application of the approach to a wide
range of fields of practice is discussed. Each reading has a
list of references.

Goldberg, Carl. ENCOUNTER: GROUP SENSITIVITY TRAINING EXPERI-
ENCE. New York: Science House, 1970. 341 p.

The author explores the social and personal conditions that bring
about the need for group training, and describes the varieties of
groups. Bion's postulate regarding the existence of a group men-
tality is the basis for his training method. The group is the primary focus. Psychodrama and specific exercises and games for
increasing personal awareness and resolving conflicts are also
examined. Guidelines for the selection of groups and trainers
are provided. The appendix presents a protocol of an actual
process group session along with explanatory footnotes. A list of
references is supplied.

Goldberg, Carl, with Merle C. Goldberg. THE HUMAN CIRCLE: AN EXIS-
TENTIAL APPROACH TO THE NEW GROUP THERAPIES. Chicago: Nelson-
Hall, 1973. xiii, 257 p.

The authors present the history and current value, in practical
terms, of therapy in groups. They concentrate on designed
groups: eight to twelve individuals committed to becoming inti-
mately acquainted and experiencing new adventures. The focus
is mainly on heterogeneous groups, although homogeneous groups
are given attention. The authors' own experience is reflected
throughout the book. Issues dealt with include socializing, goals,
resistance, and the therapist as a model.

Golembiewski, Robert T., and Blumberg, Arthur, eds. SENSITIVITY TRAIN-
ING AND THE LABORATORY APPROACH. READINGS ABOUT CONCEPTS
AND APPLICATIONS. Itasca, Ill.: F.E. Peacock, 1970. xiii, 514 p.

This collection of readings deals with the learning processes which
people undergo as members of a group, and the applications of
such processes to situations outside of the immediate group in
which the learning takes place. Each section is prefaced by an
introduction. There is no overall bibliography, but each reading
includes references.

Greenberg, Ira, ed. PSYCHODRAMA: THEORY AND THERAPY. New York:
Behavioral Publications, 1974. xvi, 496 p.

This book focuses on the therapeutic value and applied uses of
psychodrama. There are seven parts, most with papers by other

authors, introduced by the editor. Part 1 deals with Moreno's system and theory of psychodrama and its various uses. Part 2 discusses specific theoretical dimensions of psychodrama. A general theoretical overview is presented in part 3, followed by a description of the development of psychodrama to its present form. Psychodramatic techniques are applied to a range of problems in part 5, and Moreno is compared on a theoretical basis with other therapists. The editor closes the book with papers evaluating the ability of psychodrama to meet individual and societal needs.

Heckel, Robert V., and Salzberg, H.C. GROUP PSYCHOTHERAPY: A BEHAVIORAL APPROACH. Columbia: University of South Carolina Press, 1976. ix, 223 p.

The authors review the literature on both traditional and behavioral approaches to group psychotherapy. They describe typical behaviors of therapists in group settings, anticipate patients' common responses to group therapy events, and redefine therapist and patient activities in behavioral terms. They also deal with methods particular to marathon groups and to the group treatment of alcoholics. The book closes with remarks on desirable training experiences for group psychotherapists.

Kadis, Asya L., et al. A PRACTICUM OF GROUP PSYCHOTHERAPY. New York: Hoeber Medical Division, Harper and Row, 1963. viii, 195 p.

This is a handbook of group psychotherapy insofar as it provides an overview of the major practical aspects of group psychotherapy. The direction of the book is based on psychodynamics. The development of a group therapy program is described, and the selection of patients and the structuring of the first group session are discussed. A chapter is included on coping with special kinds of clinical problems. Appendix 1 presents a curriculum for a two-year part-time training program in group psychotherapy. Appendix 2 contains the schedule of a weekend workshop in group psychotherapy. References follow each chapter.

Kemp, C. Gratton. FOUNDATIONS OF GROUP COUNSELING. New York: McGraw-Hill, 1970. xii, 321 p.

This book attempts to integrate behavioral concepts from a range of fields to provide an interdisciplinary approach to group counseling. The author focuses on methodology and on meaning, on the foundational principles which clarify the process taking place in groups. Single-theory and multiple-theory approaches to group process are discussed, and there are sections on the preparation and functioning of the group counselor. The book represents an exposition of the author's belief that the meaning of life is a function of the quality of interpersonal relationships therein.

Kissen, Morton, ed. FROM GROUP DYNAMICS TO GROUP PSYCHOANAL-YSIS: THERAPEUTIC APPLICATIONS OF GROUP DYNAMIC UNDERSTAND-ING. Washington, D.C.: Hemisphere, 1976. xv, 362 p.

This textbook of selected source materials on relationships between group dynamic processes and group therapy of a psychoanalytic nature is aimed at students of graduate level and above. Inter-actions between the group as a whole and individual group mem-bers are discussed. Pertinent and comprehensive bibliographies are included.

Lakin, Martin. INTERPERSONAL ENCOUNTER: THEORY AND PRACTICE IN SENSITIVITY TRAINING. New York: McGraw-Hill, 1972. xv, 302 p.

This volume is addressed to a variety of people in and around the sensitivity group field: practitioners, consumers, and researchers. The author presents a historical account of the group movement and a conceptual framework for approaching group-individual interaction. Trainer roles and problems are dealt with, and trainee perceptions of the group experience are examined. The participant's difficulty in integrating the emotional and cognitive aspects of the group experience is discussed. Attention is given to policy, ethical, and evaluation issues in relation to groups. Current and potential applications of group training are explored.

Lieberman, Morton A.; Yalom, Irvin D.; and Miles, Matthew B. ENCOUN-TER GROUPS: FIRST FACTS. New York: Basic Books, 1973. x, 495 p.

The purpose of the encounter group is to serve as a framework within which group members can observe their own behavior and its impact on others. The authors deal with the processes involved in such groups, with the learning that occurs, the changes that are wrought, and outcome measures. Two appendixes of measure-ment techniques are included.

Malamud, Daniel I., and Machover, Solomon. TOWARD SELF-UNDERSTAND-ING: GROUP TECHNIQUES IN SELF-CONFRONTATION. Springfield, Ill.: Charles C Thomas, 1965. 288 p.

This book deals with an area which lies between the more tradi-tional fields of group psychotherapy and mental health education. It describes a workshop in self-understanding. The authors sum-marize each session, adding an interpretive commentary. The role of the workshop leader, types of member reactions which may be anticipated, and the application of various group experiments are illustrated.

Milman, Donald S., and Goldman, George D., eds. GROUP PROCESSES TODAY: EVALUATION AND PERSPECTIVE. Springfield, Ill.: Charles C Thomas, 1974. 336 p.

This set of articles comes from a psychoanalytic training program's conference. It provides a survey of the fields of contemporary group process and group psychotherapy, from both the theoretical and applied perspectives. Contributors include Emanuel K. Schwartz, Albert Ellis, Elizabeth Mintz, Seymour R. Kaplan and Max Siegel. References accompany some articles.

Mintz, Elizabeth E., with contributions by Lorelle Saretsky and Barry Sherman. MARATHON GROUPS. REALITY AND SYMBOL. New York: Appleton-Century-Crofts, 1971. xi, 286 p.

The author describes the principle of the marathon group and proposes that the power of such groups lies in their functioning simultaneously as reality experiences and symbolic experiences. They allow the honest expression of feelings and can be playgrounds and/or battlefields for the participants. The author shows how frustrations and hostilities come to be replaced by concern and loving mutual acceptance, and how open communication can result in growth in self-respect. An appendix presents suggestions for marathon leaders. References are listed at the end of each chapter.

Moreno, Jacob L. WHO SHALL SURVIVE? FOUNDATIONS OF SOCIOMETRY, GROUP PSYCHOTHERAPY AND SOCIODRAMA. Beacon, N.Y.: Beacon House, 1953. cxiv, 763 p.

This volume is made up of several "books" which trace the background and development of the method of studying human relations known as sociometry, along with its companion techniques, group psychotherapy and sociodrama. Moreno includes a set of preludes which discusses the development of these methods in his mind. Book 1 describes the sociometric system. Book 2 deals with the evolution of groups. Sociometry of a community, and of its construction and reconstruction, follows in books 3 and 4. The sociometric planning of society and further applications of sociometry are examined in books 5 and 6. A glossary and bibliography are included, as well as an index to sociograms.

Morris, Kenneth T., and Cinnamon, Kenneth M. A HANDBOOK OF NONVERBAL GROUP EXERCISES. Springfield, Ill.: Charles C Thomas, 1975. 324 p.

These nonverbal exercises are described as tools to achieve improved behavior. Groups with which they may be used are discussed and include personal growth, encounter, and marathon groups. All exercises are described in a standardized format, and those that have above average potential for achieving goals are asterisked. The material is organized into sections dealing with trust, relaxation, rejection, frustration, and sensory awareness.

_____ . A HANDBOOK OF VERBAL GROUP EXERCISES. Springfield, Ill.:
Charles C Thomas, 1974. 338 p.

> The authors have arranged the exercises according to specific
> goals, and they are structured as to primary goals, subsidiary
> goals, group application, administrative procedure, suggestions
> for facilitator process, and variations. The book helps the reader
> determine the appropriateness and effectiveness of exercises for
> specific experiences.

_____ , eds. CONTROVERSIAL ISSUES IN HUMAN RELATIONS TRAINING
GROUPS. Springfield, Ill.: Charles C Thomas, 1976. xxvii, 137 p.

> The editors and seven contributors have written on crucial and
> controversial issues in the field of human relations training groups.
> These include certification and licensing, physical contact, sex,
> roles and responsibilities of facilitators, screening, and socio-
> economic class as a factor in groups. Each chapter begins with
> specific questions on the issue followed by the responses of the
> contributors. A summary ends each chapter. A final chapter
> presents contributors' responses to issues and concerns not discussed
> in preceding chapters. The appendix describes guidelines for
> psychologists conducting growth groups, for group facilitators in
> higher education, and for the preparation of professional group
> facilitators.

Mowrer, O. Hobart, THE NEW GROUP THERAPY. Princeton, N.J.: Van
Nostrand, 1964. ix, 262 p.

> The author directs his text toward those engaged in self-help
> groups of various kinds and toward individuals who have sought
> professional help and found it lacking. The book is divided
> into four parts: historical and cultural context, definition and
> diagnosis, means and methods, and "the argument amplified,"
> which closes with a chapter on Freudianism, behavior therapy,
> and self-disclosure. The author's admitted bias is in the direc-
> tion of Christian religion and its therapeutic potential for the
> individual seeking to become a full person. A bibliography is
> supplied.

Napier, Rodney W., and Gershenfeld, Matti K. INSTRUCTOR'S MANUAL.
GROUPS: THEORY AND EXPERIENCE. Boston: Houghton Mifflin, 1973.
x, 148 p.

> This manual is intended for the professional facilitator who can
> use the activities to unlock the appropriate learning process for
> a particular group at a particular time. The authors encourage
> flexibility in the use of both their book, GROUPS: THEORY AND
> EXPERIENCE (see p. 8) and their manual, but caution that the
> facilitator must have a good sense of where the group is at any

given time in order to achieve the optimal effect from the use of the exercises. Each chapter begins with an overview of exercises, and discussion sections are included toward the close of each chapter.

Ohlsen, Merle M. GROUP COUNSELING. New York: Holt, Rinehart and Winston, 1970. xv, 303 p.

The author sets out to help practicing and prospective counselors in their work with counseling groups. The development of treatment goals cooperatively with clients, the selection of clients and initiation of the counseling process, and the features of resistance, transference, and countertransference are discussed. Practical suggestions and illustrations can be found throughout. There are chapters on counseling difficult clients, children, and adolescents. Each chapter has a summary and list of references.

Rogers, Carl R. CARL ROGERS ON ENCOUNTER GROUPS. New York: Harper and Row, 1970. vii, 172 p.

The author describes the origin of encounter groups and the process involved in an encounter group session. He discusses the changes which such group experiences can effect in individuals, in relationships, and in organizations. Potential applications are explored, as are implications for the future of encounter groups.

Rosenbaum, Max, and Snadowsky, Alvin, eds. THE INTENSIVE GROUP EXPERIENCE. New York: Free Press, 1976. xiv, 210 p.

The authors examine and evaluate various types of groups. Chapter 1 deals with the history of group psychotherapy and explores contemporary developments. Chapter 2 looks at group training labs, group interaction, and leadership. Personal growth, encounter, and self-awareness groups are examined in chapter 3, and chapter 4 deals with an intentional group with particular problems, such as alcoholics. Chapter 5 looks at communal living, its history and current forms, and internal tensions and conflicts in communes.

Ruitenbeek, Hendrik M. THE NEW GROUP THERAPIES. New York: Discus Books, 1970. 240 p.

The author has written a critical book about some of the new therapies involving groups. He discusses the basis of group psychotherapy and describes and evaluates the contributions of various approaches, including encounter marathons, the Esalen experience, addiction groups, nude groups, and theme groups. The roles of patient and therapist in the new therapies are dealt with. The reader is provided with an examination of how people in these new therapies learn to experience the impact they make on one another.

Sax, Saville, and Hollander, Sandra. REALITY GAMES. New York: Macmillan, 1972. xxvii, 277 p.

The authors present a set of games in which the players regain those areas of feeling and communication which had been divided and restricted by the demands of life. They emphasize that the games be practiced and experienced, not just read about. Two kinds of skills are taught, all other games depend on them. These are focus skills (models of ideal communication) and T-group skills (awareness of communication patterns and effects through increasing honesty and openness). The book is written for application in a variety of situations from small groups to communities.

Schein, Edgar H., and Bennis, Warren G., eds. PERSONAL AND ORGANIZATIONAL CHANGE THROUGH GROUP METHODS: THE LABORATORY APPROACH. New York: Wiley, 1965. x, 376 p.

This book describes the process known as laboratory training and seeks to construct the theoretical principles and assumptions underlying it. Parts 2 and 3 are largely by a group of contributors and deal with the uses of laboratory training as well as research on its outcomes. Appendix 1 supplies the steps necessary for running a laboratory, and appendix 2 presents a selected bibliography.

Shaffer, John B., and Galinsky, M. David. MODELS OF GROUP THERAPY AND SENSITIVITY TRAINING. Englewood Cliffs, N.J.: Prentice-Hall, 1974. xiii, 303 p.

This book is an overview of major group approaches in education, psychiatry, and social work. The methods are described without comparative evaluation. Psychotherapy groups are clearly differentiated from other kinds of groups. Approaches included are psychoanalytic, group dynamic, psychodrama, gestalt, T-groups, and encounter groups. The book is aimed at senior undergraduate and graduate students specializing in areas using group techniques.

Slavson, Samuel R. AN INTRODUCTION TO GROUP THERAPY. New York: Commonwealth Fund, 1943. xvi, 352 p.

This is an account of group therapy as a method of treating children in need of professional help. The basic principles of interpersonal therapy are outlined, and the practice of group therapy is described. Choice of clientele, the therapeutic process, and variations in group treatment are discussed. Two records of group meetings and five case studies are presented. Four appendixes give outlines for a referral summary, a progress report, integration conferences, and follow-up study. An index of group therapy terms and phrases used in the book is supplied.

_____, ed. THE PRACTICE OF GROUP THERAPY. New York: International Universities Press, 1947. 271 p.

This book of articles by medical and nonmedical psychotherapists describes the application of various kinds of group therapy to emotionally disturbed, socially maladjusted, and mental patients. The editor describes the general principles of group therapy. He and other contributors present articles on activity group therapy with a variety of patients including exceptional children and psychopathic personalities. Interview group therapy is described, with the patients ranging from psychoneurotic adults to speech disorder patients. A chapter is included on didactic group psychotherapy with psychotic patients.

Solomon, Lawrence N., and Berzon, Betty, eds. NEW PERSPECTIVES ON ENCOUNTER GROUPS. San Francisco: Jossey-Bass, 1972. xxii, 432 p.

Some of the problems raised by small group research, specifically by the study of a group by itself, are reviewed by a number of contributors. The book is divided into three sections: issues, technologies, and applications of small group experiences. A bibliography and combined subject-author index are supplied.

Stephenson, Richard M., and Scarpitti, Frank R. GROUP INTERACTION AS THERAPY. THE USE OF THE SMALL GROUP IN CORRECTIONS. Westport, Conn.: Greenwood Press, 1974. xiii, 235 p.

The authors describe an experimental program designed to intervene in the processes of delinquency and change participants' behavior to a more acceptable variety. Evaluative research on the results of the treatment is presented, and a summary of comparative research on similar programs is included. An appendix describes the measuring instruments used in the study. A selected bibliography is supplied.

Thompson, Sheila, and Kahn, J.H. THE GROUP PROCESS AS A HELPING TECHNIQUE. A TEXTBOOK FOR SOCIAL WORKERS, PSYCHIATRISTS, PSYCHOLOGISTS, FAMILY DOCTORS, TEACHERS AND OTHER WORKERS IN COMMUNITY SERVICES. New York: Pergamon Press, 1970. xvii, 158 p.

This is a brief survey of group relations as a therapeutic tool, both for those who require treatment and as a way of enriching everyone's life experience. The authors discuss the background to group work and the group situation, and distinguish between group psychotherapy, group counseling, and group discussion, including theories and settings relevant to each. A short bibliography is supplied.

Wassell, B. Bohdan. GROUP ANALYSIS. New York: Citadel Press, 1966. Originally published as GROUP PSYCHOANALYSIS. New York: Philosophical Library, 1959. xiii, 306 p.

The author describes a method for treating personality disorders, using case histories and showing how group principles reveal and begin to resolve issues which may not always emerge in the course of individual therapy. Psychoanalytic theory, drawing heavily on the Karen Horney school, is described for the benefit of the lay-man. Later portions of the book are somewhat more complex. Chapter-by-chapter notes are provided.

Weschler, I[rving].R., and Riesel, J. INSIDE A SENSITIVITY TRAINING GROUP. Los Angeles: Institute of Industrial Relations, University of California, 1959. 133 p.

The emphasis in this book is primarily on individual personality rather than group functioning. The book does, however, present a comprehensive account of thirty sessions of a sensitivity training group, using three sources: trainer recollections and comments, excerpts from diaries of group members, and observations from a psychologist who had attended the group sessions and interviewed the trainer.

Whitaker, Dorothy S., and Lieberman, Morton A. PSYCHOTHERAPY THROUGH THE GROUP PROCESS. New York: Atherton Press, 1964. vii, 305 p.

The authors examine the properties of groups and present a theory concerning the relation between these and therapeutic change. They suggest that their view, though developed in regard to therapeutic groups nevertheless has relevance for other groups. Part 1 discusses group processes in the context of therapy and deals with topics such as equilibrium and change and the development of the group. Part 2 discusses the individual's therapeutic experience and the therapeutic process. Part 3 discusses the therapist's con-tribution. Each chapter is followed by notes. A bibliography is included.

Wolberg, Lewis R.; and Aronson, Marvin L., eds; with Arlene R. Wolberg, guest ed. GROUP THERAPY 1976: AN OVERVIEW. New York: Stratton Intercontinental Medical Books, 1976. xv, 246 p.

This book, dedicated to J.L. Moreno, devotes four chapters to various aspects of the life and work of this seminal thinker. These are followed by chapters on action techniques, systems theory, and psychoanalytic group therapy. Many topics are dis-cussed under these headings, but the prevailing viewpoint is tra-ditional and analytic.

Wolf, Alexander, et al. BEYOND THE COUCH. DIALOGUES IN TEACH-
ING AND LEARNING PSYCHOANALYSIS IN GROUPS. New York: Science
House, 1969. xiv, 364 p.

> The authors describe the practice of psychoanalysis in groups and
> the interplay between individual and group activity. Methods of
> training therapists for this kind of work are also discussed, and
> the effectiveness of telephonic supervision is pointed out. Through
> the medium of the trainees' meetings, parallels between transfer-
> ence, countertransference and so-called supertransference are il-
> lustrated, and specific problems of the method are examined, such
> as the effect of the absence of face-to-face cues. A list of
> references is included.

Yalom, Irvin D. THE THEORY AND PRACTICE OF GROUP PSYCHOTHERAPY.
New York: Basic Books, 1970. xi, 398 p.

> The author brings a dual research-clinical orientation to this
> book. He discusses group therapy from the standpoint of its
> "curative factors," or the mechanisms of change that exist in
> therapy groups. The first four chapters describe the derivation
> and operation of these factors, and the next nine chapters con-
> stitute an inductive sequence describing a system of therapy based
> on these factors. The final chapter reviews the goals of the book:
> to provide a guide for the training of group therapists, and to
> describe the scientific basis of group therapy. References are
> listed at the end of each chapter.

# Chapter 7

# ORGANIZATIONAL SETTINGS

Argyris, Chris. PERSONALITY AND ORGANIZATION. THE CONFLICT
BETWEEN SYSTEM AND THE INDIVIDUAL. New York: Harper and Row,
1957. xiii, 291 p.

> The author constructs a framework within which to integrate avail-
> able research on organizational behavior. The relationship be-
> tween the formal organization and the individual is discussed,
> with the conclusion that the organization conflicts with the indi-
> vidual who thereby fails to reach full self-actualization. The
> author states his conclusions in the form of a set of propositions
> regarding organizational behavior. Chapter-by-chapter references
> are presented.

_____. UNDERSTANDING ORGANIZATIONAL BEHAVIOR. Homewood,
Ill.: Dorsey Press, 1960. xii, 179 p.

> The author approaches the study of organization by developing a
> conceptual and methodological framework. He presents data from
> empirical research based on this model. Included are proposals
> for the quantitative analysis of self-actualization. He also sets
> forth ideas on the subject of organizational change.

Bakke, E. Wight. THE FUSION PROCESS. A MAP FOR THE EXPLORA-
TION OF THE RELATIONSHIP OF PEOPLE AND ORGANIZATIONS. New
Haven, Conn.: Labor and Management Center, Yale University, 1953. iv,
58 p.

> This publication presents a model of people's behavior in and
> regarding organizations, developed at the Yale Labor and Man-
> agement Center. The description of the model, research design,
> and research problems is accomplished while keeping technical
> language to a minimum. The book is aimed both at the person
> in the organizational field and at researchers. Charts are sup-
> plied in the description of the fusion process.

Bakke, E. Wight, and Argyris, Chris. ORGANIZATIONAL STRUCTURE AND DYNAMICS. A FRAMEWORK FOR THEORY. New Haven, Conn.: Labor and Management Center, Yale University, 1954. 38 p.

> This short book is divided into two main sections: concepts used and theoretical framework, and generalizations. It sets up postulates regarding organizational processes and derives therorems from them, to arrive at a framework for theory in this area.

Blau, Peter M., and Scott, W. Richard. FORMAL ORGANIZATIONS. A COMPARATIVE APPROACH. London: Routledge and Kegan Paul, 1963. xiv, 312 p.

> This is a sociological analysis of the effect of organizations on the structure of society and the significance of organizations as work environments. Theory and research are reviewed. The nature and kinds of formal organizations, the connections between them and the rest of society, and facets of their internal structure (such as the social structure of work groups, communication, peer group and hierarchical relations, and management) are discussed. A comprehensive bibliography is supplied.

Blum, Milton L. INDUSTRIAL PSYCHOLOGY AND ITS SOCIAL FOUNDATIONS. Rev. ed. New York: Harper and Bros., 1956. xvi, 612 p.

> Blum presents industrial psychology in the interest of promoting harmonious relations by using the democratic process in industry. He examines the employers' and the employees' perspectives, dealing with topics such as motivation, job satisfaction, leadership, and communication. Psychological tests mentioned in the text are listed in the appendix. Each chapter ends with a summary and chapter bibliography.

Burke, W. Warner, and Hornstein, Harvey A., eds. THE SOCIAL TECHNOLOGY OF ORGANIZATION DEVELOPMENT. La Jolla, Calif.: University Associates, 1972. xxii, 340 p.

> This book of readings is directed at students of organization behavior and change, organization development practitioners, and organization managers. Divided into seven sections, it deals with topics such as team building, managing conflict, techno-structural intervention, data feedback, and training. Each section contains an editors' overview.

Dubin, Robert. THE WORLD OF WORK: INDUSTRIAL SOCIETY AND HUMAN RELATIONS. Englewood Cliffs, N.J.: Prentice-Hall, 1958. xiii, 448 p.

The author deals with people's behavior at work and the reasons
for it. Topics such as behavior systems, organizational structure,
motivation and morale are discussed. Dubin also attempts to
develop a theory of human interaction in industry. A chapter-
by-chapter bibliography is presented.

_____, ed. HUMAN RELATIONS IN ADMINISTRATION WITH READINGS
AND CASES. 2d ed. Englewood Cliffs, N.J.: Prentice-Hall, 1961. xix,
635 p.

This book of readings deals with the human resources of organizations and the human relations entailed in the administration of
these resources. It is divided into seven parts: administrative
perspectives, organizations, administrative personnel, administrative relationships, administrative action, internal and external
environment, and case materials on human relations in administration. Topics include motivation, informal groups, bureaucracy,
power, authority, communication, decision making, and leadership. Each reading contains a list of references.

Gardner, Burleigh B., and Moore, David G. HUMAN RELATIONS IN
INDUSTRY: ORGANIZATION AND ADMINISTRATIVE BEHAVIOR. 4th ed.
Homewood, Ill.: Richard D. Irwin, 1964. 479 p.

The authors attempt to provide guidelines for increased understanding of the patterns and processes involved when people work
together in an organization. This edition provides an introduction to business administration covering sociology, social anthropology and human relations in industry. Organizational behavior
and theory are also presented in a traditional human relations
approach.

Guest, Robert H.; Hersey, Paul; and Blanchard, Kenneth H. ORGANIZA-
TIONAL CHANGE THROUGH EFFECTIVE LEADERSHIP. Englewood Cliffs,
N.J.: Prentice-Hall, 1977. viii, 184 p.

This is a narrative case study which contains theoretical, diagnostic, and therapeutic material to help link theory with practice. The authors attempt to analyze and interpret the case
study in terms of as many relevant behavioral science theories
and frameworks as possible.

Haire, Mason, ed. MODERN ORGANIZATION THEORY. A SYMPOSIUM
OF THE FOUNDATION FOR RESEARCH ON HUMAN BEHAVIOR. New York:
Wiley; London: Chapman and Hall, 1959. x, 324 p.

The participants in this symposium included representatives of
academia and interested industries. Viewpoints presented include

a behavioral theory of organizational objectives, an interaction approach and a motivation approach to the theory of organization, and biological models of the growth of organizations. Contributors include E. Wight Bakke, Anatol Rapoport, Chris Argyris, and Dorwin Cartwright. Each paper contains a list of references.

_____. ORGANIZATIONAL THEORY IN INDUSTRIAL PRACTICE. A SYMPOSIUM OF THE FOUNDATION FOR RESEARCH ON HUMAN BEHAVIOR. New York: Wiley, 1962. x, 173 p.

This book presents papers on organization theory in action by representatives of industry. Topics include designing an organization structure, organization of the planning process, the nature and use of authority, and organizational structures in transition. Contributors include Hugh Estes, Robert C. Hood, and Harry D. Kolb.

Hickman, C. Addison, and Kuhn, Manford H. INDIVIDUALS, GROUPS, AND ECONOMIC BEHAVIOR. New York: Dryden Press, 1956. xvii, 266 p.

The authors explore the nature, causes, and consequences of role conflict and role ambiguity. Role stress is viewed from the varying but complementary perspectives of organizational process, interpersonal relations, and personality processes. A national survey and an intensive study were conducted, and results from these are tabulated in a set of appendixes. A bibliography is also supplied.

Katz, Daniel, and Kahn, Robert L. THE SOCIAL PSYCHOLOGY OF ORGANIZATIONS. New York: Wiley, 1966. 498 p.

The authors discuss group behavior beginning at the point where small group studies stop: the behavior of people in organizations and institutions. An open-system theory is developed, in which the assumption of entropy (the necessary dependence of an organization on its environment) is emphasized. This open-system view is then used for the study of large-scale organizations.

Kelly, Joe. ORGANIZATIONAL BEHAVIOUR. Homewood, Ill.: Richard D. Irwin, 1969. xvi, 666 p.

This book is intended an an introduction to organizational psychology. It traces the development of the field from industrial psychology through human relations to organizational behavior. Personality, the group, and the organization are dealt with, followed by studies of executive behavior and a section on applications. The author closes with a look to the future. Most chapters are summarized and include a glossary of terms. Readings and cases appear throughout the book in boxes. A bibliography is supplied.

Likert, Rensis. THE HUMAN ORGANIZATION: ITS MANAGEMENT AND VALUE. New York: McGraw-Hill, 1967. ix, 258 p.

This book deals with the application of quantitative research results to improve the management of the human resources of an enterprise. The science-based system of management is described. The author focuses on the systemic nature of the enterprise and the motivational forces at work. Appendixes provide tables of organizational variables and profiles of organizational characteristics, with a correlation matrix of organizational and performance characteristics of different management systems based on a comparative analysis discussed in the book. A bibliography is included.

Loveday, Peter, and Campbell, Ian. GROUPS IN THEORY AND PRACTICE. Sydney Studies in Politics 1. Sydney: F.W. Cheshire, 1962. 98 p.

This is the first of a monograph series based on research in progress in the department of government, University of Sydney, Australia. It contains two studies on political groups: Loveday surveys group theories of politics; Campbell discusses some political groups in Australia at the turn of the century, particularly the role of pressure groups in relation to the parties and in the economic field. References are supplied for each article.

Maier, Norman R.F. PRINCIPLES OF HUMAN RELATIONS. APPLICATIONS TO MANAGEMENT. New York: Wiley, 1952. ix, 474 p.

This book discusses human relations problems in industry, techniques for dealing with them, and problems arising in training people to practice effective techniques. Although the examples and applications are of an industrial nature, the principles apply to individuals or groups. Topics include role playing, group decision processes, democratic supervision, problem solving, and nondirective counseling. Some case material is presented. A bibliography is included.

Melman, Seymour. DYNAMIC FACTORS IN INDUSTRIAL PRODUCTIVITY. Oxford: Basil Blackwell, 1956. xiii, 238 p.

The author explores two parallel processes in business-managed industrial firms, emphasizing the similarities in the decision-making activities involved in each. The two processes are the rise of administrative overhead and the mechanization of production. The author describes the methods of investigation used and the results. The book is divided into four parts: determinants of changes in production methods, determinants of manpower utilization, determinants of productivity levels, and implications of the productivity process. References are supplied throughout the book.

Miller, Eric J., ed. TASK AND ORGANIZATION. New York: Wiley, 1976. xviii, 379 p.

This volume of readings deals with the interrelationship between the individual, the different groups to which he or she belongs, and the organizational settings within which the person and the group operate. Part 1 explores the individual and the organization; part 2 discusses the design of organization for task performance in different kinds of institutions; and part 3 describes strategies for change, through external intervention, education, and internal initiative. Each part has an introductory article; each chapter contains a reference list. There is an introductory essay by the editor on role perspectives.

Miller, Eric J., and Rice, A. Kenneth. SYSTEMS OF ORGANIZATION. THE CONTROL OF TASK AND SENTIENT BOUNDARIES. London: Tavistock, 1967. xviii, 286 p.

The authors set out to develop a theory of organization that deals with organization, human activities and tasks within one framework. Part 1 describes the conceptual framework. Part 2 examines transactions across enterprise boundaries, using as examples a service industry and a sales force. Part 3 uses a family business to illustrate disentanglement of coincident task boundaries. Temporary and transitional task systems and the elimination of organizational boundaries within enterprises are discussed. The final section is concerned with task and sentient systems and their boundary controls. References are supplied.

Rackham, Neil; Honey, Peter; and Colbert, Michael J. DEVELOPING INTERACTIVE SKILLS. Northampton, Engl.: Wellens, 1971. 191 p.

This book presents an account of the authors' effort to improve the nature of the interactive capabilities of personnel management in two large organizations. They describe the development and use of a methodology for identifying and obtaining behavioral data of relevance to the interpersonal situation, feeding back and diagnosing those data to training participants, and thereafter designing practice sessions and plans by which individuals can improve their interpersonal behavior as the data describe. The training technique of varying group composition is discussed along with the influence of group mix on helping individuals change their behavior.

Rice, A. Kenneth. THE ENTERPRISE AND ITS ENVIRONMENT. A SYSTEM THEORY OF MANAGEMENT ORGANIZATION. London: Tavistock, 1963. xiv, 364 p.

The author discusses a particular consulting position in an organization and the initiation and implementation of change which this entailed. The concepts and assumptions employed are described as being linked in a broad conceptual framework that relates institutions, groups, and individuals. The theory which develops out of the work described here is elaborated in the last part of the book. Its essence lies in treating enterprises as living organisms. Appendixes provide charts illustrating relationships between parts of the system. A bibliography is supplied.

Roethlisberger, Fritz J., and Dickson, William J. MANAGEMENT AND THE WORKER. Cambridge, Mass.: Harvard University Press, 1939. 615 p.

An account of the series of studies on the human effects of work and working conditions done at the Hawthorne Plant of the Western Electric Company. Included are five parts: working conditions and employee efficiency, a plan for the improvement of employee relations, a conceptual scheme for the understanding of employee dissatisfaction, social organization of employees, and applications to practice of research results.

Sayles, Leonard R. BEHAVIOR OF INDUSTRIAL WORK GROUPS: PREDICTION AND CONTROL. New York: Wiley, 1958. viii, 182 p.

The author bases this discussion on field investigation of a variety of informal work-group behaviors. He deals with membership characteristics and types of leadership which enhance the ability of such work groups to meet their needs. The implications of group activity for research on work groups, as well as for union and management are explored. The research method employed in the book is presented in an appendix.

Scott, Ellis L. LEADERSHIP AND PERCEPTIONS OF ORGANIZATION. Research Monograph no. R-82. Columbus: Bureau of Business Research, Ohio State University, 1956. 122 p.

In an organizational setting, each person's perception of the structure of the organization unit of which he or she is a member is compared with an organization chart drawn up for the unit. The data are analyzed with respect to discrepancies between charted and perceived organization and correspondences or reciprocations between the perceptions of subordinates, peers, and superiors. The relationship of these findings to variables such as unit effectiveness and morale is discussed.

Selekman, Benjamin M. LABOR RELATIONS AND HUMAN RELATIONS. New York: McGraw-Hill, 1947. xi, 255 p.

The author views the path to successful collective bargaining as
lying along the road of sound human relations, focusing on cooperation while recognizing differences. What such relationships
require in terms of day-to-day function among workers is the
question the book seeks to answer. It explores the course of
interacting influence on the existing network of relationships
when a union comes on the scene and it deals with the problems
posed for leaders on both sides. The content of collective bargaining is discussed as a social process. Footnotes appear throughout the book.

Simon, Herbert A. ADMINISTRATIVE BEHAVIOR: A STUDY OF DECISION-
MAKING PROCESS IN ADMINISTRATIVE ORGANIZATION. 3d ed. New
York: Free Press, 1976. 364 p.

This book, first published in 1945, focuses on organizational
decision making, taking into account the relation of organization
structure to decision making and the decision making of management science and operations research. This edition incorporates
the first edition and adds six new chapters. Authority, communication processes, and loyalty to group and goals or identifications
are discussed. Bibliographical references are contained in footnotes throughout the text.

Stogdill, Ralph M. INDIVIDUAL BEHAVIOR AND GROUP ACHIEVEMENT.
A THEORY. THE EXPERIMENTAL EVIDENCE. New York: Oxford University Press, 1959. xi, 352 p.

The author develops a theory of organization achievement based
on the assumption that what happens in groups can be described
in terms of the interactions between the members. The book
deals with group structure, performance, purpose, and achievement. Each chapter presents definitions and theoretical discussion followed by sections on research. A list of references is
included.

Tannenbaum, Robert; Weschler, Irving R.; and Massarik, Fred. LEADERSHIP
AND ORGANIZATION: A BEHAVIORAL SCIENCE APPROACH. New York:
McGraw-Hill, 1961. xiv, 456 p.

The authors divide their work into three sections, each with its
own introduction. Part 1 deals with leadership and the influence
process and covers the issues of subordinate participation and
organizational change, among other topics. Part 2 deals with
sensitivity training and leadership development, and part 3 presents studies in organization. A list of Human Relations Research
Group publications, 1950-60, is included as well as a selected,
annotated bibliography of works on related topics.

Thelen, Herbert A. DYNAMICS OF GROUPS AT WORK. Chicago: University of Chicago Press, 1954. vii, 379 p.

> Some concepts commonly discussed in the field of group behavior
> are presented as background material. These include leadership
> development and needs of group members. The author presents
> practical suggestions for leaders, members, and organizers of
> groups in the following areas: human relations, education, pub-
> lic meetings, citizen action, administration and management, and
> faculty self-training. A short list of selected readings is included.

U.S. Research and Development Board, Committee on Human Resources. Panel on Human Relations and Morale. SYMPOSIUM ON RESEARCH IN GROUP BEHAVIOR. Washington, D.C.: 1952. v, 106 p.

> This symposium centers around the problems of the armed forces,
> in order to improve their management methods and develop prin-
> ciples of group behavior that can be applied to situations to
> which any group may be exposed, in and out of combat. The
> papers deal with criterion research, experimental research, and
> applied research. Contributors include Donald Baier, Solomon E.
> Asch, David C. McClelland, and George W. Baker.

Viteles, Morris S. MOTIVATION AND MORALE IN INDUSTRY. New York: W.W. Norton, 1953. xvi, 510 p.

> Several British and American experimental studies and attitude
> surveys are described and evaluated. The focus is on the deter-
> minants of morale and the sources of motivation in industry.
> Attention is paid to the application of findings in order to bring
> about increased morale, job satisfaction, and productivity. Refer-
> ences are listed at the end of each chapter.

Weiss, Robert S. PROCESS OF ORGANIZATION. Ann Arbor: Survey Research Center, Institute for Social Research, University of Michigan, 1956. ix, 117 p.

> This is a report of a study carried out in a particular organization.
> It describes the workings of that organization and presents a con-
> ceptual scheme for the analysis of organizations in general.
> Organizational functions, structure, and coordination are exam-
> ined, as are processes of allocation and adaptation. Technical
> material pertaining to the study is contained in the appendixes.
> A bibliography is included.

Zaleznick, Abraham; Christensen, C.R.; and Roethlisberger, F[ritz].J. THE MOTIVATION, PRODUCTIVITY, AND SATISFACTION OF WORKERS: A PREDICTION STUDY. Boston: Division of Research, Graduate School of Business Administration, Harvard University, 1958. xxii, 442 p.

The authors report research on the factors influencing motivation, productivity, and satisfaction of individuals in an industrial work situation. Clinical and analytical methods are used in the investigation. The authors draw up theories, derive hypotheses, and test them against a set of predicted and actual outcomes.

# Chapter 8

# EDUCATIONAL SETTINGS

Amidon, Edmund J., and Hough, John B., eds. INTERACTION ANALYSIS: THEORY, RESEARCH, AND APPLICATION. Reading, Mass.: Addison-Wesley, 1967. xiii, 402 p.

This book of readings deals with one of the recent developments in analyzing the instructional process. Many of the articles were previously published, but some were written specifically for this volume. Part 1 describes the background to the field and its theoretical foundations. Part 2 considers procedures and research on teaching patterns, and part 3 discusses the application of interaction analysis to problems of teacher education. Each part is introduced by an overview. References are provided.

Bany, Mary A., and Johnson, Lois V. CLASSROOM GROUP BEHAVIOR. GROUP DYNAMICS IN EDUCATION. New York: Macmillan, 1964. xii, 412 p.

This volume was written to give teachers some understanding of the dynamic forces that affect the class as a group. The characteristics of classroom groups are described in terms of cohesiveness, interaction and structure, norms, and goals. Techniques for changing group behavior are also discussed. Actual incidents of classroom behavior are reported and analyzed to illustrate the application of what is known in the field of group psychology. Questions for study and discussion and lists of suggested readings appear at the end of each chapter.

Henry, Nelson B., ed. THE DYNAMICS OF INSTRUCTIONAL GROUPS. SOCIOPSYCHOLOGICAL ASPECTS OF TEACHING AND LEARNING. THE FIFTY-NINTH YEARBOOK OF THE NATIONAL SOCIETY FOR THE STUDY OF EDUCATION. Part 2. Chicago: National Society for the Study of Education, 1960. xi, 186 p.

Originally intended to be a study of the class as a group, this collection of readings broadened to include such areas as the role functions of the teacher, the unique aspects of the classroom as a human group, the social structure of the class, group norms, and the diagnosis and guidance of instructional groups. Each reading has footnotes, and a general index is included.

Jennings, Helen H. SOCIOMETRY IN GROUP RELATIONS. A MANUAL FOR TEACHERS. 2d ed. Westport, Conn.: Greenwood Press, 1973. xi, 105 p.

This book was originally developed as a work guide for elementary and secondary school teachers. The author hopes to enhance sociometric work in the classroom, believing in the importance of our self-esteem in influencing our ability to work and learn. The use of sociometric procedures can facilitate social relationships to the benefit of all concerned. A chapter on the psychological theory of sociometric choices is included.

Miles, Matthew B. LEARNING TO WORK IN GROUPS: A PROGRAM GUIDE FOR EDUCATIONAL LEADERS. New York: Horace Mann Institute of School Experimentation, Teachers College, Columbia University, 1959. xiv, 285 p.

This is a comprehensive collection of available materials on the topic of helping individuals to learn better in groups. The author deals with a number of key processes: specific training activities, problems relating to the assumption of the trainer role, and difficulties concerning the evaluation process. Appendixes supply a list of published accounts of training sessions and a selected library of resources.

Newman, Ruth G. GROUPS IN SCHOOLS. A BOOK ABOUT TEACHERS, PARENTS, AND CHILDREN. New York: Simon and Schuster, 1974. 286 p.

This book describes the group dynamics of the classroom, including how the interaction of groups influences the learning process, and how the dynamics of group action, group relations, and group thinking can facilitate or hinder a child's progress in school. The author supplies an analysis of the "games" that children play among themselves, and demonstrates that by understanding the dynamics of these games we can effect a transformation of our present educational system. A bibliography is included.

# Chapter 9

# SOCIAL WORK GROUP SETTINGS

Bernstein, Saul, ed. EXPLORATIONS IN GROUP WORK: ESSAYS IN THEORY AND PRACTICE. Boston: Charles River Books, 1976. xv, 136 p.

This book deals with social work groups, or groups whose members are served by agencies, and in which the primary focus is on development of the members. The contributors discuss how groups are started and what the group worker's expectations should be of the stages of progression, as well as the processes of conflict and decision making. The twin themes of diagnosis and of worker's intervention are emphasized throughout. References are listed at the end of each article.

_____. FURTHER EXPLORATIONS IN GROUP WORK. Boston: Milford House, 1973. xiii, 179 p.

The editor and contributors present a set of applications of some theories of groups in social casework settings. They have selected dimensions of group properties and use these as a focus, rather than trying to deal with a complete social system. Some of these dimensions are goals and values, stages, and composition. The life of the group is related to the functioning of members outside of the group. Real groups rather than those in laboratory settings are considered. Psychiatric care, children, and scapegoating are among the areas of application. Bibliographies follow each of the six readings.

Douglas, Tom. GROUPWORK PRACTICE. New York: International Universities Press, 1977. 224 p.

The author discusses the use of groups in social work and the practical problems of starting, running, and terminating a social work group. The book includes charts, checklists, analysis sheets, methods of recording, and details of observing. Contract, client partnership, conflict and confrontation, and leadership are explored. A glossary of terms used in groupwork and an annotated reading list are supplied, along with references in the text.

Hartford, Margaret E. GROUPS IN SOCIAL WORK: APPLICATION OF SMALL GROUP THEORY AND RESEARCH TO SOCIAL WORK PRACTICE. New York: Columbia University Press, 1972. viii, 297 p.

This book draws together small group theory, research findings, and experiences with groups. The author offers a framework to help social workers in their decisions to use groups, in their efforts to create and form groups, and in their intervention and activity with them. Two main uses of groups are discussed: where the individual is the target (for the benefit of group participants), and where the institution, community, or society is the target (for social change and amelioration of crises).

Northen, Helen. SOCIAL WORK WITH GROUPS. New York: Columbia University Press, 1969. vii, 270 p.

This book describes the theory that underlies the method and procedures by which social workers employ specially designed groups to help persons. The emphasis is on the role of the social worker in influencing movement toward mutually determined goals, and the ways whereby the group itself and its interaction with other social systems affect workers' actions and clients' movements.

Sullivan, Dorothea F., ed. THE PRACTICE OF GROUP WORK. New York: Association Press, 1947. x, 230 p.

This is a set of articles written mainly by the leaders in the United States and Canada of the nineteen groups described. Group work is viewed as a way of achieving personality development. The book concludes with a chapter on criteria for group work; these include group criteria and individual factors.

_____. READINGS IN GROUP WORK. New York: Association Press, 1952. xvi, 438 p.

This collection of articles, many reprinted from journals, focuses on the group process in its relational aspects. It is aimed at the group worker, in the human relations area. A short bibliography is supplied along with definitions of group work, the function of the group worker, and basic principles of social group work.

# Chapter 10

# GENERAL APPLIED SETTINGS

Berne, Eric L.  THE STRUCTURE AND DYNAMICS OF ORGANIZATIONS
AND GROUPS.  New York:  Grove Press, 1963.  x, 260 p.

The author offers the book as a framework for the therapy of
organizations and groups.  The four-part division covers the
following:  first, a simple group meeting is analyzed; second,
a group model is set up and its practical applications outlined;
third, the individual as group member is studied, using the principles of transactional analysis; fourth, a chapter for group therapists and some applications of the system to the help of organizations and groups is provided.  One appendix deals with group
dynamics literature, the other with a classification of social
aggregates.  A glossary is provided.

Bonner, Hubert.  GROUP DYNAMICS:  PRINCIPLES AND APPLICATIONS.
New York:  Ronald Press, 1959.  531 p.

The dynamics of small group behavior are presented through the
aspects of group structure, cohesion, learning, leadership, problem solving, and intergroup tensions.  Bonner examines the applications of group dynamics to industry, education, political behavior, community relations, and group psychotherapy.  The book
concludes with a critical evaluation of the assumptions involved
in group dynamics.

Colman, Arthur D., and Bexton, W. Harold, eds.  GROUP RELATIONS
READER.  Sausalito, Calif:  Grex, 1975.  xii, 370 p.

This collection of original papers and reprints constitutes an interdisciplinary survey of materials in the theory and practice of
group relations.  The readings are divided into sections dealing
with theory, method, and applications.  In the latter part, fields
covered include clinical work, education and professional training, organizational consultation, and architecture, design, and
planning.  Papers include the writings of Bion, Rice, and Miller,
along with later American studies, most of which are in the application field.  A bibliography is included.

Dunphy, Dexter C. THE PRIMARY GROUP. A HANDBOOK FOR ANALYSIS AND FIELD RESEARCH. New York: Appleton-Century-Crofts, 1972. ix, 301 p.

> This is a study of one particular kind of small group: the primary group. By this the author means families, peer groups, informal groups within organizational settings, and resocialization groups such as therapeutic or rehabilitation groups. The book focuses on ways of thinking about and studying such groups. In part 1, the author develops a primary group model; part 2 deals with key variables in primary group systems and how to measure them. Each chapter is annotated, and an author and subject index is supplied.

Dyer, William G., ed. MODERN THEORY AND METHOD IN GROUP TRAINING. New York: Van Nostrand Reinhold, 1972. xiv, 251 p.

> This book of readings is divided into five sections dealing with the personal style of the trainer, theory of intervention, new designs, ethical issues, and the relation of group methods to organizational consultations. Most of the articles are original. The volume is directed toward potential and practicing professionals in the group training field.

Festinger, Leon; Schacter, Stanley; and Back, Kurt [W.]. SOCIAL PRESSURES IN INFORMAL GROUPS. A STUDY OF HUMAN FACTORS IN HOUSING. New York: Harper and Bros., 1950. Reissue. Stanford, Calif.: Stanford University Press, 1963. x, 197 p.

> This study was precipitated by the necessity for understanding the needs of families in the housing market at the time when mass-production techniques made houses more readily available. The satisfaction of the occupants with the lifestyle possible in their homes is considered an important determinant of where and how they choose to live. Group formation, standards, and structure are dealt with. Two additional chapters, by Catherine Bauer and Robert Woods Kennedy, explore practical application problems. These chapters are omitted from the 1963 reissue. The appendix describes the methodology of the field study.

Gibbard, Graham S; Hartman, John J.; and Mann, Richard D., eds. ANALYSIS OF GROUPS. CONTRIBUTIONS TO THEORY, RESEARCH, AND PRACTICE. San Francisco: Jossey-Bass, 1974. xxiv, 444 p.

> This set of readings examines the operation of different sorts of small experimental groups in classroom, sensitivity training, and psychotherapeutic settings. The book is divided into five parts: part 1 deals with strategies of observation and analysis, part 2 with group process and development, part 3 with the relationship

between the individual and the group, part 4 with shared fantasy and myth, and part 5 with the dynamics of leadership. Each part has an introductory article. There is a bibliography.

Henderson, George. HUMAN RELATIONS. FROM THEORY TO PRACTICE. Norman: University of Oklahoma Press, 1974. x, 450 p.

The author directs the book at those actively engaged in attempting to improve human relationships. There are four sections: foundations, strategies for change, programs for change, and new techniques. Chapters on psychotherapy, T-groups, and encounter groups are included, as well as readings on transactional analysis and simulations and games. Appendixes supply individual, group, and community-change questionnaires. A list of suggested readings appears after each chapter.

Jacobs, Alfred, and Spradlin, Wilford, eds. THE GROUP AS AGENT OF CHANGE. New York: Behavioral Publications, 1974. xxvii, 463 p.

This collection examines the use of group methods of intervention for producing change in organizations and individuals. The contributors' view is that intervention involves educative and learning processes. Their articles are divided into four sections: perspectives and overview, innovative treatment strategies and programs, theory and conceptualization, and data and research. The social settings range from home, kindergarten, and psychiatrist's office to hospital ward and community at large.

Jones, John E., and Pfeiffer, J. William, eds. ANNUAL HANDBOOK FOR GROUP FACILITATORS. Iowa City, Iowa: University Associates, 1975. viii, 289 p.

This is the fourth annual published in the series, and it continues the focus of the previous volumes on the practicality and usefulness of human relations training materials. Theoretical positions, techniques, experiences, and suggestions for applications are reflected in the contents. Each section is introduced, and a short set of book reviews is included. Author biographies are supplied.

_____. THE 1977 ANNUAL HANDBOOK FOR GROUP FACILITATORS. Iowa City, Iowa: University Associates, 1977. 290 p.

This is a resource tool for group leaders. The section on structured experiences covers a range of training topics: organization decision making, force-field analysis, leadership, feelings, and trust. The instrumentation section presents scales, applicable in consultation and training. Lecturettes concentrate on topics such as communication, personal growth, and conflict. Theory and practice papers present the work of practitioners in human relations training, and the resources section includes bibliographies on small-group training, and nonverbal communication.

_____. THE 1978 ANNUAL HANDBOOK FOR GROUP FACILITATORS. Iowa City, Iowa: University Associates, 1978. 290 p.

This is a resource tool for group leaders. The section on structured experiences covers a range of training topics, including feelings, leadership, and trust. The instrumentation section presents scales applicable in consultation and problem solving. Lecturettes concentrate on communication, intervention, and contracting. Theory and practice papers present the work of practitioners in human relations training. The resource section includes a directory of graduate programs in applied behavioral sciences as well as an article on selecting workshop sites.

Kaplan, Martin F., and Schwartz, Steven. HUMAN JUDGEMENT AND DECISION PROCESSES IN APPLIED SETTINGS. New York: Academic Press, 1977. 304 p.

The authors present a set of conceptual and methodological tools for scientifically based decision-making theory in areas such as mass transportation, the criminal justice system, conflict resolution, and personnel. They demonstrate the use of decision-making frameworks such as information-integration theory, social judgment theory, and expectancy theory. The book is intended for anyone in the business of managing, planning, teaching, researching, or policy making.

Leslie, Robert C. SHARING GROUPS IN THE CHURCH. Nashville, Tenn.: Abingdon, 1971. 224 p.

The author presents an introduction to the dynamics and principles of small group work in the church. The book is aimed at helping sharing groups to develop trust and experience reconciliation and personality growth of members. The author shows how small group work can be strategic in church renewal.

Lifton, Walter M. WORKING WITH GROUPS: GROUP PROCESS AND INDIVIDUAL GROWTH. 2d ed. New York: Wiley, 1966. xii, 288 p.

The author views competent group work as important in preventing many problems now the concern of the helping professions. Group settings are seen as effective learning experiences. The issues involved in group process are summarized, followed by descriptions of group situations which Lifton considers instructional. He further supplies resumes with interpretations different from his own. The educational setting is given special emphasis. Each chapter has a summary/discussion section and bibliography.

Lippitt, Ronald. TRAINING IN COMMUNITY RELATIONS: A RESEARCH EXPLORATION TOWARD NEW GROUP SKILLS. New York: Harper, 1949. xiv, 286 p.

This is an account of a two-week workshop for intergroup relations workers. Various techniques are illustrated, among them

role playing, role reversal, soliloquizing, and analysis of a
chairman's role. Evaluation data is included, and interview
schedules are presented in the appendix.

Newstetter, Wilber I.; Feldstein, Marc J.; and Newcomb, Theodore M.
GROUP ADJUSTMENT: A STUDY IN EXPERIMENTAL SOCIOLOGY.
Cleveland: School of Applied Social Sciences, Western Reserve University,
1938. xv, 154 p.

This is a report of activities at the Wawokiye Camp Research
Project in which a group of thirty boys was gathered for experimental group work purposes. The authors make use of a personal
preference technique and describe a technique for measuring some
aspects of interaction through behavior observations. Appendixes
give details of the methods used, and thirty-one tables and six
charts are supplied.

Pfeiffer, J. William; Helsin, Richard; and Jones, John E. INSTRUMENTA-
TION IN HUMAN RELATIONS TRAINING: A GUIDE TO 92 INSTRUMENTS
WITH WIDE APPLICATION TO THE BEHAVIORAL SCIENCES. 2d ed. Iowa
City, Iowa: University Associates, 1976. 328 p.

This handbook is designed for use by practitioners in human relations training. It presents an introduction to the theory, methodology, and development of measurement tools. The authors
describe why a particular instrument is appropriate for a particular group, and suggest how instrument feedback can be applied
in an effective manner. Practical ideas are provided on incor-
porating paper-and-pencil devices into laboratories, workshops,
courses, and other training events.

Pfeiffer, J. William, and Jones, John E., eds. A HANDBOOK OF STRUC-
TURED EXPERIENCES FOR HUMAN RELATIONS TRAINING. 3 Vols.
Iowa City, Iowa: University Associates, 1973-74.

These handbooks are collections of techniques, ideas, and forms
for use in various human relations training designs. The structured experiences are of varying levels of sophistication. The
exercises include studying group process, increasing skills in interpersonal communication, and studying assumptions underlying
human relations training. Bibliographies of additional sources are
provided.

_____. THE 1972 ANNUAL HANDBOOK FOR GROUP FACILITATORS.
Iowa City, Iowa: University Associates, 1972. viii, 271 p.

This handbook is directed toward practitioners in the various
fields using small groups. It contains articles on topics such as
types of growth groups, organizational development, contracts in

human relations groups, and transactional analysis. The book, in the form of a looseleaf notebook, presents sections on instruments, structured experiences, lecturettes, and book reviews. It includes guides to human relations training resource materials and a section on professional organizations involved in the human potential movement.

Pollack, Gertrude K.  LEADERSHIP OF DISCUSSION GROUPS.  CASE MATERIAL AND THEORY.  New York:  Wiley, 1975.  391 p.

This book is aimed at group leaders who need help in dealing with the problems of reaching and holding the group.  It also presents methods for leading group therapy in groups comprised of teenagers, adults, and older people.  Recordings of actual discussions are supplied accompanied by the author's comments, which emphasize the techniques of guiding group discussions into productive areas and reveal the underlying theory.  The use of content outlines, evaluation sheets, and other tools for the leader is demonstrated.

Rothman, Jack, ed.  PROMOTING SOCIAL JUSTICE IN THE MULTIGROUP SOCIETY:  A CASEBOOK FOR GROUP RELATIONS PRACTITIONERS.  New York:  Association Press, 1971.  253 p.

The contributors present a variety of source materials illustrating aspects of group relations practice.  This is a sourcebook with a casebook approach.  Divided into four parts, it deals with group rights, group identity and power, intergroup attitudes and relations, and group welfare.  Social groups include ethnic, religious, and classes, and problem-program areas range from alcoholism and education to riot control and management.  The concern throughout is with matters of group aspiration, identity, status, conflict, power relations, and accommodations.  A bibliography is supplied.

Short, James F., Jr., ed.  GANG DELINQUENCY AND DELINQUENT SUBCULTURES.  New York:  Harper and Row, 1968.  viii, 328 p.

This collection of articles deals with a number of aspects of delinquent gangs.  Some phenomena of group life such as leadership, status, and cohesiveness are applied to the gang and to delinquent subcultures in order to better understand their functioning.  Notes to the chapters are supplied.

Short, James F., Jr., and Strodtbeck, Fred L.  GROUP PROCESS AND GANG DELINQUENCY.  Chicago:  University of Chicago Press, 1965.  xv, 294 p.

The authors approach the problem of gang delinquency from a basic group process perspective.  The book describes a study of streetcorner gangs, examining values, behavior dimensions, racial differentials, sources of threat, and group norms, and attempting some explanations of gang action. The group process perspective is placed in the context of recent theoretical developments, especially those concerning social exchange. References are included throughout the book, and data is presented in tables.

# Chapter 11

# BIBLIOGRAPHICAL REFERENCE WORKS

## A. GENERAL REFERENCE WORKS

In addition to works cited below, the user is also referred to AMERICAN DOCTORAL DISSERTATIONS (Ann Arbor University Microfilms), AMERICAN LIBRARY RESOURCES (American Library Association), AMERICAN REFERENCE BOOKS ANNUAL (Libraries Unlimited), BIBLIOGRAPHIC INDEX (Wilson), BOOK REVIEW DIGEST (Wilson), BOOK REVIEW INDEX (Gale Research), COMPREHENSIVE DISSERTATION INDEX (Ann Arbor University Microfilms), CURRENT NATIONAL BIBLIOGRAPHIES (Greenwood), DISSERTATION ABSTRACTS INTERNATIONAL (Ann Arbor University Microfilms), DISSERTATION ABSTRACTS INTERNATIONAL: RETROSPECTIVE INDEX (Ann Arbor University Microfilms), GOVERNMENT PUBLICATIONS AND THEIR USE (Brookings Institute), GUIDE TO REFERENCE BOOKS (American Library Association), INDEX TO AMERICAN AUTHOR BIBLIOGRAPHIES (Scarecrow), IRREGULAR SERIALS AND ANNUALS (Bowker), MONTHLY CATALOG OF UNITED STATES GOVERNMENT PUBLICATIONS, (Superintendent of Documents), A POPULAR GUIDE TO GOVERNMENT PUBLICATIONS (Columbia University), THE STANDARD PERIODICAL DIRECTION (Oxbridge), and A WORLD BIBLIOGRAPHY OF BIBLIOGRAPHIES (Rowman and Littlefield).

AMERICAN BEHAVIORAL SCIENTIST GUIDE TO RECENT PUBLICATIONS IN THE SOCIAL AND BEHAVIORAL SCIENCES. New York: ABS, 1965. xxi, 781 p.

> This publication lists the monthly new studies citations appearing in back issues of the AMERICAN BEHAVIORAL SCIENTIST. It covers the period almost to the end of 1964. Later citations can be found in the monthly issues of the ABS, or in their bi-monthly publication NEW STUDIES IN THE SOCIAL AND BEHAVIORAL SCIENCES.

AN ANNOTATED BIBLIOGRAPHY OF RESEARCH, 1947-60. Compiled by Lewis E. Durham and Jack R. Gibb. Research Reprint Series no. 2. Arlington, Va.: National Training Laboratories, 1960. Unpaged.

This is a listing of forty-nine publications which resulted from
research carried out in whole or in part at the National Training
Laboratories during 1947-60. Included are books, journal articles,
dissertations, and mimeographed manuscripts. For each citation,
the laboratory in which the research occurred and the year in
which data were collected is shown.

ANNUAL REVIEW OF PSYCHOLOGY. Stanford, Calif.: Annual Reviews,
1950--. Annual.

These volumes provide frequent summaries in order to serve as a
reliable record of progress in the field. Fifteen to twenty areas
are focused on. The original plan adopted in 1958 was to review some topics each year, some in alternate years, and others
every third or fourth year, but greater flexibility in handling
topics evolved over the years. The time lag for inclusion is
very short. Bibliographies are appended which cite nearly three
thousand books and articles on the field. These constitute a
current set of basic contributions to research.

BEHAVIORAL SCIENCE TECHNIQUES. AN ANNOTATED BIBLIOGRAPHY
FOR HEALTH PROFESSIONALS. Compiled by Monique K. Tichy. New
York: Praeger, 1975. x, 118 p.

This volume presents the behavioral and social psychological
techniques relevant for the team delivery of health care. Part 1
deals with basic behavioral science research. The books and
articles in part 2 describe the application of behavioral science
knowledge and techniques. Part 3 lists general references, in-
dicating the location in this book where the entries have been
reviewed. The annotations are subdivided into content and
critique sections.

BIBLIOGRAPHIC GUIDE TO PSYCHOLOGY: 1975. Boston: G.K. Hall,
1976. 182 p.

This is one of a series of subject guides by this publisher which
brings together all publications cataloged during 1975 by the
Research Libraries of the New York Public Library, with further
entries from Library of Congress MARC tapes. They serve as
annual supplements to New York Public Library catalogs. All
types of material are included (books, nonbooks, and serials),
as are all languages. Main entries supply complete cataloging
information; secondary and subject entries provide abridged information.

BIBLIOGRAPHY OF BIBLIOGRAPHIES IN PSYCHOLOGY, 1900-27. Compiled
by Chauncey M. Louttit. Bulletin 65. Washington, D.C.: National Research Council, 1928. Reprint. New York: Burt Franklin, 1970. 108 p.

This volume lists 2,134 bibliographies in books or articles that contain at least fifty references, have a high rating for complete coverage of the subject, and provide good historical orientation. Part 1 presents a list of the general works and periodical searched, and part 2 continues with abstracts, indexes, and review journals. The main list of bibliographies, arranged by author, appears in part 3. Part 4 is the subject index, heavily cross-referenced.

CHOICE. Chicago: American Library Association, Association of College and Research Libraries, 1964--. 11 times a year.

This publication is a channel for reviewing new books in time to be useful for the development of undergraduate college library collections. It screens and authoritatively reviews the current output of books. The reviews are prepared with the help of some one thousand specialists and focus on appraising the professional merits of the books and their place in the literature of the field. General and reference works are added as a special area. Author and title index cumulates annually in February.

CURRENT CONTENTS: BEHAVIORAL, SOCIAL AND MANAGEMENT SCIENCES. Philadelphia: Institute for Scientific Information, 1969--. Weekly.

This publication lists tables of contents in their original format from over seven hundred foreign and domestic journals, compiled with specialist assistance. Delay is minimal; listings sometimes appear before publication of the journals. It is designed to accelerate the flow of information by providing a vehicle for increasing awareness of available information in periodical literature.

DICTIONARY OF MODERN SOCIOLOGY. Prepared by Thomas Ford Hoult. Totowa, N.J.: Littlefield, Adams, 1969. xviii, 408 p.

The author presents a list of definitions, many with accompanying quotations illustrating the usage of the terms. The main dictionary section is followed by a section in which entries are classified by specialty. The final section is an author index.

DICTIONARY OF PSYCHOLOGY. New rev. ed. Prepared by J.P. Chaplin. New York: Dell, 1975. xxix, 576 p.

This dictionary presents a list of definitions of technical terms in psychology and related terms from psychiatry, psychoanalysis, and biology. Entries for the central concepts of psychology, and for eminent contributors to the field, are encyclopedic rather than lexicographic. Appendixes, which precede the list of definitions, provide information on common abbreviations, Hull's symbolic constructs, Rorschach scoring symbols, Greek letter symbols, prefixes, suffixes, and combining forms, and statistical formulas commonly used in psychology.

A DICTIONARY OF SOCIOLOGY. Prepared by Geoffrey D. Mitchell. Chicago: Aldine, 1968. 224 p.

 The author examines some three hundred terms whose connotations
 are too technical to be adequately defined by general dictiona-
 ies. Each term is given a short definition or description, followed by historical reference to its uses and, when possible, citation
 of works to put the term in context. Length of entries varies
 from a sentence or two to two or three pages. Longer entries
 are initialed by contributors.

DIRECTORY OF SOCIAL STUDIES/SOCIAL SCIENCE ORGANIZATIONS. Compiled by Frances Haley and Regina McCormick. Boulder, Colo.: ERIC Clearinghouse for Social Studies/Social Science Education and Social Science Education Consortium, 1975. 43 p.

 This volume lists 111 social science/social studies service organizations, describing the services offered, purpose, educational
 level, current projects, and geographical area served. The cross-
 references include acronyms, directors, grade level, area served,
 and service and subject fields. A list of the publishers of social
 science curriculum materials is supplied.

ENCYCLOPEDIA OF ASSOCIATIONS. 13th ed. 3 vols. Edited by Nancy Yakes and Denise Akey. Detroit: Gale Research Co., 1979.

 Volume 1 of this set lists national associations of the United States,
 arranged by group, such as "Trade, Business and Commercial" and
 then by specific type, such as accountants. The information provided includes addresses, membership size, officers, publications,
 and statement of purpose and activities. A section on inactive,
 defunct, or former names is included, as is a list of citizen
 action groups. Associations are alphabetically indexed. Volume
 2 is a geographic-executive index to the material in volume 1.
 Volume 3 is a loose-leaf listing of quarterly reports on associations newly formed or newly identified by the editors.

GOVERNMENT REFERENCE BOOKS, A BIENNIAL GUIDE TO U.S. GOVERN- MENT PUBLICATIONS. Edited by Sally Wyncoop. Littleton, Colo.: Libraries Unlimited, 1970--. Biennial.

 This series locates and reviews reference books published by the
 U.S. government. Titles are annotated individually or in groups.
 Most of the one hundred subjects covered are in the social
 sciences. Appendixes provide major bibliographic sources and
 ordering procedures, and a directory of issuing agencies is included.

A GUIDE TO BOOK REVIEW CITATIONS; A BIBLIOGRAPHY OF SOURCES. Compiled by Richard A. Gray. Ohio State University Libraries Publication 2. Columbus: Ohio State University Press, 1969. 221 p.

This volume identifies and describes 512 sources of book reviews
for various subjects, roughly half of them in the social sciences.
For inclusion, a source "must cite reviews from more than one
journal or periodical, and . . . must cite book reviews in con-
tradistinction to critical studies." Five indexes accompany the
classified arrangement: subject, personal name, title, chronology,
and country-of-origin.


GUIDE TO REFERENCE MATERIALS. Vol. 2: SOCIAL AND HISTORICAL
SCIENCES, PHILOSOPHY AND RELIGION. 3d ed. Edited by Albert J.
Walford. London: Library Association, 1975. Distributed by American
Library Association, Chicago. 674 p.

This volume contains entries for some 4,500 titles, along with
several hundred subsumed entries. The annotations derive a critical flavor from the inclusion of remarks from many reviewing
journals. There are a number of cross-references to volume 1
of the GUIDE. Cut-off date for inclusion was April 1974, but a
few titles published later are presented.


HANDBOOK OF EVALUATION RESEARCH. 2 vols. Edited by Elmer L.
Struening and Marcia Guttentag. Beverly Hills, Calif.: Sage, 1975.

The editors have assembled two volumes of readings on evaluation
research. The first volume presents expert opinions on the various stages involved in such research and provides for the consid-
eration of alternative approaches so that the most appropriate
may be adopted. Volume 2 surveys the literature in selected
content areas, notably mental health programs. A cumulative
bibliography appears in volume 2.


THE HARVARD LIST OF BOOKS IN PSYCHOLOGY. 4th ed. Compiled by
the psychologists at Harvard University. Cambridge, Mass.: Harvard University Press, 1971. viii, 108 p.

This new edition has forty more entries than the third, with over
fifty percent new entries from the previous edition. It is selective rather than comprehensive, the annotated entries representing
fundamental works in the areas covered.


HUMANITIES INDEX. New York: H.W. Wilson, 1975--. Quarterly, with
annual cumulation.

Supersedes in part SOCIAL SCIENCES AND HUMANITIES INDEX
(see p. 126).


INDEX BIBLIOGRAPHICUS. 4th ed. 4 vols. Edited by Federation Internationale de Documentation. The Hague: FID, 1959-64.

These volumes are designed to serve as a selective directory of currently published abstracting and bibliographic services for retracing literature in a given field. This edition is a complete revision of the 1951 edition. Entries are arranged according to the Universal Decimal Classification. They include foreign language publications and services. Volume 1 deals with science and technology, and volume 2 with social sciences, volume 3 covers humanities, and volume 4 presents general bibliographies.

INDEX TO PSYCHOLOGY, MULTIMEDIA. Los Angeles: National Information Center for Educational Media, University of Southern California, 1972. x, 461 p.

This index is a bibliographic guide to nonbook media in psychology. It is divided into three main sections: a subject guide to psychology preceded by a subject heading outline, an alphabetical guide to media in psychology, and a directory of producers and distributors. Materials represented include 35mm filmstrips, 8mm motion cartridges, 16mm motion pictures, video tapes, records, and audio tapes. A wide range of topics is covered in clinical, developmental, educational, and social psychology.

INTERNATIONAL BIBLIOGRAPHY OF SOCIOLOGY. Paris: UNESCO, 1952–61. Chicago: Aldine, 1962. Annual.

This publication of three hundred to five hundred entries in English and French comprises a classified listing of books, periodical articles, pamphlets, and official government publications in many languages. Indexes are provided in English and French.

INTERNATIONAL ENCYCLOPEDIA OF PSYCHIATRY, PSYCHOLOGY, PSYCHOANALYSIS AND NEUROLOGY. 12 vols. Edited by Benjamin B. Wolman et al. New York: Aesculapius Publishers, 1977.

This is a cross-disciplinary reference work containing nearly two thousand articles written by over fifteen-hundred leading figures in these fields. It brings up to date the areas of research, theory, and practice for professionals, therapists, researchers, and others with an interest in the human mind, its functions, ills, and treatment.

INTERNATIONAL ENCYCLOPEDIA OF THE SOCIAL SCIENCES. 17 vols. Edited by David L. Sills. New York: Macmillan, 1968.

This encyclopedia provides information on topics and people in the social sciences, embracing concepts, theories, and methods in a range of disciplines including anthropology, economics, law, political science, psychology, and sociology. Analytical and comparative aspects of the topics are emphasized. Biographies of about six hundred persons are included. A selected bibliography follows each article, providing documentation for the article and suggestions for further reading.

INTERNATIONAL INDEX: A GUIDE TO PERIODICAL LITERATURE IN THE SOCIAL SCIENCES AND HUMANITIES. Vols. 1-18. New York: H.W. Wilson. 1907/15-April 1964/March 1965. Quarterly. March 1913--. Bimonthly except July. With annual and quadrennial cumulations. Title varies: 1907/15-1916/19, Readers' guide to periodical literature supplement; 1920/23-1952/55, International index to periodicals. Ceased publication with Vol. 18.

Superseded by SOCIAL SCIENCES AND HUMANITIES INDEX (see p. 126).

Library of Congress. CATALOG OF BOOKS REPRESENTED BY LIBRARY OF CONGRESS PRINTED CARDS ISSUED TO JULY 31, 1942. 167 vols. Ann Arbor, Mich.: Edwards Brothers, 1942-46.

These volumes are in the process of being replaced by THE NATIONAL UNION CATALOG: PRE-1956 IMPRINTS (see p. 124). Only those volumes covering entries beginning with "Luce" to the end of the alphabet need be consulted.

Library of Congress. NATIONAL REFERRAL CENTER FOR SCIENCE AND TECHNOLOGY. SOCIAL SCIENCES: A DIRECTORY OF INFORMATION RESOURCES IN THE UNITED STATES. Rev. ed. Washington, D.C.: Government Printing Office, 1973. 700 p.

This volume contains a list of public and private organizations that have specialized information about some aspect of the social sciences and that can provide this knowledge on request. "Social science" is here very broadly defined, ranging from philosophy to business. Each listing supplies the organization's address, areas of concern, information services, and publications.

MATHEMATICAL SOCIOLOGY: A SELECTIVE ANNOTATED BIBLIOGRAPHY. Compiled by Janet Holland and M.D. Steuer. New York: Schocken Books, 1969. vii, 109 p.

This volume contains 451 annotated entries for articles and books dating from 1950 for the articles, earlier for books. Entries are grouped under headings which direct the reader to the appropriate numbered entries. In the annotated listings section, articles are followed by books, arranged alphabetically by author. Topics include attitudes, communication, decision making, small and large groups, influence, and sociometry.

A MODERN DICTIONARY OF SOCIOLOGY. Prepared by George A.
Theodorson and Achilles G. Theodorson. New York: Thomas Y. Crowell,
1969. viii, 469 p.

> This dictionary was written primarily for undergraduate and gradu-
> ate students, but it is also directed toward professionals in related
> fields as well as the general public. The authors seek to be
> inclusive in their choice of entries and draw on various concep-
> tual levels and historical periods and from several theoretical and
> methodological approaches. Concepts from related fields are
> included. Entries are cross-referenced, and short discussions
> accompany some definitions.

THE NATIONAL UNION CATALOG: A CUMULATIVE AUTHOR LIST REPRE-
SENTING LIBRARY OF CONGRESS PRINTED CARDS AND TITLES REPORTED
BY OTHER AMERICAN LIBRARIES, 1968-72. Ann Arbor, Mich.: J.W.
Edwards, in progress since 1974.

> Ninety volumes have been published (through "Stu"). When com-
> pleted, this set will replace the annual cumulations which the
> Library of Congress has published for the years 1968-72. The
> latter must still be consulted for entries after "Stu." Materials
> published in 1972 or later are listed in the paperbound quarterly
> cumulations of the National Union Catalog Author Lists.

THE NATIONAL UNION CATALOG, 1956 THROUGH 1967: A CUMULA-
TIVE AUTHOR LIST REPRESENTING LIBRARY OF CONGRESS PRINTED CARDS
AND TITLES REPORTED BY OTHER AMERICAN LIBRARIES. 125 vols. Totowa,
N.J.: Rowman and Littlefield, 1970-72.

> This is a complete cumulation for the years indicated.

THE NATIONAL UNION CATALOG: PRE-1956 IMPRINTS: A CUMULA-
TIVE AUTHOR LIST REPRESENTING LIBRARY OF CONGRESS PRINTED CARDS
AND TITLES REPORTED BY OTHER AMERICAN LIBRARIES. Compiled and
edited with the cooperation of the Library of Congress and the National Union
Catalog Subcommittee, Resources Committee, Resources and Technical Services
Division, American Library Association. London: Mansell, in progress since
1968.

> This is a projected 610-volume master cumulation of all Library
> of Congress catalogs. As of 1974, 344 volumes had been issued.
> When completed, this edition (usually referred to as "Mansell")
> will contain printed cards for all books cataloged by the Library
> of Congress and by other American libraries participating in the
> National Union Catalog, published through 1956.

NEW YORK TIMES BOOK REVIEW INDEX, 1896-1970. 5 vols. New York:
New York Times/Arno Press, 1973.

This is the only book review index to a major American news-
paper. It contains references to reviews of books not listed in
BOOK REVIEW DIGEST. The five volumes are arranged by author,
title, byline, subject, and category, respectively.

PSYCHOLOGICAL ABSTRACTS. Lancaster, Pa.: American Psychological
Association, 1927. Monthly.

This abstract index to current literature in psychology was a bimonthly publication before 1966. It presents an annual total of
some 16,000 abstracts of books, periodical articles, dissertations,
and other literature in the psychological field. Entries are
arranged under subject categories such as group motivation, educational and methodological research, group dynamics and therapies, group structure, group effectiveness and influence, group
process and interaction. The time lag between publication of a
book or article and appearance of its abstract is about six months.

PSYCHOSOURCES: A PSYCHOLOGY RESOURCE CATALOG. Compiled by
the editors of Communications/Research/Machines, Inc. New York: Bantam
Books, 1973. 215 p.

This reference book covers 215 topics, discussed under eleven
headings. Among them are learning, roles, communication,
organization, and access information. Detailed information is
provided on books, journals, films, and their sources.

READER'S GUIDE TO PERIODICAL LITERATURE. New York: Wilson, 1905.

This is the standard cumulated periodical index. Frequency of
permanent cumulations varies. It indexes U.S. periodicals of a
popular, general, and nontechnical character in the social sciences,
humanities, literature, and science. Arrangement is that of a
dictionary catalog containing subject and author entries, and
title entries where authorship cannot be established.

REFERENCE BOOKS IN PAPERBACK. AN ANNOTATED GUIDE. 2d ed.
Edited by Bohdan S. Wynar. Littleton, Colo.: Libraries Unlimited, 1976.
317 p.

This book provides material on a wide variety of topics under
thirty-seven chapter headings, including education, psychology,
social sciences and area studies, and sociology. Each chapter
is subdivided by type of material, such as dictionaries, bibliographies, and directories, or by particular topics in the area.
Each entry supplies full bibliographic information and an evaluative annotation. Many more related titles are referred to in the
annotations.

# Bibliographical Reference Works

RESEARCH MATERIALS IN THE SOCIAL SCIENCES. 2d ed. Compiled by Jack A. Clarke. Madison: University of Wisconsin Press, 1967. viii, 56 p.

This selective and annotated bibliography is intended for graduate students who are about to carry out research in the social sciences. It updates its 1959 predecessor. The compiler includes the major abstracting journals and bibliographies for each social science. Materials are arranged in sections, including indexes to periodicals, publications of learned societies, newspapers, government publications, bibliographies, and guides to the resources of American libraries. There are 215 entries.

SERIALS IN PSYCHOLOGY AND ALLIED FIELDS. 2d ed. Compiled by Margaret Tompkins and Norma Shirley. Troy, N.Y.: Whitston, 1976. 472 p.

The authors present a listing of eight hundred titles. Only English-language periodicals and those that have abstracts or tables of contents in English are included. Information on entries includes publication schedule, date of first issue, the sponsoring organization, a statement of editorial objectives, and a profile of requirements and contents of the serial.

SOCIAL SCIENCE RESEARCH HANDBOOK. Prepared by Raymond G. McInnis and James W. Scott. New York: Barnes and Noble, 1975. xix, 395 p.

This volume provides the reader with a guide to sources of information in the social sciences. In each section, only a select number of the more important and widely used books on that particular subject are presented, with an evaluative description. Part 1 of the book presents a section on each of the various disciplines in the social sciences; part 2 contains sections on each major area of the world. A section-by-section bibliography is included at the back.

SOCIAL SCIENCES AND HUMANITIES INDEX. New York: Wilson, 1965--. Quarterly.

This is a author and subject index to a changing list of over two hundred periodicals. The criterion for inclusion is wide usage. Areas covered include sociology, anthropology, area studies, and political science. Cumulations are annual and biennial. This index continues INTERNATIONAL INDEX (see p. 123) after 1965. It ceased publication with Volume 26, 1973, and superseded by SOCIAL SCIENCES INDEX (see below) and HUMANITIES INDEX (see p. 121).

SOCIAL SCIENCES INDEX. New York: Wilson, 1975--. Quarterly, with annual cumulation.

Supersedes in part SOCIAL SCIENCES AND HUMANITIES INDEX (see above).

SOCIOLOGICAL ABSTRACTS. New York: 1952--. Number varies, 4 to 6 times a year.

> These volumes abstract over 140 sociological journals and include abstracts from an additional 400 social science journals. Papers prepared for meetings of national and international sociological societies are also abstracted and appear as supplements. Total number of items is over six thousand per year, which is increasing with inclusion of non-English-language works. Abstracts are arranged in broad professional interest areas. The last issue of each volume, the cumulative index, is usually delayed about nine months.

SOCIOLOGY OF AMERICA: A GUIDE TO INFORMATION SOURCES. Edited by Charles Mark. American Studies Information Guide Series, vol. 1. Detroit: Gale Research, 1976. 454 p.

> This is a selective bibliography containing 1,861 numbered entries, almost 80 percent of them annotated. They are mainly scholarly works on American society and on specific aspects of American life and culture. Most of the entries date from 1960, but some classics published prior to that date are included. Criteria for inclusion involve significance of the entry in question and frequency of consultation or citation. Many works on theoretical and applied sociology are intentionally omitted.

SOURCES OF INFORMATION IN THE SOCIAL SCIENCES: A GUIDE TO THE LITERATURE. 2d ed. Prepared by Carl M. White and associates. Chicago: American Library Association, 1973. xviii, 702 p.

> This guide covers eight fields in the social sciences. Each section is written by a specialist who selects, organizes, and reviews monographic materials, followed by a list of reference works. Annotations are included, sometimes on a group basis. There is an initial section on social science literature in general.

SUBJECT GUIDE TO MAJOR UNITED STATES GOVERNMENT PUBLICATIONS. Compiled by Ellen Jackson. Chicago: American Library Association, 1968. x, 175 p.

> Titles included are those of permanent interest from the earliest period to the present. Subject headings follow Library of Congress practice, with some modifications. Each entry provides full title, publication date, pagination, note of illustrations and charts, a series note where applicable, and the classification number as employed in the MONTHLY CATALOG OF UNITED STATES GOVERNMENT PUBLICATIONS. Agency of issue is listed following collation. Explanatory notes and annotations are supplied where the publication's title does not sufficiently convey its nature. There is a section on guides, catalogs, and indexes by W.A. Katz.

SUBJECT GUIDE TO PERIODICAL INDEXES AND REVIEW INDEXES. Prepared by Jean S. Kujoth. Metuchen, N.J.: Scarecrow Press, 1969. 129 p.

> In part 1 the academic-subject index lists periodical indexes by title under broad subjects roughly corresponding to major academic departments. Letter symbols indicate the type of information provided by the index. Part 2 lists indexes alphabetically by title and gives a description of each in terms of form, content, and subjects. A set of summary tables with titles and type of information is supplied at the end.

THESAURUS OF PSYCHOLOGICAL INDEX TERMS. Edited by Robert G. Kinkade. Washington, D.C.: American Psychological Association, 1974. iii, 362 p.

> This book is divided into three parts. The first part lists all official vocabulary terms, with broader, narrower, and other related terms for each; it then lists unofficial terms, directing the reader to its official equivalent. The second part is an alphabetical listing of the official vocabulary. The third part orders the terms in topical outline form.

ULRICH'S INTERNATIONAL PERIODICALS DIRECTORY: A CLASSIFIED GUIDE TO CURRENT PERIODICALS, FOREIGN AND DOMESTIC. New York and London: R.R. Bowker, 1932--. Biennial.

> The fifteenth edition contains entries for approximately 55,000 current periodicals and 1,800 titles that have ceased or suspended publication since the fourteenth edition. Each entry gives full title and subtitle, date publication commenced (where known), frequency, publisher, editor, price, and titles of indexes or abstracting services in which it is listed.

U.S. Office of Education. EDUCATIONAL RESOURCES INFORMATION CENTER. SOCIAL STUDIES AND SOCIAL SCIENCE EDUCATION: AN ERIC BIBLIOGRAPHY. New York: Macmillan, 1973. xiii, 598 p.

> This bibliography includes the acquisitons of the ERIC Clearinghouse for Social Studies/Social Science Education from September 1970 through December 1972 as well as relevant documents acquired by other ERIC Clearinghouses from 1966 through 1972. Also included are journal articles indexed in CURRENT INDEX TO JOURNALS IN EDUCATION from 1970 through 1972. Entries are organized in four sections: ERIC documents, ERIC journal articles, subject index, and author index.

## B. GROUP BEHAVIOR SOURCES

ADDITIONS TO A BIBLIOGRAPHY ON THE PRESENT STATUS OF ROLE
THEORY. 2 vols. Compiled by Bruce J. Biddle. Technical Report No. 6,
Contract Nonr 2296(02). Washington, D.C.: Group Psychology Branch,
Office of Naval Research, 1962, 1964. 38 p.

> This work includes books, journal articles, doctoral dissertations,
> and papers read at conferences. They cover any field in which
> role theory is used. Volume 1 contains 564 entries; volume 2
> contains 339 entries. Both are in alphabetical order without
> further division.

"An Annotated Review and Classification of Selected Research Relevant to
Group Work." Prepared by Marvin D. Feit and Errol Koesterich. Master's
thesis, Columbia University School of Social Work, 1965. 216 p. Mimeographed. Indexes.

> This volume describes the materials available in the social work
> field, organized by time, locus, and focus. The literature sur-
> veyed by the authors is presented and annotated in an appendix
> of 219 entries. Annotations examine each entry under the head-
> ings of objective, method, and findings. Studies are indexed
> according to content emphasis, setting, and year.

BIBLIOGRAPHY OF GROUP PSYCHOTHERAPY, 1906–56 (1906 through 1955).
Compiled by Raymond J. Corsini and Lloyd J. Putzey. Beacon, N.Y.:
Beacon House, 1957. 75 p.

> This volume brings together all the then-known books, chapters
> of books, articles, and theses in the field of group psychotherapy,
> totaling 1,747 entries. Most of the research reports included
> were published between 1950 and 1955.

"Bibliography of Small Group Research: From 1900 through 1953." Compiled
by Fred L. Strodtbeck and A. Paul Hare. SOCIOMETRY 17 (May 1954):
107-78.

> This was the first comprehensive bibliography on small group
> research, containing 1,407 entries arranged by author. Included
> are research reports whose main focus is the nature and conse-
> quences of face-to-face interaction in small groups. Articles
> and monographs considered to be important methodological and
> substantive contributions are starred. The bibliography is updated
> by Hare in his HANDBOOK OF SMALL GROUP RESEARCH (see
> p. 4).

"Bibliography of Small Group Research: 1959-69." Compiled by A. Paul
Hare. SOCIOMETRY 35 (1972): 1-50.

# Bibliographical Reference Works

The materials in this bibliography are included in the author's HANDBOOK OF SMALL GROUP RESEARCH (see p. 4).

COLLECTIVE BEHAVIOR: A BIBLIOGRAPHY. Compiled by Denton E. Morrison and Kenneth E. Hornback. New York: Garland, 1976. 534 p.

This volume provides just over 5,000 entries on mostly contemporary American phenomena, centered on the attempts of the powerless to acquire power in political, economic, or religious arenas by uniting. The works included are generally scientific, and psychological or social-psychological in approach. No annotations are supplied.

COMMUNICATION IN ORGANIZATIONS: AN ANNOTATED BIBLIOGRAPHY AND SOURCEBOOK. Compiled by Robert M. Carter. Management Information Guide Series, 25. Detroit: Gale Research, 1972. ix, 272 p.

This bibliography is aimed at both the practicing manager and the student of communication. It includes books, portions of books, and periodical articles. Information on some films and other media is also supplied. Materials are grouped under headings such as theories and systems of organizational communication, barriers to organizational communication, vertical and horizontal communication, and organizational change. Within each section, entries are listed chronologically.

GROUP PSYCHOTHERAPY: A BIBLIOGRAPHY OF THE LITERATURE FROM 1956 THROUGH 1964. Compiled by Bernard Lubin and A.W. Lubin. Lansing: Michigan State University Press, 1966. 186 p.

This is the sequel to Corsini and Putzey's 1957 BIBLIOGRAPHY OF GROUP PSYCHOTHERAPY (see p. 129) and lists more items for the nine years 1956–64 than the earlier work does for fifty. Research reports are also proportionately more numerous in this volume. Listing is chronological.

GROUP WORK IN THE HELPING PROFESSIONS: A BIBLIOGRAPHY. Compiled by David G. Zimpfer. Washington, D.C.: Association for Specialists in Group Work, 1976. vii, 452 p.

This volume presents books, journal articles, dissertations, and unpublished documents about group dynamics up to June 1975. It constitutes a general survey of social group work. About seventy-two periodicals were systematically searched and several more scanned for relevant materials. Group procedures in counseling and guidance, in psychotherapy and in educational settings are covered. The bibliography is organized into two sections: a topical listing and an author listing.

LEADERSHIP: ABSTRACTS AND BIBLIOGRAPHY, 1904-74. Compiled by Ralph M. Stogdill. Columbus: College of Administrative Science, Ohio State University, 1977. v, 829 p.

> This is a collection of 3,690 abstracts which the author prepared for the publication of his HANDBOOK OF LEADERSHIP (see p. 73). As such, they served as a framework for analyzing and summarizing the main research on leadership and focus on statements of findings rather than specifics of research design. Major journals are abstracted through 1974. The items emphasize the efforts of professional scholars and researchers in understanding leadership.

ORGANIZATIONAL COMMUNICATION: A BIBLIOGRAPHY. Compiled by Henry Voos. New Brunswick, N.J.: Rutgers University Press, 1967. 251 p.

> The author has surveyed the literature on group communication from 1958-1966. The groups involved vary from dyads to larger groups, and they are looked at from both psychological and managerial points of view. The literature search is selective, and the 315 entries are annotated. The fields covered are primarily those of the social and technological sciences.

The following are texts on small group behavior which include extensive bibliographical sections.

Argyle, Michael. THE SCIENTIFIC STUDY OF SOCIAL BEHAVIOUR. London: Methuen and Co.; New York: Philosophical Library, 1957. viii, 239 p.

> This book deals specifically with one aspect of social psychology: the study of social interaction. As such, its bibliography of 500 entries is useful for students of group behavior.

Bass, Bernard M. LEADERSHIP, PSYCHOLOGY, AND ORGANIZATIONAL BEHAVIOR. New York: Harper and Row, 1960. xiii, 584 p.

> This book includes a 1,155-item bibliography on topics related to leadership. It features a number of articles taken from foreign journals, thus presenting information on research outside the United States, both in the leadership area and in related areas of the small group field.

Hare, A. Paul. HANDBOOK OF SMALL GROUP RESEARCH. 2d ed. New York: Free Press, 1976. xvi, 781 p.

> This bibliography of 6,037 entries includes all the references from the 1962 edition of the book and the entries from the author's 1972 "Bibliography of Small Group Research: 1959-69" (see p. 129). Research in the field is extended to December 1974.

Hare, A. Paul; Borgatta, Edgar F.; and Bales, Robert F. SMALL GROUPS:
STUDIES IN SOCIAL INTERACTION. New York: Alfred A. Knopf, 1955.
xv, 666 p.

> This book presents a list of 594 articles, mostly taken from the
> 1954 bibliography by Fred L. Strodtbeck, and A. Paul Hare,
> "Bibliography of Small Group Research: From 1900 through
> 1953" (see p. 129). Each article is abstracted, and the focus
> is on original contributions dealing specifically with small groups.
> A topical index to the bibliography is supplied.

Hollander, Edwin P., and Hunt, Raymond G., eds. CURRENT PERSPECTIVES
IN SOCIAL PSYCHOLOGY. 4th ed. New York: Oxford University Press,
1976. xiv, 590 p.

> Although this is a social psychology text, it approaches the field
> with a focus on group behavior so that much of its bibliography
> is relevant in this regard. It presents almost one thousand entries.

McGrath, Joseph E., and Altman, Irwin. SMALL GROUP RESEARCH: A
SYNTHESIS AND CRITIQUE OF THE FIELD. New York: Holt, Rinehart and
Winston, 1966. ix, 601 p.

> In the course of describing a system of classification of social
> science knowledge, the authors present almost 250 annotated ex-
> amples to which they apply this system. A further bibliography
> of 2,699 entries is provided.

Raven, Bertram H. A BIBLIOGRAPHY OF PUBLICATIONS RELATING TO
THE SMALL GROUP. Technical Report No. 1. Contract Nonr 253 (54)
(NR 171-350). Los Angeles: Department of Psychology, University of Cali-
fornia, 1959.

> A card system was designed for the author's use, from which the
> materials for this bibliography were taken. Many of the items
> came from the Hare et al. 1955 bibliography (see above), but
> additional journal articles were added as received. All entries
> are cross-referenced by means of a coding system based on the
> content of the articles.

Senn, Peter R. SOCIAL SCIENCE AND ITS METHODS. Boston: Holbrook,
1971. x, 357 p.

> The appendix of this book provides information on where to look
> for published materials in the social sciences. It is divided into
> several parts dealing with general bibliographic aids, encyclo-
> pedias and handbooks, surveys and other guides to the literature,
> indexes, abstracts, bibliographies, and a selected list of journals.
> Social science disciplines include behavioral science, education,
> psychology, social work, and sociology.

Stogdill, Ralph M. HANDBOOK OF LEADERSHIP: A SURVEY OF THEORY
AND RESEARCH. New York: Free Press, 1974. viii, 613 p.

The bibliography accompanying this volume numbers some three
thousand entries covering four decades of research on leadership.
Books and journals are included. The journals most widely used
in the bibliography are listed at the beginning, with their abbreviations. No annotations are supplied, but a comprehensive
annotated bibliography on the field can be found in LEADERSHIP:
ABSTRACTS AND BIBLIOGRAPHY, 1904-74 by the same author
(see p. 131).

_____. INDIVIDUAL BEHAVIOR AND GROUP ACHIEVEMENT: A THEORY.
THE EXPERIMENTAL EVIDENCE. New York: Oxford University Press, 1959.
xi, 352 p.

The bibliography included here deals mainly with achievement in
groups, studies of organizations, leadership, and individual and
group performance effectiveness. There are 794 entries.

Thibaut, John W., and Kelley, Harold H. THE SOCIAL PSYCHOLOGY OF
GROUPS. New York: Wiley, 1959. xiii, 313 p.

The authors present a bibliography of over three hundred items
on groups from a social-psychological point of view.

Triandis, Harry C. INTERPERSONAL BEHAVIOR. Monterey, Calif.: Brooks/
Cole, 1977. xiii, 329 p.

This text is designed for undergraduate students in fields concerned with social behavior. The author attempts to summarize
the literature on interpersonal behavior and presents over four
hundred references.

# Chapter 12
# PERIODICALS

ACADEMY OF MANAGEMENT JOURNAL. Quarterly. $20. Edited by John B. Miner. Editorial address: Academy of Management Journal, Department of Management, Georgia State University, 33 Gilmer Street, Atlanta, Ga. 30303. Business address: Robert Henderson, University of Tampa, Fla. 33606. Sponsor: Academy of Management. First issue: 1958.

> Objectives: It is through its meetings and scholarly publications that the Academy of Management maintains a climate conducive to management research. Through its Institute for Management Research it also acts as a liaison between members who have research skills and organizations which have projects to be developed.

ACTA PSYCHOLOGICA (AMSTERDAM): EUROPEAN JOURNAL OF PSYCHOLOGY. (English text). Bimonthly. $33.20. Editorial address: P.A. Vroon, Psychological Institute, Hooigracht 15, Leiden, The Netherlands. Business address: North Holland Publishing Co., P.O. Box 1270, Amsterdam, The Netherlands. First issue: 1935 (suspended 1942-48).

> Objectives: "Devoted to the publication of psychonomic studies which are defined as the field of psychological research that is fundamental rather than applied, quantitative rather than verbal."

ADMINISTRATIVE SCIENCE QUARTERLY. Quarterly. $14 Individuals; $22 Institutions. Edited by Karl E. Weick. Editorial and business address: ASQ, Malott Hall, Cornell University, Ithaca, N.Y. 14853. Publisher: Graduate School of Business and Public Administration at Cornell University. First issue: 1956.

> Objectives: This is a multidisciplinary journal which seeks to extend the knowledge and understanding of administration by means of theoretical analysis and empirical investigation.

ADOLESCENCE. Quarterly. $16 Individuals; $20 Institutions. Editor-in-chief: William Kroll. Editorial and business address: Libra Publishers, P.O. Box 165, 391 Willets Road, Roslyn Heights, N.Y. 11577. First issue: 1956.

Objectives: This research journal seeks to coordinate the activities of a variety of disciplines which study the adolescent. It thus presents a range of perspectives on the adolescent's personality and behavior in society.

ADVANCES IN EXPERIMENTAL SOCIAL PSYCHOLOGY. Irregular biennial. $14.50–$17.50. Edited by Leonard Berkowitz. Editorial address: Department of Psychology, University of Wisconsin, Madison, Wis. 53706. Business address: Academic Press, 111 Fifth Avenue, New York, N.Y. 10003. First issue: 1964.

Objectives: "To deal primarily with experimental research by integrating the data in such a way that the observed events can be shown to be cases of a more general phenomenon."

AMERICAN BEHAVIORAL SCIENTIST. Bimonthly. $18 Individuals; $30 Institutions. International Editorial Advisory Board. Editorial and business address: Sage Publications, 275 South Beverly Drive, Beverly Hills, Calif. 90212. First issue: 1957.

Objectives: Presents studies on human behavior and social problems, from an interdisciplinary perspective. The emphasis is on the methodology employed. In 1977, to mark the twentieth anniversary of the journal's existence, a series of special issues commenced in which each issue is devoted to a particular topic.

AMERICAN JOURNAL OF NURSING. Monthly. $12. Edited by Thelma M. Schorr. Editorial and business address: American Journal of Nursing, 10 Columbus Circle, New York, N.Y. 10019. Publisher: American Journal of Nursing Co. Sponsor: American Nurses' Association. First issue: 1900.

Objectives: "All aspects of professional nursing."

AMERICAN JOURNAL OF OCCUPATIONAL THERAPY. 10 times a year. $10.50 Individuals; $12.50 Institutions. Acting Editor: Elaine Viseltear. Editorial and business address: 6000 Executive Building, Rockville, Md. 20852. Publisher: American Occupational Therapy Association. First issue: 1947.

Objectives: This journal presents papers which deal with occupational therapy in a professional and scientific setting. Included are professional trends, development of theory, research, and educational activities, and new approaches and techniques.

AMERICAN JOURNAL OF ORTHOPSYCHIATRY. 5 times a year. $16. Edited by Eli M. Bower and Editorial Board. Editorial address: Editor, American Journal of Orthopsychiatry, 1775 Broadway, New York, N.Y. 10019. Business address: AOA Publications Sales Office, 49 Sheridan Avenue, Albany, N.Y. 12210. First issue: 1930.

Objectives: This journal is published in an effort to further the understanding of human behavior and to increase the effectiveness of behavior disorder treatment. The emphasis is on therapeutic work with children, preventive and social psychiatry, and research in dynamic interpersonal relationships which affect human personality.

AMERICAN JOURNAL OF PSYCHIATRY. (Formerly AMERICAN JOURNAL OF INSANITY). Monthly. $18. Edited by Francis J. Braceland. Editorial and business address: 1700 Eighteenth Street, N.W., Washington, D.C. 20009. Sponsor: American Psychiatric Association. First issue: 1844.

Objectives: "To publish articles dealing with significant new research in some area of psychiatry not being considered for publication elsewhere."

AMERICAN JOURNAL OF PSYCHOANALYSIS. Quarterly. $16 Individuals; $26 Institutions. Edited by Helen A. DeRosis. Editorial address: 329 East 62nd Street, New York, N.Y. 10021. Business address: APS Publications, 150 Fifth Avenue, New York, N.Y. 10011. Publisher: Association for the Advancement of Psychoanalysis. First issue: 1941.

Objectives: The journal is directed toward all who have an interest in the understanding and therapy of problems of an emotional nature. Articles seek to communicate modern concepts of psychoanalytic practice and theory, and allied investigations in related fields.

AMERICAN JOURNAL OF PSYCHOLOGY. Quarterly. $15. Edited by Lloyd G. Humphreys and Editorial Board. Editorial address: Department of Psychology, University of Illinois, Champaign, Ill. 61820. Business address: University of Illinois Press, Urbana, Ill. 61801. First issue: 1887.

Objectives: "To report on original experiments and publish information on experimental psychology."

AMERICAN JOURNAL OF PSYCHOTHERAPY. Quarterly. $20. Editor-in-chief: Stanley Lesse. Editorial address: 114 East 78th Street, New York, N.Y. 10021. Business address: Erika R. Hyde, 119-121 Metropolitan Avenue, Jamaica, N.Y. 11415. Sponsor: Association for the Advancement of Psychotherapy. First issue: 1947.

Objectives: This journal has an eclectic nature. It deals with all features of psychotherapy and its relationships with organic medicine, the social sciences, and various schools of psychodynamics.

AMERICAN JOURNAL OF SOCIOLOGY. Bimonthly. $15 Individuals; $20 Institutions. Edited by Charles E. Bidwell and Editorial Board. Editorial address: 1130 East 59th Street, University of Chicago, Chicago, Ill. 60637. Business address: University of Chicago Press, 5801 Ellis Avenue, Chicago, Ill. 60637. First issue: 1895.

Objectives: This journal publishes fundamental sociological theory, research, and analysis. It seeks to disseminate the most up-to-date thinking and empirical work in the sociological field. All areas of human relations, social principles, and social action are covered.

AMERICAN PSYCHOLOGIST. Monthly. $18. Edited by Charles A. Kiesler. Editorial and business address: American Psychological Association, 1200 Seventeenth Street, N.W., Washington, D.C. 20036. Publisher/sponsor: American Psychological Association. First issue: 1946.

Objectives: This is the official journal of the American Psychological Association. It publishes articles on current issues in psychology and also theoretical, practical, and empirical articles on broad aspects of the field.

AMERICAN SOCIOLOGICAL REVIEW. Bimonthly. $10 Members; $15 Nonmembers; $30 Institutions. Edited by Morris Zelditch, Jr. Editorial address: Department of Sociology, Stanford University, Stanford, Calif. 94305. Business address: American Sociological Association, 1722 N Street, N.W., Washington, D.C. 20036. Sponsor: American Sociological Association. First issue: 1936.

Objectives: This journal publishes articles on a wide range of research and scholarship, relevent to both sociologists and social scientists in related fields. These include areas such as social psychology, education, race relations, medical sociology, and marriage and the family.

AMERICAN SOCIOLOGIST. Quarterly. $8 Members; $12 Nonmembers; $16 Institutions. Edited by Allen Grimshaw. Editorial address: Institute for Social Research, 1022 East Third Street, Bloomington, Ind. 47401. Business address: American Sociological Association, 1722 N Street, N.W., Washington, D.C. 20036. Sponsor: American Sociological Association. First issue: 1965.

Objectives: This journal publishes major articles which analyze sociology as a discipline and as a profession. These include reports on practices and standards in teaching, publication, research, and the application of sociological knowledge.

ANNUAL REVIEW OF PSYCHOLOGY. Annual. $10. Edited by Mark R. Rosenzweig and Lyman W. Porter. Business address: 4139 El Camino Way, Palo Alto, Calif. 94306. First issue: 1950.

Objectives: This review publishes articles on a number of aspects of psychology. Subjects over the years have included methodology, behavior disorders, personality, group dynamics, perception, and industrial relations.

# Periodicals

ARCHIVES OF GENERAL PSYCHIATRY. (Formerly ARCHIVES OF NEUROL-
OGY AND PSYCHIATRY). Monthly. $18 Individual. Edited by Daniel
X. Freedman. Editorial address: University of Chicago, Department of
Psychiatry, 950 East 59th Street, Chicago, Ill. 60637. Business address:
American Medical Association, 535 North Dearborn Street, Chicago, Ill.
60610. Publisher/sponsor: American Medical Association. First issue: 1959.

> Objectives: The ARCHIVES publishes articles from any discipline
> that is related to the study of human behavior in illness and in
> health. These include approaches of a psychological, psychiatric,
> sociological, anthropological, morphological, biochemical, or
> psychosmatic nature.

AUSTRALIAN AND NEW ZEALAND JOURNAL OF PSYCHIATRY. Quarterly.
$10. Edited by Roger C. Buckle. Editorial and business address: Maudsley
House, 107 Rathdowne Street, Carlton, Victoria 3053, Australia. Sponsor:
Australian and New Zealand College of Psychiatrists. First issue: 1967.

> Objectives: "To report on research and all aspects of psychiatric
> work being done in southeast Asia."

AUSTRALIAN AND NEW ZEALAND JOURNAL OF SOCIOLOGY. 3 times a
year. $7.50 Individual; $10 Institutions. Edited by Lois Bryson. Editorial
and business address: Sociological Association of Australia and New Zealand,
Department of Anthropology and Sociology, Monash University, Clayton,
Victoria 3168, Australia. First issue: 1965.

> Objectives: "To publish articles covering the broad field of
> sociology."

AUSTRALIAN JOURNAL OF PSYCHOLOGY. 3 times a year. $8.50.
Edited by R.A. Champion, Department of Psychology, University of Sydney,
Sydney, N.S.W. 20006, Australia. Business address: Australian Psychol-
ogical Society, National Science Centre, 191 Royal Parade, Parkville,
Victoria 3052, Australia. First issue: 1949.

> Objectives: "To publish original contributions in psychology."

AUSTRALIAN PSYCHOLOGIST. 3 times a year. $7.10. Edited by Clive
Williams. Editorial address: Counselling Services, University of Sydney,
Sydney, N.S.W. 2006, Australia. Business address: Australian Psychological
Society, National Science Centre, 191 Royal Parade, Parkville, Victoria
3052, Australia. Publisher: University of Queensland Press. First issue:
1966.

> Objectives: "To publish articles of a broad and general nature
> in the field of psychology both descriptive and experimental."

BEHAVIOR. Weekly. $35. Business address: National Technical Information Service, U.S. Department of Commerce, 5285 Port Royal Road, Springfield, Va. 22151. First issue: 1973.

> Objectives: This publication reports on a variety of topics, including social concerns, education, attitudes, motivation, job training, and employment. Publications cited are produced by U.S. government agencies, and by private organizations and individuals on federal contracts or grants.

BEHAVIORAL SCIENCE. Bimonthly. $21 Individuals; $35 Institutions. Edited by James G. Miller. Editorial and business address: University of Louisville, P.O. Box 1055, Louisville, Ky. 40201. Sponsor: Society for General Systems Research and the Institute of Management Sciences. First issue: 1958.

> Objectives: This journal publishes articles on general theories of behavior and on empirical research which is oriented toward these theories in particular. The focus is on research in mental health and disease.

BEHAVIOR RESEARCH METHODS AND INSTRUMENTATION. Bimonthly. $10 Individuals; $20 Institutions. Edited by Joseph B. Sidowski. Editorial address: Department of Psychology, University of South Florida, Tampa, Fla. 33620. Business address: Psychonomic Society, 1108 West 34th Street, Austin, Texas 78705. First issue: 1968.

> Objectives: This journal reports on the methods of research in experimental psychology. Topics covered include experimental designs and methods, laboratory techniques and instrumentation, and computer technology. The proceedings of the Annual Conference on The Use of On-Line Computers in Psychology are published here.

BRITISH JOURNAL OF MEDICAL PSYCHOLOGY. (Formerly MEDICAL SECTION OF BRITISH JOURNAL OF PSYCHOLOGY). Quarterly. $39.50. Edited by Arthur H. Crisp and J.P. Watson. Editorial address: J.P. Watson, Department of Psychiatry, Guy's Hospital Medical School, London Bridge, London, England. Business address: Cambridge University Press, 32 East 57th Street, New York, N.Y. 10022. Sponsor: British Psychological Society. First issue: 1920.

> Objectives: This journal publishes articles which have a psychological approach to mental illness and physical diseases with psychological components. Many disciplines in the field of mental health are included.

BRITISH JOURNAL OF PSYCHIATRY. (Formerly JOURNAL OF MENTAL SCIENCE). Monthly. $100 Individuals; $125 Institutions. Edited by J.L.

Crammer. Editorial address: Royal College of Psychiatrists, 17 Belgrave Square, London, England. Business address: Headley Brothers Ltd., Ashford, Kent, England. Sponsor: Royal College of Psychiatrists. First issue: 1855 (as THE ASYLUM JOURNAL).

> Objectives: "To deal with 'mental science' in its practical, that is, its sociological point of view and to cover 'mental physiology and pathology,' with their vast range of inquiry into insanity, education, crime and all things that tend to preserve mental health or to cause mental disease."

BRITISH JOURNAL OF PSYCHOLOGY. Quarterly. $60. Edited by A.D.B. Clarke, Department of Psychology, The University, Hull, England. Business address: Cambridge University Press, 32 East 57th Street, New York, N.Y. 10022. Sponsor: British Psychological Society. First issue: 1904.

> Objectives: This journal publishes articles which have as their concern the experimental approach to all major areas in psychology.

BRITISH JOURNAL OF SOCIAL AND CLINICAL PSYCHOLOGY. Quarterly. $57. Edited by Halla Beloff and H.R. Beech. Editorial addresses: Halla Beloff (Social Psychology Editor), Department of Psychology, University of Edinburgh, 60 the Pleasance, Edinburgh, Scotland; H.R. Beech (Clinical Psychology Editor), Department of Psychiatry, Withington Hospital, West Didsbury, Manchester, England. Business address: Cambridge University Press, 32 East 57th Street, New York, N.Y. 10022. Sponsor: British Psychological Society. First issue: 1962.

> Objectives: This journal publishes articles in a wide range of clinical and psychological areas including personality mechanisms and dimensions, abnormal psychology, and environmental psychology.

BRITISH JOURNAL OF SOCIOLOGY. Quarterly. $22. Edited by Angus Stewart and Editorial Board. Editorial address: London School of Economics and Political Science, Houghton Street, Aldwych, London, England. Business address: Routledge and Kegan Paul, Broadway House, Newton Rd., Henley on Thames RG9 1EN, England; U.S. address: 9 Park Street, Boston, Mass. 02108. Sponsor: London School of Economics and Political Science. First issue: 1950.

> Objectives: "Sociological theory and study of diverse social problems in Great Britain and abroad."

CALIFORNIA JOURNAL OF EDUCATIONAL RESEARCH. Quarterly. $10. Edited by Robert Smith. Editorial and business address: Department of Educational Psychology, University of Southern California, Waite Phillips Hall, Room 403, Los Angeles, Calif. 90004. Sponsor: University of Southern California. First issue: 1950.

Objectives: This journal publishes a range of articles including original research in education and critical reviews of past research. It also reports demonstration projects based on concepts devised for research.

CANADIAN COUNSELLOR. Quarterly. $9. Edited by Myrne B. Nevison. Editorial address: Faculty of Education, University of British Columbia, Vancouver, 8 B.C., Canada. Business address: 1000 Yonge Street, Ste. 302, Toronto M4W 2K1, Ontario, Canada. Sponsor: Canadian Guidance and Counseling Association. First issue: 1967.

Objectives: This journal publishes research and other papers in Canada generally focusing on the underlying philosophies regarding social, economic, and educational goals. Papers concentrate on how these philosophies related to the individual's freedom and responsibility. The journal seeks to keep its readers informed about recent developments in human understanding.

CANADIAN JOURNAL OF BEHAVIORAL SCIENCE. (Text in English; Summaries in French). Quarterly. $25. Edited by P.O. Davidson. Editorial address: Department of Psychology, University of British Columbia, Vancouver, B.C. V6T 1W5, Canada. Business address: Canadian Psychological Association, 1390 Sherbrooke Street W., Montreal, Quebec H3G 1K2, Canada. Publisher: University of Toronto Press. Sponsor: Canadian Psychological Association. First issue: 1969.

Objectives: "To publish research and theoretical articles mainly in the applied areas of psychology."

CANADIAN PSYCHOLOGICAL REVIEW [PSYCHOLOGIE CANADIENNE]. (Formerly [1974] CANADIAN PSYCHOLOGIST). (Articles in English and French). Quarterly. $25. Edited by David Gibson. Editorial address: Department of Psychology, The University, Calgary, Alberta T2N 1N4, Canada. Business address: Canadian Psychological Association, 1390 Sherbrooke Street W., Montreal, Quebec H3G 1K2, Canada. Publisher/sponsor: Canadian Psychological Association. First issue: 1950.

Objectives: This journal (up to 1974) published the official papers and proceedings of CPA. It also presented comments and notes on psychological affairs, evaluative reviews, and "psychological theory of technological significance." Policy since 1975 has been to emphasize critical review and theoretical statements in any psychological area. Interdisciplinary approaches are especially favored.

CATALOG OF SELECTED DOCUMENTS IN PSYCHOLOGY. Quarterly. $6 Members; $14 Nonmembers. Edited by Janet T. Spence. Editorial and business address: Journal Supplement Abstract Service, American Psychological Association, 1200 Seventeenth Street, N.W., Washington, D.C. 20036. Sponsor: American Psychological Association. First issue: 1971.

Objectives: "To provide ready access to diverse materials unavailable through existing journals."

CHILD PSYCHIATRY AND HUMAN DEVELOPMENT. Quarterly. $40. Edited by John C. Duffy. Editorial address: 7111 44th Street, Chevy Chase, Md. 20015. Business address: Human Sciences Press, 72 Fifth Avenue, New York, N.Y. 10011. First issue: 1970.

Objectives: This journal is designed to serve a variety of related professional groups: specialists in the fields of social science, psychology, child psychiatry, and human development. Articles focus on defining the developing child and adolescent in conflict and in health.

CHILDREN TODAY. (Formerly CHILDREN). Bimonthly. $6.10. Edited by Judith Reed. Editorial address: "Children Today" Office of Child Development, Children's Bureau, P.O. Box 1182, Washington, D.C. 20013. Subscription address: Superintendent of Documents, U.S. Government Printing Office, Washington, D.C. 20402. First issue: 1954.

Objectives: This journal publishes material on a variety of fields related to child development and services for children and youth. Included are articles on child welfare, psychology, social work, and maternal and child health.

CLINICAL SOCIAL WORK JOURNAL. Quarterly. $12 Individual; $30 Institutions. Edited by Mary L. Gottesfeld. Editorial address: 285 West End Avenue, New York, N.Y. 10023. Publisher and business address: Human Sciences Press, 72 Fifth Avenue, New York, N.Y. 10011. Sponsor: National Federation of Societies for Clinical Social Work. First issue: 1973.

Objectives: This journal publishes materials on clinical practice from a number of viewpoints: practice-oriented, theoretical, and historical. It seeks to be interdisciplinary on content, scope, and authorship. Its aim is to deepen and broaden the skill and understanding of the teacher and practitioner of clinical social work whether their concern be with families, couples, individuals, or groups.

COLLEGE STUDENT JOURNAL. (Formerly COLLEGE STUDENT SURVEY). Quarterly. $7.50 Individual; $10 Institutions. Edited by Russell N. Cassel. Editorial and business address: Project Innovation, Box 566, Chula Vista, Calif. 92010. First issue: 1967.

Objectives: The focus of this journal is undergraduate college students and all aspects of their lives. Theoretical papers and original investigations are published on topics such as college student learning, opinions, attitudes, and values.

COMMUNITY MENTAL HEALTH JOURNAL. Quarterly. $12 Individual; $30 Institutions. Edited by L.A. Baler. Editorial address: University of Michigan School of Public Health, Community Mental Health Program, Room M5108 SPH 11, Ann Arbor, Mich. 48104. Business address: Behavioral Publications, 72 Fifth Avenue, New York, N.Y. 10011. First issue: 1965.

Objectives: The journal defines mental health as more or less congruent with the concept of social well-being. Within this definition, it publishes articles on emergent approaches in mental health practice, research, and theory as they relate to the community.

CONTEMPORARY PSYCHOANALYSIS. Quarterly. $14 Individual; $34 Institutions. Edited by Arthur H. Feiner. Editorial address: 20 West 74th Street, New York, N.Y. 10023. Business address: Academic Press, 111 Fifth Avenue, New York, N.Y. 10003. Sponsor: William Alanson White Institute and William Alanson White Psychoanalytic Society. First issue: 1964.

Objectives: The journal publishes contributions to the post-Freudian study of personality and to the principles and practice of psychoanalysis. The intellectual tradition followed is that of the founders, among them Erich Fromm and Harry Stack Sullivan.

CONTEMPORARY PSYCHOLOGY. Monthly. $10 Members; $25 Nonmembers. Edited by Janet T. Spence. Editorial address: Department of Psychology, University of Texas, Austin, Tex. 78712. Business address: American Psychological Association, 1200 Seventeenth Street, N.W., Washington, D.C. 20036. First issue: 1956.

Objectives: This is a journal of critical reviews of materials in psychology, including books, tapes, and films. Although most of the inclusions are discussed at some length, there is also a short section at the end of each issue where items are commented on briefly. Materials are selected to represent an international cross-section of psychological works. Approximately seven hundred books are reviewed each year.

COUNSELING PSYCHOLOGIST. Quarterly. $9 Students; $12 Institutions. Edited by John M. Whiteley. Editorial and business address: Counseling Psychologist, Washington University, Box 1180, St. Louis, Mo. 63130. Publisher/sponsor: Division of Counseling Psychology, American Psychological Association. First issue: 1969.

Objectives: This journal publishes critical reviews and evaluation of professional issues in the field. Each issue contains a lead article on an important issue in counseling and psychotherapy, followed by a series of critiques and reviews.

DISSERTATION ABSTRACTS INTERNATIONAL. (Formerly, 1969, DISSERTA-TION ABSTRACTS). Monthly. $205. (Two Sections: A--The Humanities and Social Sciences; B--The Sciences and Engineering. Each $125). Edited by Patricia Colling. Editorial and business address: University Microfilms, International, P.O. Box 1764, Ann Arbor, Mich. 48106. First issue: 1938.

Objectives: The ABSTRACTS publishes a monthly listing of doctoral theses that have been submitted for publication and are available in either xerographic copy or microfilm. They appear in abstracted journal form. Since 1969, dissertations from European universities are included. Issues of the ABSTRACTS are also available in microfilm beginning with 1966.

EDUCATION. Quarterly. $10 Individual; $14 Institutions. Edited by Russell N. Cassel. Editorial and business address: "Education," P.O. Box 566, Chula Vista, Calif. 92010. First issue: 1880.

Objectives: This journal publishes original materials of an empirical or theoretical nature which deal with innovations in teaching, learning, and education. Articles deal with all areas and levels of education. The primary focus is on innovations in the school, actual or proposed, and evaluative or theoretical.

ENVIRONMENT AND BEHAVIOR. Quarterly. $14 Individual; $24 Institutions. Edited by Gary H. Winkel. Editorial address: Environmental Psychology Program, City University of New York, 33 West 42nd Street, New York, N.Y. 10036. Business address and publisher: Sage Publications, 275 South Beverly Drive, Beverly Hills, Calif. 90212. First issue: 1969.

Objectives: This journal publishes rigorous theoretical and experimental work. The focus is on the influence of the physical environment on human behavior. Articles deal with individual, group, and institutional levels.

EUROPEAN JOURNAL OF SOCIAL PSYCHOLOGY. (Text in English; Summaries in French, German, and Russian). Quarterly. $18.50 Individual; $27.50 Institutions. Editorial Board. Editorial address: Psychologisch Laboratorium der Katholieke Universiteit, Erasmuslaan 16, Nijmegen, The Netherlands. Business address: Mouton and Co., P.O. Box 482. The Hague, The Netherlands. Sponsor: Netherland Organization for the Advancement of Pure Research. First issue: 1971.

Objectives: This journal seeks to provide information on current theoretical developments and empirical research. It serves as a common forum for European social psychologists.

FAMILY PROCESS. Quarterly. $12 Individuals; $20 Institutions. Edited by Donald A. Bloch. Editorial and business address: "Family Process," 149 East 78th Street, New York, N.Y. 10021. Sponsor: Mental Research Institute and the Nathan W. Ackerman Family Institute of New York. First issue: 1962.

Objectives: The journal publishes original articles on the theory and practice of family treatment. Particular attention is paid to family mental health and family psychotherapy, as well as related topics.

GROUP ANALYSIS. 3 times a year. £10 Individual; £15 Institutions. Edited by P.B. deMare. Editorial address: The Trust for Group Analysis, 1 Bickenhall Mansions, Bickenhall Street, London, England. Publisher: The Trust for Group Analysis on behalf of the Group-Analytic Society (London) and the Institute of Group Analysis.

Objectives: The journal seeks to promote the free exchange of information and views among people who are actively interested in the development of techniques and methods of group analysis. These can be applied to group-analytic psychotherapy and allied areas, such as family theory.

GROUP LEADER'S WORKSHOP. Monthly. $35. Edited by Jim Elliott. Editorial and business address and publisher: Jim Elliott, P.O. Box 1254, Berkeley, Calif. 94701. Sponsor: Explorations Institute. First issue: 1969.

Objectives: The journal publishes articles dealing with encounter groups, experiential groups, laboratory training, organization development, psychotherapy groups, and sensitivity training.

GROUP PROCESS. Biannual. $12 Individual; $24 Institutions. Edited by Max Rosenbaum. Editorial address: Box 1078, Grand Central Station, New York, N.Y. 10017. Business address and publisher: Gordon and Breach, One Park Avenue, New York, N.Y. 10016. Sponsor: Association for Group Psychoanalysis and Process. First issue: 1968.

Objectives: "Present stimulating articles and issues that capture the significant group processes of our time and day."

GROUP PSYCHOTHERAPY, PSYCHODRAMA AND SOCIOMETRY. (Formerly SOCIATRY). (Title was Group Psychotherapy up to 1971). Quarterly. $14. Edited by Zerka T. Moreno. Editorial and business address: Beacon House. 259 Wolcott Avenue, Beacon, N.Y. 12508. Sponsor: American Society of Group Psychotherapy and Psychodrama. First issue: 1947.

Objectives: This journal is the official organ of the society. It seeks to provide information, research methods, and the latest findings in group and action methods.

HOSPITAL AND COMMUNITY PSYCHIATRY. Monthly. Members $12. Non-members $15. Edited by D.W. Hammersley. Editorial and business address and sponsor: American Psychiatric Association, 1700 Eighteenth Street, N.W., Washington, D.C. 20009. First issue: 1950.

Objectives: This journal provides for a multidisciplinary exchange of information about programs in community facilities and hospitals which treat alcoholism, drug abuse, mental illness, and mental retardation.

HUMANITAS. 3 times a year. $10. Edited by Adrian Van Kaam. Editorial address: Institute of Man, Duquesne University, Pittsburgh, Pa. 15219. Business address: Publication Manager, Institute of Man, Duquesne University, Pittsburgh, Pa. 15219. First issue: 1965.

Objectives: "Presented as a thoughtful collaboration between contemporary scholars and authors who explore from their own point of view various aspects of the central theme directing each issue, i.e., 'creativity,' 'the human body,' 'love,' 'violence.'"

HUMAN ORGANIZATION. Quarterly. $17 Individuals; $25 Institutions. Edited by H. Russell Bernard. Editorial address: Institute of Behavioral Science No. 1, University of Colorado, Boulder, Colo. 80302. Business address and sponsor: Society for Applied Anthropology, 1703 New Hampshire Avenue, N.W., Washington, D.C. 20009. First issue: 1941.

Objectives: "Developmental change viewed from the individual neighborhood, community, regional, national and international perspective."

HUMAN RELATIONS. Bimonthly. $32.50 Individuals; $65 Institutions. Edited by E.L. Trist. Editorial address: University of Pennsylvania, Wharton School, Management and Behavioral Science Center, Philadelphia, Pa. 19174. Business address: Plenum Publishing Co., 227 West 17th Street, New York, N.Y. 10011. First issue: 1947.

Objectives: This journal seeks to present articles from a number of social sciences in order to demonstrate the relatedness of their theoretical and practical problems. It publishes theoretical and review articles and research reports. Contributors include anthropologists, economists, geographers, planners, political scientists, psychologists, and sociologists.

HUMBOLDT JOURNAL OF SOCIAL RELATIONS. Semi-annual. $9. Edited by Samuel P. Oliner and Carol Harris. Editorial and business address: 211

Administration Building, Humboldt State University, Arcata, Calif. 95521.
First issue: 1973.

Objectives: "To publish original papers from all the social sciences dealing with current social issues."

INTERNATIONAL JOURNAL OF GROUP PSYCHOTHERAPY. Quarterly. $20 Individual; $30.75 Institutions. Edited by Saul Scheidlinger. Editorial address: P.O. Box 230, 150 Christopher Street, New York, N.Y. 10014. Publisher: International Universities Press, 239 Park Avenue South, New York, N.Y. 10003. Sponsor: American Group Psychotherapy Association. First issue: 1951.

Objectives: This journal presents reports and interpretations of practice and research in group psychotherapy. Work in the United States and other countries is discussed. Articles seek to elucidate and extend the scope of group psychotherapy as an emerging technique in the field of psychotherapy in general.

INTERNATIONAL JOURNAL OF GROUP TENSIONS. Quarterly. $20. Edited by Benjamin B. Wolman. Editorial address: Florence Denmark, Graduate Center of the City University of New York, 33 West 42nd Street, New York, N.Y. 10036. Business address: 10 West 66th Street, New York, N.Y. 10023. Sponsor: International Organization for the Study of Group Tensions. First issues: 1974.

Objectives: This is the official publication of the organization. It is an interdisciplinary journal of behavioral sciences concerned with the study of violence and conflict in human relations. Studies of ethnic, political, racial, religious, and socio-economic conflicts are presented.

INTERNATIONAL JOURNAL OF PSYCHOLOGY [JOURNAL INTERNATIONALE DE PSYCHOLOGIE]. (Articles in English or French). Quarterly. $12. Edited by J. Leroux. Editorial address: Dunod, 70 rue de Saint-Mande B.P. 119-93104 Montreuil Cedex, Belgium. Publisher: International Union of Psychology and Science. First issue: 1966.

Objectives: This journal concentrates on cross-cultural comparisons of psychological phenomena in both general and social psychology. Materials are published also which deal with the opposition of theory and method encountered by professionals from a variety of countries, because of differences in their training and culture.

INTERNATIONAL JOURNAL OF SOCIAL PSYCHIATRY. Quarterly. $10 Individuals; $14 Institutions. Edited by Joshua Bierer. Editorial and Business address: Avenue Publishing Co., 18 Park Avenue, London, England. American contributions: Marvin K. Opler, Departments of Anthropology and Psychiatry, State University of New York at Buffalo, 4242 Ridge Lea Road, Buffalo, N.Y. 14226. First issue: 1955.

Objectives: This journal is interdisciplinary in nature and is directed toward anthropologists, psychiatrists, psychologists, and other professionals in the fields of sociological theory, social services, and mental health. Materials deal with various aspects of the behavioral and social sciences.

INTERNATIONAL JOURNAL OF SPORT PSYCHOLOGY. (Articles in English and in French). 3 times a year. $10 Members; $16 Nonmembers. Edited by Ferruccio Antonelli. Editorial address: Via della Camilluccia, 195-00135, Rome, Italy. Business address: Edizioni Luigi Pozzi, Via Panama, 68-00198, Rome, Italy. Sponsor: International Society of Sports Psychology. First issue: 1969.

Objectives: This journal focuses on the psychological aspects of sport and physical activities. It seeks to further the development of sports psychology as a branch of applied psychology, and as a scientific field in its own right. It publishes original papers, dealing with the psychosocial, psychophysiological, and psychopathological aspects of sports and physical activities. It is the official journal of the International Society of Sports Psychology.

INTERPERSONAL DEVELOPMENT. Quarterly. $26. Edited by F. Massarik and Editorial Board. Editorial address: 6245 Scenic Avenue, Hollywood, Calif. 90028. Business address: S. Karger, 25 Arnold-Boecklin Strasse, Ch. 25-4011, Switzerland. First issue: 1970.

Objectives: The journal presents a variety of materials ranging from rigorous inquiry, reporting, and observation, to an occasional selection from the belles-lettres.

JOURNAL FOR THE THEORY OF SOCIAL BEHAVIOR. Semiannual. $12.50 Individual. $20 Institutions. Edited by Paul Secord. Editorial address: Urban Studies, Queens College, CUNY, Flushing, N.Y. 11367. Business address: Blackwell's, 108 Cowley Road, Oxford, England. First issue: 1971.

Objectives: This journal publishes theoretical papers by behavioral scientists and philosophers. Topics range around the field of social behavior. Papers deal with critical reviews of ideas, innovative procedures and methods, and analyses of concepts.

JOURNAL OF ABNORMAL PSYCHOLOGY. (Formerly JOURNAL OF AB-NORMAL AND SOCIAL PSYCHOLOGY). Bimonthly. $25. Edited by Leonard D. Eron. Editorial address: Department of Psychology, Box 4348, University of Illinois, Chicago Circle, Chicago, Ill. 60680. Business address:

American Psychological Association, 1200 Seventeenth Street, N.W., Washington, D.C. 20036. Publisher and sponsor: American Psychological Association. First issue: 1906.

> Objectives: Articles include topics on basic theory and research in the field, covering the determinants and correlates of abnormal behavior.

JOURNAL OF APPLIED BEHAVIORAL SCIENCE. Quarterly. $19. Edited by Leonard D. Goodstein. Editorial and business address: NTL Institute, P.O. Box 9155, Rosslyn Station, Arlington, Va. 22209. Sponsor: NTL Institute for Applied Behavioral Science. First issue: 1965.

> Objectives: Articles deal with furthering the reader's knowledge of the goals, processes, and outcomes of social innovation and planned change. These phenomena are examined with regard to persons, groups, and larger systems.

JOURNAL OF APPLIED PSYCHOLOGY. Bimonthly. $12 Members; $30 Nonmembers. Edited by Edwin A. Fleishman. Editorial address: Department of Psychology, Elliott Hall, University of Minnesota, Minneapolis, Minn. 55455. Business address and sponsor: American Psychological Association, 1200 Seventeenth Street, N.W., Washington, D.C. 20036. First issue: 1917.

> Objectives: This journal focuses on original works dealing with any area of applied psychology except clinical psychology.

JOURNAL OF APPLIED SOCIAL PSYCHOLOGY. Quarterly. $19.50 Individual; $42 Institutions. Edited by Peter Suedfeld and Siegfried Struefert. Editorial address: Department of Psychology, University of British Columbia, 2075 Wesbrook Place, Vancouver B.C., V6T 1W5, Canada. Business address: 1511 K Street, N.W., Washington, D.C. 20005. First issue: 1917.

> Objectives: "Devoted to applications of experimental behavioral science research to problems of society."

JOURNAL OF COMMUNICATION. Quarterly. $15. Edited by George Gerbner. Editorial and business address: Annenberg School of Communications, International Communication Association, 3620 Walnut Street, Philadelphia, Pa. 19174. Publisher: Annenberg School Press. First issue: 1951.

> Objectives: This journal publishes articles that contain insights into the ways in which methods of communication and media affect our society and our lives.

JOURNAL OF COMMUNITY PSYCHOLOGY. Quarterly. $25. Edited by J.R. Newbrough. Editorial address: Journal of Community Psychology, George Peabody College, Box 319, Nashville, Tenn. 37203. Business address:

Clinical Psychology Publishing Co., 4 Conant Square, Brandon, Vt. 05733.
First issue: 1973.

> Objectives: This journal publishes articles dealing with human
> behavior in community settings. They can be of an assessment,
> evaluation, intervention, research, or review nature. There is
> an emphasis on the community as supporting the development and
> growth of its residents and meeting their needs.

JOURNAL OF CONFLICT RESOLUTION. Quarterly. $16.80 Individual;
$28 Institutions. Edited by Bruce M. Russett. Editorial address: Sage Pub-
lications, 275 Beverly Drive, Beverly Hills, Calif. 90212. First issue: 1957.

> Objectives: This journal publishes articles dealing with aspects
> of general social conflict and war and peace problems. Special
> attention is paid to the analysis of causes, prevention, and solu-
> tions.

JOURNAL OF CONSULTING AND CLINICAL PSYCHOLOGY. (Formerly
JOURNAL OF CONSULTING PSYCHOLOGY). Bimonthly. $12 Members;
$30 Nonmembers. Edited by Brendan A. Maher. Editorial address: 1120
William James Hall, Harvard University, 33 Kirkland Street, Cambridge,
Mass. 02138. Business address and sponsor: American Psychological Associa-
tion, 1200 Seventeenth Street, N.W., Washington, D.C. 20036. First
issue: 1937.

> Objectives: This journal publishes original research in clinical
> psychology. This includes formulations of clinical concepts or
> theory and applications of psychological principles to clinical
> practice.

JOURNAL OF COUNSELING PSYCHOLOGY. Bimonthly. $8 Members;
$20 Nonmembers. Edited by Samuel H. Osipow. Editorial address: Depart-
ment of Psychology, Ohio State University, 1945 North High Street, Columbus,
Ohio 43210. Business address and sponsor: American Psychological Association, 1200 Seventeenth Street, N.W., Washington, D.C. 20036. First issue:
1954.

> Objectives: This journal publishes material on theory, research
> and practice in the field of counseling, as well as related activ-
> ities of personnel workers and counselors. There is some empha-
> sis on articles which deal with counseling from a developmental
> viewpoint, as well as on therapeutic, remedial, group, and diag-
> nostic approaches. Tests are reviewed periodically.

JOURNAL OF CRIMINAL LAW AND CRIMINOLOGY. (Published 1951-1972
as JOURNAL OF CRIMINAL LAW, CRIMINOLOGY AND POLICE SCIENCE).
Quarterly. $15 Individual; $18.50 Institutions. Chief editor: Francine
Rissman. Editorial address: 357 East Chicago Avenue, Chicago, Ill. 60611.
Business address: 428 East Preston Street, Baltimore, Md. 21202. Publisher:
Williams and Wilkins Co. for Northwestern University School of Law. First
issue: 1910.

Objectives: "To provide a scholarly review of developments and issues in criminal law and criminology."

JOURNAL OF CROSS-CULTURAL PSYCHOLOGY. (Text in English; Summaries in English, French, and German). Quarterly. $13.50 Individual; $22.50 Institutions. Edited by Walter J. Lonner and Editorial Board. Editorial address: Department of Psychology, Western Washington State College, Bellingham, Wash. 98225. Business address: Sage Publications, 225 South Beverly Drive, Beverly Hills, ·Calif. 90212. Sponsor: International Association for Cross-Cultural Psychology. First issue: 1970.

Objectives: This journal publishes behavioral and social research of a cross-cultural nature. Articles are preferred that focus on the conditioning of psychological phenomena by cultures or subcultures, as well as research that treats the individual as a member of the cultural groups.

JOURNAL OF EDUCATIONAL PSYCHOLOGY. Bimonthly. $30. Edited by Joanna Williams. Editorial address: P.O. Box 238, Teachers College, Columbia University, New York, N.Y. 10027. Business address and sponsor: American Psychological Association, 1200 Seventeenth Street, N.W., Washington, D.C. 20036. First issue: 1910.

Objectives: This journal reports theoretical papers and original investigations dealing with problems of learning and teaching. Articles also cover the individual's psychological development, adjustment, and relationships.

JOURNAL OF EMPLOYMENT COUNSELING. Quarterly. $2 Members; $4 Nonmembers. Edited by John A. Bailey. Editorial address: Department of Counseling and Guidance Personnel Services, University of Nevada, Reno, Nev. 89507. Business address: American Personnel and Guidance Association, 1607 New Hampshire Avenue, N.W., Washington, D.C. 20009. Publisher: National Employment Counselors Association. First issue: 1963.

Objectives: This journal publishes articles on industrial and occupational psychology, vocational counseling, and employment counseling in both private and public agencies. It aims to enlighten its readership regarding the theory and practice of employment counseling. Materials may be based on a survey of the literature, on research, or on personal experience.

JOURNAL OF EXPERIMENTAL PSYCHOLOGY: GENERAL. (From 1975, one of four sections of JOURNAL OF EXPERIMENTAL PSYCHOLOGY). Quarterly. $6 Members; $16 Nonmembers. All four sections: $60. Edited by Gregory A. Kimble. Editorial address: Department of Psychology, University of Colorado, Boulder, Colo. 80309. Business address: American Psychological Association, 1200 Seventeenth Street, N.W., Washington, D.C. 20036. First issue: 1975.

Objectives: "Comprehensive and integrative research reports of
new research leading to a substantial advance in knowledge
which are of interest to the entire community of experimental
psychologists."

JOURNAL OF EXPERIMENTAL SOCIAL PSYCHOLOGY. Bimonthly. $12
Individual; $40 Institutions. Edited by Anthony N. Doob. Editorial address:
Department of Psychology, University of Toronto, Toronto, Ontario, Canada.
Business address: Academic Press, 111 Fifth Avenue, New York, N.Y. 10003.
First issue: 1965.

Objectives: This journal publishes articles on current research in
a number of social-psychological areas. The emphasis is on investigations of social interaction and related themes. Mostly experimental research is included, but papers of other kinds are presented provided they are relevant to the interests of professionals
in the field.

JOURNAL OF GENERAL PSYCHOLOGY. Quarterly. $30. Edited by
Powell Murchison and Editorial Board. Editorial and business address: Journal
Press, Box 543, 2 Commercial Street, Provincetown, Mass. 02657. First
issue: 1928.

Objectives: "Devoted to experimental, physiological, and comparative psychology."

JOURNAL OF HEALTH AND SOCIAL BEHAVIOR. (Formerly JOURNAL OF
HEALTH AND HUMAN BEHAVIOR). Quarterly. $8 Members; $12 Non-
members; $16 Institutions. Edited by Mary E.W. Goss. Editorial address:
Department of Public Health, A-623, Cornell University Medical College,
1300 York Avenue, New York, N.Y. 10021. Business address: American
Sociological Association, 1722 N Street, N.W., Washington, D.C. 20036.
First issue: 1960.

Objectives: The papers published by this journal use sociology
as their chief method of defining and analyzing problems of
human welfare. They also consider the occupations and institutions which deal with the diagnosis and management of these
problems.

JOURNAL OF HUMANISTIC PSYCHOLOGY. Quarterly. $10 Individual;
$14 Institutions. Edited by Thomas C. Greening. Editorial address: 1314
Westwood Boulevard, Suite 205, Los Angeles, Calif. 90024. Business address:
JHP Circulation Office, 325 Ninth Street, San Francisco, Calif. 94103.
Sponsor: Association for Humanistic Psychology. First issue: 1961.

Objectives: This journal publishes research studies, theoretical
papers, experiential reports, and applications of humanistic psychology and humanistic analyses of contemporary culture. Topics
include authenticity, commitment, encounter, identity, love,
search for meaning, self-actualization, psychological health, and
values.

JOURNAL OF INTERGROUP RELATIONS. Quarterly. $11. Edited by
J. Griffin Crump. Editorial address: 8924 Battery Road, Alexandria, Va.
22308. Business address: 701 West Walnut Street, Louisville, Ky. 40203.
Sponsor: National Association of Human Rights Workers. First issue: 1958.

> Objectives: The journal publishes articles in the interest of in-
> creasing acceptance of the principles and goals of intergroup re-
> lations work. It seeks also to improve the standards of profes-
> sional intergroup relations practice, and to advance intergroup
> relations in general.

JOURNAL OF MARRIAGE AND THE FAMILY. (Formerly, 1963, MARRIAGE
AND FAMILY LIVING). Quarterly. $20. Edited by Felix M. Berardo.
Editorial address: Department of Sociology, University of Florida, Gaines-
ville, Fla. 32611. Business address: 1219 University Avenue, S.E., Minneapolis,
Minn. 55414. Sponsor: National Council on Family Relations. First issue:
1939.

> Objectives: "Medium for the presentation of original theory,
> research interpretation and critical discussion of materials related
> to marriage and the family."

JOURNAL OF NEGRO EDUCATION. Quarterly. $7.50. Editor-in-chief:
Charles A. Martin and Editorial Board. Editorial and business address: Bureau
of Educational Research, Howard University, Washington, D.C. 20059.
Publisher: Howard University under auspices of Bureau of Educational Research.
First issue: 1932.

> Objectives: The journal seeks to further the collection and dis-
> semination of information about the education of black people.
> It publishes discussions which critically appraise practices and
> proposals regarding the education of black people.

JOURNAL OF PERSONALITY. Quarterly. $18. Edited by Philip R.
Costanzo. Editorial address: P.O. Box GM, Duke Station, Durham, N.C.
27706. Business address: Duke University Press, Box 6697, College Station,
Durham, N.C. 27708. First issue: 1932.

> Objectives: The journal publishes scientific studies of personality.
> The emphasis is now on personality-related consistencies in per-
> ception and learning, experimental investigations of character
> structure and behavior dynamics, and personality development in
> its cultural context.

JOURNAL OF PERSONALITY AND SOCIAL PSYCHOLOGY. Monthly. $25
Members; $60 Nonmembers. Edited by Anthony G. Greenwald. Editorial
address: Ohio State University, 404C West Seventeenth Avenue, Columbus,
Ohio 43210. Business address: American Psychological Association, 1200
Seventeenth Street, N.W., Washington, D.C. 20036. Sponsor: American
Psychological Association. First issue: 1965.

Objectives: This journal publishes both theoretical and research articles. The focus is on how people affect social processes and are affected by them. Topics include attitudes, social interaction, communication, influences, socialization, social motivation, normal psychodynamic processes, and psychological aspects of social structure.

JOURNAL OF PERSONALITY AND SOCIAL SYSTEMS. Quarterly. $12 Individuals; $24 Institutions. Edited by John L. Johnson. Associate editors: Margaret J. Rioch and David L. Singer. Editorial and business address: 1610 New Hampshire Avenue, N.W., Washington, D.C. 20009. Sponsor: A.K. Rice Institute. First issue: 1977.

Objectives: This journal publishes theoretical contributions on the interaction between the individual and groups and social systems. Studies which are empirical or descriptive in nature are included provided they integrate data with theoretical constructs. Organizational and clinical applications are also considered.

JOURNAL OF PSYCHOANALYSIS IN GROUPS. Annual. $4. Edited by Jerome Steiner and Samuel Slip. Editorial address: 211 Central Park West, New York, N.Y. 10024. Business address: David Halperin, 257 West 86th Street, New York, N.Y. 10024. Publisher: DeWereld, The Netherlands. First issue: 1965.

Objectives: This journal presents papers drawn from all fields of group treatment and dynamics directed to psychiatrists."

JOURNAL OF PSYCHOLOGY. Bimonthly. $45. Managing Editor: Powell Murchison. Business and editorial address: Managing Editor, Journal Press, Box 543, 2 Commercial Street, Provincetown, Mass. 02657. First issue: 1935-36.

Objectives: "To supply immediate publication for psychologists in all fields of psychology."

JOURNAL OF PSYCHOSOMATIC RESEARCH. Bimonthly. $25 Individual; $60 Institutions. Edited by Denis Leigh and Editorial Board. Editorial address: Maudsley Hospital, London, England. Business address: Pergamon Press, Maxwell House, Fairview Park, Elmsford, N.Y. 10523. First issue: 1956.

Objectives: This journal publishes articles from world-wide contributors on psychosomatic medicine. They deal with experimental and clinical studies along with studies from marginal fields, such as anthropology, biology, and sociology.

JOURNAL OF SOCIAL ISSUES. Quarterly. $14 Individual; $20 Institutions. Edited by Jacqueline D. Goodchilds, Department of Psychology, University of California, Los Angeles, Calif. 90024. Business address: P.O. Box 1248,

Ann Arbor, Mich. 48106. Sponsor: Society for the Psychological Study of Social Issues, American Psychological Association. First issue: 1945.

Objectives: The journal publishes articles which bring theory and practice into focus on human problems of the group, the community, the nation, and the world. It aims to communicate scientific findings and interpretations in a nontechnical fashion while maintaining professional standards.

JOURNAL OF SOCIAL PSYCHOLOGY. Bimonthly. $45. Managing Editor: Powell Murchison. Editorial and business address: Journal Press, Box 543, 2 Commercial Street, Provincetown, Mass. 02657. First issue: 1930.

Objectives: Articles published by this journal focus mainly on studies of persons in group settings, and of personality and culture. Cross-cultural notes and articles are given special attention.

JOURNAL OF SOCIAL SERVICE RESEARCH. Quarterly. $20 Individual; $35 Institutions. Chairman of Editorial Board: S.K. Khinduka. Editorial address: George Warren Brown School of Social Work, Washington University, St. Louis, Mo. 63130. First issue: 1977.

Objectives: This journal aims to foster research in social welfare and social work. Papers deal with a range of topics from empirical policy studies to clinical research. They are intended to provide a source of research-based investigation of theory and problems related to the design, delivery, and management of social services.

JOURNAL OF VOCATIONAL BEHAVIOR. Bimonthly. $35 Institutions. Edited by Lenore W. Harmon. Editorial address: Educational Psychology Department, 777 Enderis Hall, University of Wisconsin-Milwaukee, Milwaukee, Wis. 53201. Business address: Academic Press, 111 Fifth Avenue, New York, N.Y. 10003. First issue: 1971.

Objectives: This journal presents theoretical, methodological, and empirical material on the factors which underlie vocational development, implementation, long-term effectiveness, satisfaction, and selection. Discussion is also devoted to obstacles in career development because of sexual, ethnic, and national boundaries.

MERRILL-PALMER QUARTERLY OF BEHAVIOR AND DEVELOPMENT. (Title varies: MERRILL-PALMER QUARTERLY). Quarterly. $11. Edited by Martin L. Hoffman. Editorial address: Department of Psychology, University of Michigan, Ann Arbor, Mich. 48104. Business address: Merrill-Palmer Institute, 71 East Ferry Avenue, Detroit, Mich. 48202. Sponsor: Merrill-Palmer Institute. First issue: 1954.

Objectives: This journal publishes articles in a variety of disciplines dealing with human development. They include completed research reports, illustrative case material, results of exploratory research, and conceptual analyses of problems under examination.

OPERATIONS RESEARCH. Bimonthly. $30. Edited by George L. Nemhauser, Upson Hall, Cornell University, Ithaca, N.Y. 14853. Business address: Operations Research Society of America, 428 East Preston Street, Baltimore, Md. 21202. Publisher and sponsor: Operations Research Society of America. First issue: 1952.

Objectives: The articles in this journal apply the principles of industrial management, engineering, and analysis to discussion, problem solving, and practical application of problems in other disciplines.

ORGANIZATIONAL BEHAVIOR AND HUMAN PERFORMANCE. Bimonthly. $30. Edited by James C. Naylor. Editorial address: Department of Psychological Sciences, Purdue University, West Lafayette, Ind. 47907. Business address: Academic Press, 111 Fifth Avenue, New York, N.Y. 10003. First issue: 1966.

Objectives: "Empirical research and theoretical developments in all areas of human performance theory and organizational psychology."

PERCEPTUAL AND MOTOR SKILLS. Bimonthly. 2 vols. a year. $91.40. Edited by Robert B. and Carol H. Ammons. Editorial and business address: Box 9229, Missoula, Mont. 59807. First issue: 1949.

Objectives: This journal publishes theoretical and experimental articles on motor skills and perception, particularly as these are affected by experience. An interdisciplinary approach is employed, including such areas as time and motion study, physical therapy and education, and anthropology.

PERSONALITY AND SOCIAL PSYCHOLOGY BULLETIN. Quarterly. $5 Individual; $15 Institutions. Edited by Clyde Hendrick. Editorial address: Department of Psychology, Kent State University, Kent, Ohio 44242. Business address: Alan E. Gross, Managing Editor, Department of Psychology, University of Missouri, St. Louis, Mo. 63121. Sponsor: Division of Personality and Social Psychology, American Psychological Association. First issue: 1975.

Objectives: This publication presents short reports in all areas of social psychology and personality. Included are theoretical articles, research reports, field studies, innovations, and criticism and rebuttals.

PERSONNEL. Bimonthly. $12 Members; $15 Nonmembers. Editor-in-chief: Ernest C. Miller. Editorial and business address: 135 West 50th Street, New York, N.Y. 10020. Publisher and sponsor: American Management Associations, Saranac Lake, N.Y. 12983. First issue: 1919.

Objectives: "To provide operating managers in all functional areas of business with timely and useful information about the management of people on the job."

PERSONNEL AND GUIDANCE JOURNAL. 10 times a year. $20. Edited by Leo Goldman. Editorial and business address: 1607 New Hampshire Avenue, N.W., Washington, D.C. 20009. Publisher and sponsor: American Personnel and Guidance Association. First issue: 1921.

Objectives: "To present current information on significant developments in all areas of counseling and guidance."

PERSONNEL PRACTICE BULLETIN. Quarterly. $4.10. Editorial and business address: Assistant Director, Sales and Distribution Section, Australian Government Publishing Service, P.O. Box 84, Canberra, A.C.T. 2600, Australia. Publisher: Australian Government Printing Service, Canberra, Australia. Sponsor: Department of Labor and Immigration. First issue: 1945.

Objectives: This journal presents current Australian information on personnel management, directed toward those concerned with human relationships in commerce and industry. Articles include reports on developments in industrial training and welfare, and departmental studies in industrial psychology and personnel practice.

PERSONNEL PSYCHOLOGY. Quarterly. $18. Edited by Milton D. Hakel. Editorial address: Department of Psychology, Ohio State University, 404-C West Seventeenth Avenue, Columbus, Ohio 43210. Business address: P.O. Box 6965. College Station, Durham, N.C. 27708. First issue: 1948.

Objectives: This journal publishes "reports of research methods, and results, or applications of research results to the solution of personnel problems in business, industry, and government."

PROCEEDINGS OF THE ANNUAL CONVENTION OF THE AMERICAN PSYCHOLOGICAL ASSOCIATION. (Ceased publication 1973). Annual. $15. Edited by the Division Chairpersons and Editor of Special Publications. Editorial and business address: American Psychological Association, 1200 Seventeenth Street, N.W., Washington, D.C. 20036. Publisher and sponsor: American Psychological Association. First issue: 1965.

Objectives: This publication makes available papers which were presented at the annual convention, at an earlier date than their appearance in research journals.

PROFESSIONAL PSYCHOLOGY. Quarterly. $18. Edited by Donald K. Freedheim. Editorial and business address: American Psychological Association, 1200 Seventeenth Street, N.W., Washington, D.C. 20036. Publisher and sponsor: American Psychological Association. First issue: 1969.

Objectives: This journal spans the variety of psychological specialities concerned with promoting human welfare. It seeks to be responsive to the needs of all those who work to meet human needs on a community, group, or individual basis.

PSYCHIATRY. Quarterly. $12.50 Individual; $20 Institutions. Edited by Donald L. Burnham. Editorial and business address: 1610 New Hampshire Avenue, N.W., Washington, D.C. 20009. Publisher and sponsor: William Alanson White Psychiatric Foundation. First issue: 1938.

Objectives: This journal aims to discourage insularity in the fields which study human individual and collective problems. It thus hopes to promote understanding among the disciplines by providing a medium for interdisciplinary communication.

PSYCHOANALYTIC STUDY OF THE CHILD. Annual. Price varies; $10 Vols. 1-20; $12 Vols. 21-25. Editorial and business address: Yale University Press, 92A Yale Station, New Haven, Conn. 06520. First issue: 1945.

Objectives: Articles published here focus on psychoanalytic hypotheses regarding the study of the child, the clinical application of psychoanalytic theory, and its relevance for theories of development, normal and abnormal.

PSYCHOLOGIA: AN INTERNATIONAL JOURNAL OF PSYCHOLOGY IN THE ORIENT. (Text in English). Quarterly. $16 Individual; $22 Institutions. Edited by Ryoji Osaka. Editorial and business address: Department of Educational Psychology, Kyoto University, 606 Japan. First issue: 1957.

Objectives: This journal creates a communication channel from East to West, and seeks to provide a forum for discussion on an international basis. Articles are published from Japan, India, and other parts of Asia.

PSYCHOLOGICAL ABSTRACTS. Monthly. $190. Executive Editor: Lois Granick. Editorial and business address: American Psychological Association, 1200 Seventeenth Street, N.W., Washington, D.C. 20036. Publisher and sponsor: American Psychological Association. First issue: 1927.

Objectives: This journal presents "non-evaluative, informative summaries of the world's literature in psychology and related disciplines." Cumulative subject and author indexes are supplied in separate volumes.

PSYCHOLOGICAL BULLETIN. Bimonthly. $30. Edited by R.J. Herrnstein.
Editorial address: Harvard University, 33 Kirkland Street, Cambridge, Mass.
02138. Business address: American Psychological Association, 1200 Seventeenth Street, N.W., Washington, D.C. 20036. Publisher and sponsor:
American Psychological Association. First issue: 1904.

   Objectives: The BULLETIN is designed to help bridge the gap
   between the typical research psychologist and the technical statis-
   tician. Articles consist of critical evaluative summaries of research literature in many areas in psychology.

PSYCHOLOGICAL ISSUES. Irregular. $15. Edited by Herbert J. Schlesinger.
Editorial address: University of Colorado Medical Center, 4200 East Ninth
Avenue, Denver, Colo. 80220. Business address: International Universities
Press, 315 Fifth Avenue, New York, N.Y. 10016. First issue: 1959.

   Objectives: This monograph series publishes basic psychological
   studies along with varied source materials on a psychoanalytic
   theory of behavior. It strives to create a theory of relevance
   to all theoretical stands in psychiatry, psychology, and allied
   areas. Each monograph is devoted to a particular topic.

PSYCHOLOGICAL MONOGRAPHS. (Title varies: Vols. 1–55, PSYCHOLOGI-
CAL REVIEW. Ceased publication with Vol. 80, 1966). Irregular. Price varies.
Edited by Gregory A. Kimble. Editorial address: Department of Psychology,
Duke University, Durham, N.C. 27706. Business address: American Psycho-
logical Association, 1200 Seventeenth Street, N.W., Washington, D.C.
20036. First issue: 1895.

   Objectives: This serial publishes comprehensive experimental en-
   quiries and other studies in the psychological field which can
   not be adequately presented as journal articles. Each monograph
   is completely understandable by itself, being given over to one
   topic.

PSYCHOLOGICAL RECORD. Quarterly. $6 Individual; $10 Institutions.
Edited by Charles E. Rice. Editorial and business address: Kenyon College,
Gambier, Ohio 43022. First issue: 1937.

   Objectives: The RECORD publishes articles of an experimental
   and theoretical nature. It also includes descriptions of research
   which is in the planning stages or in progress. Commentary on
   current developments in the field is presented.

PSYCHOLOGICAL REPORTS. Bimonthly. 2 vols. a year. $91.40. Edited
by Robert B. and Carol H. Ammons. Editorial and business address: Box
9229, Missoula, Mont. 59807. First issue: 1955.

   Objectives: "To encourage scientific originality and creativity
   in the field of general psychology."

PSYCHOLOGICAL RESEARCH. (Formerly, 1974, PSYCHOLOGISCHE FOR-SCHUNG). Quarterly. $62.50. Editorial Board. Editorial address for the United States and Canada: H.W. Leibowitz, Penn State University, Department of Psychology, 614 Moore Building, University Park, Pa. 16802. Business address: Springer Verlag, 175 Fifth Avenue, New York, N.Y. 10010. First issue: 1921.

Objectives: This journal publishes articles dealing with topics in general experimental psychology. Papers are particularly welcome where they focus on the theoretical implications of the research reported. The areas of perception, learning, communication, and related topics form the core of materials published.

PSYCHOLOGICAL REVIEW. Bimonthly. $8 Members; $20 Nonmembers. Edited by W.K. Estes. Editorial address: Rockefeller University, New York, N.Y. 10021. Business address and sponsor: American Psychological Association, 1200 Seventeenth Street, N.W., Washington, D.C. 20036. First issue: 1894.

Objectives: Original articles are presented which involve critical discussions of issues of a theoretical nature, or which propose theoretical developments and ideas. The journal also republishes papers which have theoretical significance for any area within the psychological spectrum.

PSYCHOLOGY. Quarterly. $7. Edited by John A. Blazer. Editorial and business address: Box 6495 Station C, Savannah, Ga. 31405. First issue: 1964.

Objectives: This journal publishes material dealing with human behavior from the standpoint of theory, research, or techniques. Articles discuss topics such as alcohol addiction, home environment, race riots, and students.

PSYCHOLOGY TODAY. Monthly. $12. Editor-in-chief: Jack Nessel. Editorial address: One Park Avenue, New York, N.Y. 10016. Business address: P.O. Box 2990, Boulder, Colo. 80302. First issue: 1967.

Objectives: This publication presents material from psychological research in an effort to increase communication between the layman and the professional. Social science thinking and findings are thus made available to the general public.

PSYCHOMETRIKA. Quarterly. $30. Managing Editor: Bert F. Green, Jr. Editorial and business address: Department of Psychology, Johns Hopkins University, Baltimore, Md. 21218. First issue: 1936.

Objectives: "Devoted to the development of psychology as a quantitative rational science."

PSYCHOPHYSIOLOGY. Bimonthly. $22 Individual; $30 Institutions. Edited by William F. Prokasy. Editorial address: 205 Spencer Hall, University of Utah, Salt Lake City, Utah 84112. Business address: The Society for Psychophysiological Research, 2879 Fernwood, Ann Arbor, Mich. 48102. First issue: 1964.

> Objectives: This journal seeks to promote investigations on the relationships between the psychological and physiological aspects of behavior. It also publishes research findings on the neurology and physiology of normal humans as it relates to their behavior.

PSYCHOSOCIAL PROCESS: ISSUES IN CHILD MENTAL HEALTH. Semiannual. $7. Edited by Donald I. Meyers. Editorial and business address: Jewish Board of Guardians, 120 West 57th Street, New York, N.Y. 10019. First issue: 1970.

> Objectives: This publication is directed toward those in professions which concern the treatment process. It presents materials that arise from the practical problems of psychological treatment of children and their parents. These include critical discussion, original theory, interpretation, and research.

PSYCHOSOMATIC MEDICINE. Bimonthly. $17.50 Individual; $30 Institutions. Editor-in-chief: Herbert Weiner. Editorial address: 265 Nassau Road, Roosevelt, N.Y. 11575. Business address: American Elsevier Publishing Company, 52 Vanderbilt Avenue, New York, N.Y. 10017. Sponsor: American Psychosomatic Society. First issue: 1938.

> Objectives: Materials published in this journal deal with the interrelationship of physical and mental processes. Sociological, experimental, and clinical studies are all included.

PSYCHOSOMATICS. Bimonthly. $15. Edited by Wilfred Dorfman, Editorial address: 1921 Newkirk Avenue, Brooklyn, N.Y. 11226. Business address: Psychosomatics, 922 Springfield Avenue, Irvington, N.J. 07111. Sponsor: Academy of Psychosomatic Medicine. First issue: 1960.

> Objectives: This journal seeks to further scientific knowledge, and to relate the practice of medicine and dentistry to the interaction of body, mind, and environment, through clinical and laboratory research, and study. It supplies a forum for discussing these issues and for presenting research results.

PSYCHOTHERAPY: THEORY, RESEARCH, AND PRACTICE. Quarterly. Free to members; $17 Nonmembers. Edited by Arthur L. Kovacs and Editorial Board. Business address: California School of Professional Psychology, 3755 Beverly Boulevard, Los Angeles, Calif. 90004. Sponsor: Division of Psychotherapy, American Psychological Association. First issue: 1964.

Objectives: The journal publishes a variety of articles ranging
from theoretical contributions and research studies to case reports
and discussions of actual practice. The aim is to encourage the
interaction of these areas. Many orientations are represented.

PUBLIC PERSONNEL MANAGEMENT. Bimonthly. $15. Edited by John W.
Moore. Editorial and business address: Room 240, 1313 East 60th Street,
Chicago, Ill. 60637. Publisher: International Personnel Management Associa-
tion. First issue: 1940.

Objectives: "To publish original articles on personnel management and human resources in many occupational fields."

QUARTERLY JOURNAL OF STUDIES ON ALCOHOL. Quarterly. $20.
Edited by Mark Keller. Editorial and business address: Rutgers Center for
Alcohol Studies, Smithers Hall, New Brunswick, N.J. 08903. Publisher:
Journal of Studies on Alcohol. First issue: 1940.

Objectives: This journal publishes in two parts. Part A presents
scholarly and scientific materials on all aspects of alcohol and
alcohol problems. Part B covers international literature on the
subject and presents book reviews, bibliographies, and abstracts
of contemporary literature.

RACE. Quarterly. $12.50. Edited by Simon Abbott and Editorial Board.
Editorial and business address: Institute of Race Relations. 247-9 Penton-
ville Road, London, England. Publisher: Oxford University Press for Institute
of Race Relations. First issue: 1959.

Objectives: This journal concentrates on the United States,
Africa, and the United Kingdom. Its articles explore the international social situation and problems as they concern race.
Many disciplines employed include psychology, anthropology,
history, law, and business.

REPRESENTATIVE RESEARCH IN SOCIAL PSYCHOLOGY. Semiannual. $4
Individual; $12 Institutions. Edited by Christopher G. Wetzel, Richard E.
Sands, and Editorial Board. Editorial and business address: Department of
Psychology, Davie Hall, University of North Carolina, Chapel Hill, N.C.
27514. First issue: 1970.

Objectives: This publication seeks to present a relatively un-
biased selection of materials on a variety of psychological phenomena by publishing negative as well as positive replications of
work in the field. The general aim is to foster methodological
improvement and theoretical clarification.

RESOURCES IN EDUCATION. (Formerly, 1974, RESEARCH IN EDUCATION).
Monthly. $42.70. Edited by Educational Resources Information Center

(ERIC). Editorial address: ERIC, National Institute of Education, Washington, D.C. 20208. Business address: Superintendent of Documents, U.S. Government Printing Office, Washington, D.C. 20402. Sponsor: National Institute of Education and ERIC. First issue: 1966.

> Objectives: This journal announces recently completed research and research-related reports in the field of education. It is composed of resumes, and indexes which cite the contents by subject, author, and institution.

REVIEW OF EDUCATIONAL RESEARCH. 5 times a year. Free to members; $10 Nonmembers. Editor-in-chief: Samuel Messick. Editorial address: Box 2604, Educational Testing Service, Princeton, N.J. 08540. Business address: American Educational Research Association, 1126 Sixteenth Street, N.W., Washington, D.C. 20036. Sponsor: American Educational Research Association. First issue: 1931.

> Objectives: This journal publishes materials by areas of interest. It treats research studies in a manner designed to synthesize findings and conclusions so as to encourage further research.

RURAL SOCIOLOGY. Quarterly. $24. Edited by James H. Copp. Editorial address: Department of Rural Sociology, Texas A and M University, College Station, Tex. 77843. Business address and sponsor: Rural Sociological Society, 306-A Comer Hall, Auburn University, Auburn, Ala. 36830. First issue: 1936.

> Objectives: "To promote communication of research findings and relevant educational ideas among persons interested in the field of rural sociology."

SCIENCE. Weekly. $50. Edited by Philip H. Abelson. Editorial and business address: 1515 Massachusetts Avenue, N.W., Washington, D.C. 20005. Publisher: American Association for the Advancement of Science. First issue: 1883.

> Objectives: This publication presents issues related to the advancement of science. Discussions include conflicting or minority standpoints, rather than relying solely on consensual opinions.

SIMULATION AND GAMES. Quarterly. $15 Individual; $28 Institutions. Edited by Garry D. Brewer. Editorial address: Box 1A, School of Organization and Management, Yale University, 1891 Yale Station, New Haven, Conn. 06520. Business address: Sage Publications, 275 South Beverly Drive, Beverly Hills, Calif. 90212. First issue: 1970.

> Objectives: This journal publishes empirical and theoretical materials on man, man-machine, and machine simulations of social processes. Empirical studies and technical papers focus on new gaming techniques. Theoretical papers deal with simulations in teaching and research.

SMALL GROUP BEHAVIOR. (Formerly COMPARATIVE GROUP STUDIES).
Quarterly. $13.50 Individual; $22.50 Institutions. Edited by William
Fawcett Hill. Editorial address: Department of Behavioral Sciences, Califor-
nia State Polytechnic University, 3801 West Temple Avenue, Pomona, Calif.
91768. Business address: Sage Publications, 275 South Beverly Drive, Beverly
Hills, Calif. 90212. First issue: 1970.

> Objectives: This is an interdisciplinary journal of worldwide scope
> publishing articles on research and theory. All kinds of groups
> are covered, including treatment and therapy groups. The jour-
> nal seeks to further the development of a comparative social
> science of group work.

SMITH COLLEGE STUDIES IN SOCIAL WORK. 3 times a year. $4.50.
Edited by Roger R. Miller and Editorial Board. Editorial and business address:
Smith College School for Social Work, Lilly Hall, Northampton, Mass. 01060.
Sponsor: Smith College School for Social Work. First issue: 1930.

> Objectives: "To make available articles and research reports
> relevant to the practice of casework."

SOCIAL BEHAVIOR AND PERSONALITY. Semiannual. $15 Institutions.
Edited by Robert A.C. Stewart. Editorial address: Society for Personality
Research, Editorial Services Ltd., Box 6443, Wellington, New Zealand. First
issue: 1973.

> Objectives: This publication presents articles of both a theoreti-
> cal and research nature, gathered from all over the world. The
> focus is on all areas of personality and social psychology.

SOCIAL CASEWORK. 10 times a year. $12. Edited by Margaret M.
Mangold. Editorial and business address: 44 East 23rd Street, New York,
N.Y. 10010. Publisher and sponsor: Family Service Association of America.
First issue: 1920.

> Objectives: This journal publishes materials which deal with
> current social problems. This includes professional research or
> experimentation as well as topics concerning social work theory
> and practice. It is designed mainly for social work practitioners
> and educators.

SOCIAL FORCES. Quarterly. $10 Individual; $12 Institutions. Edited by
Everett K. Wilson. Editorial address: 168 Hamilton Hall, University of
North Carolina, Chapel Hill, N.C. 27514. Business address: University of
North Carolina Press, Box 2288, Chapel Hill, N.C. 27514. First issue: 1922.

> Objectives: "To publish scholarly papers and book reviews in the
> field of sociology and in closely related areas."

SOCIAL PROBLEMS. 5 times a year. $20 Individual; $30 Institutions.
Edited by Arlene Kaplan Daniels. Editorial address: Department of Sociology,
Northwestern University, Evanston, Ill. 60201. Business address: Rebecca B.
Aurbach, "Social Problems," 208 Rockwell Hall, State University College,
1300 Elmwood Avenue, Buffalo, N.Y. 14222. Sponsor: Society for the
Study of Social Problems. First issue: 1953.

> Objectives: "Publication of scholarly research on a wide range
> of social problems."

SOCIAL PSYCHIATRY. (Text in English, French, and German). Quarterly.
$12. Edited by S. Fleck. Editorial address: Department of Psychiatry,
Yale University, 333 Cedar Street, New Haven, Conn. 06510. Business
address: Springer-Verlag, 175 Fifth Avenue, New York, N.Y. 10010. First
issue: 1966.

> Objectives: This journal publishes topics which involve the ef-
> fects of social conditions upon human behavior and the relation-
> ship between the social environment and psychiatric disorder.

SOCIAL SCIENCE RESEARCH. Quarterly. $40. Edited by Peter H. Rossi.
Editorial address: Department of Sociology, University of Massachusetts,
Amherst, Mass. 01002. Business address: Academic Press, 111 Fifth Avenue,
New York, N.Y. 10003. First issue: 1972.

> Objectives: This journal publishes methodological studies and
> quantitative research reports in the social sciences. Included are
> papers in a variety of areas, such as sociology, social psychology,
> anthropology, economics, and political science.

SOCIAL WORK. Bimonthly. $20. Editor-in-chief: Donald Brieland.
Edited by Beatrice N. Saunders. Editorial and business address: National
Association of Social Workers, 2 Park Avenue, New York, N.Y. 10016.
First issue: 1956.

> Objectives: This journal publishes current articles dealing with
> social action, social issues, and social services. It is devoted
> to furthering knowledge and improving practice in the social
> welfare area.

SOCIAL WORK IN HEALTH CARE. Quarterly. $17 Individual; $34 Institutions. Edited by Sylvia S. Clarke. Editorial address: Director, Social
Work Department, Roosevelt Hospital, New York, N.Y. 10019. Business
address: Haworth Press, 149 Fifth Avenue, New York, N.Y. 10010. First
issue: 1975.

> Objectives: This journal is directed toward medical and psychi-
> atric social workers in health care facilities, hospital social work

directors, and allied health professionals and health planners.
It seeks to inform about the changes taking place in U.S. health
care and the humanizing role of the social worker in health care
delivery.

SOCIOLOGICAL ABSTRACTS. 5 times a year. $120. Edited by Leo P.
Chall. Editorial and business address: P.O. Box 22206, San Diego, Calif.
92122. Co-Sponsored by American Sociological Association, Eastern Sociological Society, International Sociological Association, and Midwest Sociological Society. First issue: 1953.

Objectives: The ABSTRACTS provides representative and complete
selections of sociological information sources by means of abstracting international periodical literature.

SOCIOLOGICAL REVIEW. Quarterly. $17.25 Individual; $23 Institutions.
Managing Editor: Ronald Frankenberg. Editorial and business address:
University of Keele, Keele, Staffordshire, England. First issue: 1908.

Objectives: "All aspects of sociology."

SOCIOLOGY. 3 times a year. $28. Edited by Philip Abrams. Editorial
address: Department of Sociology and Social Administration, Elvet Riverside,
New Elvet, Durham, England. Business address: Oxford University Press,
Press Road, Neasden, London, England. Sponsor: British Sociological Association. First issue: 1967.

Objectives: This journal publishes materials on the sociology of
race relations, economic development, urban and rural life, education, population, industry, family, political relations, and
leisure occupations. Articles also appear which deal with the
application of sociology in social administration, medicine, and
other areas.

SOCIOLOGY AND SOCIAL RESEARCH. Quarterly. $9. Edited by Martin
H. Neumeyer. Editorial and business address: University of Southern California, University Park, Los Angeles, Calif. 90007. Publisher: University
of California Press. First issue: 1921.

Objectives: In this journal are "articles dealing with sociology,
social research, and general social science subjects."

SOCIOLOGY OF WORK AND OCCUPATIONS. Quarterly. $15 Individual;
$26 Institutions. Edited by Marie Haug. Editorial address: Department of
Sociology, Haydn Hall, Case Western Reserve University, Cleveland, Ohio
44106. Business address: Sage Publications, 275 South Beverly Drive,
Beverly Hills, Calif. 90212. First issue: 1974.

Objectives: This journal is an international forum for theory and research on the interrelationships and structures of work, occupations, and leisure.

SOCIOMETRY. Quarterly. $8 members; $12 nonmembers; $16 Institutions. Edited by Howard Schuman. Editorial address: Department of Sociology, 3012 L.S.A. Building, University of Michigan, Ann Arbor, Mich. 48109. Business address and sponsor: American Sociological Association, 1722 N Street, N.W., Washington, D.C. 20036. First issue: 1937.

Objectives: This journal is interdisciplinary in the publication of materials by both psychologists and sociologists. It seeks to impart the full variety of problems and interests represented by social-psychological research.

SOVIET PSYCHOLOGY. (Formerly part of SOVIET PSYCHOLOGY AND PSY-CHIATRY, 1962-66). Quarterly. $20 Individuals; $70 Institutions. Edited by Michael Cole. Editorial and business address: M.E. Sharpe, 901 North Broadway, White Plains, N.Y. 10603. First issue: 1966.

Objectives: This publication presents unabridged translations of selected articles from all major Soviet journals in psychological fields. The articles selected are chosen as best representing developments in Soviet psychology, and as being of greatest interest to professionals in the field.

STUDIA PSYCHOLOGICA. Quarterly. $18.45. Editorial address: Institute of Experimental Psychology, Slovak Academy of Sciences, Bratislava, Czechoslovakia. Business address: John Benjamins, N.V., 54 Warmolsstraat, Amsterdam, Netherlands. Sponsor: Institute of Experimental Psychology. First issue: 1956.

Objectives: "Publishes results of basic experimental research in psychological sciences from Central and East European countries."

TEACHERS COLLEGE RECORD. 4 times a year from September to May. $14 Individual; $18 Institutions. Edited by Douglas Sloan. Editorial and business address: Teachers College, Columbia University, 525 West 120th Street, New York, N.Y. 10027. Sponsor: Teachers College. First issue: 1900.

Objectives: This publication is concerned with education through the institutions of the culture at large. It presents articles which deal with current thought in the behavioral sciences and humanities as they shed light on the process of education.

# Chapter 13

# ORGANIZATIONS AND ASSOCIATIONS

See also the ENCYCLOPEDIA OF ASSOCIATIONS and the DIRECTORY OF SOCIAL STUDIES/SOCIAL SCIENCE ORGANIZATIONS in chapter 11, section A.

ACADEMY OF PSYCHOLOGISTS IN MARITAL AND FAMILY THERAPY. (Formerly, 1975, Academy of Psychologists in Marital Counseling). 314 Broadway, Union, N.J. 07083. Founded: 1958.

> Membership consists of licensed or certified psychologists who practice marital and family therapy and who are members of the American Psychological Association. There are four committees: ethics, publications, research, and standards. The publications of the Academy are a quarterly newsletter and THE RELATION-SHIP issued four to five times a year. It meets annually with the American Psychological Association.

AMERICAN ACADEMY OF PSYCHOTHERAPISTS (AAP). 6363 Roswell Road, N.E., Atlanta, Ga. 30328. Founded: 1955.

> This is a society of professionals engaged in the practice of psy-chotherapy. It aims to encourage and facilitate interdisciplinary work in psychotherapy. It maintains a library of recorded tapes and sponsors workshops and lectures. Publications include a quarterly journal and a newsletter, issued three times a year. An annual meeting is held.

AMERICAN ASSOCIATION OF MARRIAGE AND FAMILY COUNSELORS (AAMFC). (Formerly, 1970, American Association of Marriage Counselors). 225 Yale Avenue, Claremont, Calif. 91711. Founded: 1942.

> This is a professional society of marriage and family counselors. It has ten accredited training centers across the United States and offers a counseling referral service from its national office. It publishes a quarterly journal, a quarterly newsletter, and a semi-annual membership directory. Its convention is held annually.

# Organizations and Associations

AMERICAN BOARD OF PROFESSIONAL PSYCHOLOGY (ABPP). (Formerly 1968, American Board of Examiners in Professional Psychology). c/o Margaret Ives, 2025 I Street, N.W., Suite 405, Washington, D.C. 20006. Founded: 1947.

> This is a certification board which carries on oral examinations and presents diplomas to specialists with at least five years of practical experience in clinical psychology, counseling psychology, school psychology, or industrial and organizational psychology. The board also makes an annual award for distinguished professional achievement. Its publications include the annual MANUAL FOR ORAL EXAMINATIONS. Its annual meeting is held with the American Psychological Association.

AMERICAN EDUCATIONAL RESEARCH ASSOCIATION (AERA). (Formerly, 1930, National Association of Directors of Educational Research). 1230 Seventeenth Street, N.W., Washington, D.C. 20036. Founded: 1915.

> Members consist of researchers, professors, and students concerned with the development and application of educational research. The association presents annual awards. It has eight divisions and six publications. Its convention is held annually.

AMERICAN FOUNDATION FOR PSYCHOANALYSIS AND PSYCHOANALYSIS IN GROUPS. c/o Louis E. DeRosis, 40 East 89th Street, New York, N.Y. 10028. Founded: 1961.

> This is an association of psychiatrists which raises funds to further education and research in the area of psychoanalytic medicine. It provides a lecture service, conducts symposia, offers patient placement services, and produces motion pictures on therapy for educational purposes. The foundation is affiliated with the Association of Medical Group Psychoanalysts (see p. 173).

AMERICAN GROUP PSYCHOTHERAPY ASSOCIATION (AGPA). 1995 Broadway, 14th Floor, New York, N.Y. 10023. Founded: 1942.

> The membership of this association is limited to mental health professionals who meet specific professional and educational requirements. It has eleven committees, presents awards, and publishes the quarterly INTERNATIONAL JOURNAL OF GROUP PSYCHOTHERAPY, a semiannual newsletter, a biennial directory, and a consumers guide, brochure, brief history, and guidelines. The annual convention is held each February.

AMERICAN INSTITUTES FOR RESEARCH IN THE BEHAVIORAL SCIENCES (AIR). 1055 Thomas Jefferson Street, N.W., Suite 200, Washington, D.C. 20007. Founded: 1946.

> This scientific and educational research organization conducts programs of development and research on behavioral science

170

problems of social importance. It attempts to reach general principles to further understanding of many aspects of human behavior. Its support comes from grants and contracts from government agencies, foundations, and industry. The library contains 2,500 volumes and 20,000 technical reports on educational research and applied psychology. Other offices are in Palo Alto, Calif., Pittsburgh, Pa., and Cambridge, Mass.

AMERICAN MANAGEMENT ASSOCIATION (AMA). 135 West 50th Street, New York, N.Y. 10020. Founded: 1923 as National Personnel Association.

The American Management Association is composed of professional management executives in a variety of organizations. The educational program provides conferences, seminars, courses, and workshops on all aspects of management. The association maintains management centers in North and South America and Europe. It comprises several divisions and publishes eight serials as well as briefings and survey reports. The annual meeting takes place in September in New York City.

AMERICAN PERSONNEL AND GUIDANCE ASSOCIATION (APGA). 1607 New Hampshire Avenue, N.W., Washington, D.C. 20009. Founded: 1952.

This is a professional organization for those working in personnel and guidance in schools, communities, business, and government. It maintains a specialized library and a placement service for members. The APGA has eight committees and twelve divisions. It brings out twelve publications, among them PERSONNEL AND GUIDANCE JOURNAL, JOURNAL OF EMPLOYMENT COUNSELING, and HUMANIST EDUCATOR. The APGA meets annually.

AMERICAN PSYCHOLOGICAL ASSOCIATION (APA). 1200 Seventeenth Street, N.W., Washington, D.C. 20036. Founded: 1892.

This professional and scientific society of psychologists and educators aims to further psychology as a science, a profession, and a way of promoting human welfare. It embraces seven boards and thirty-seven divisions dealing with all areas of psychology. It publishes twenty-two journals and periodicals, along with a biographical directory and membership register. It is affiliated with Psi Chi, the national honorary society in psychology. Its convention is annual.

AMERICAN SOCIETY OF GROUP PSYCHOTHERAPY AND PSYCHODRAMA (ASGPP). 39 East 20th Street, New York, N.Y. 10003. Founded: 1942.

Membership consists of professionals interested in the fields. The society sponsors international congresses and publishes GROUP PSYCHOTHERAPY. The convention of the society is held annually.

# Organizations and Associations

AMERICAN SOCIOLOGICAL ASSOCIATION (ASA). (Formerly American Sociological Society). 1772 N Street, N.W., Washington, D.C. 20036. Founded: 1905.

> This professional society is made up of those interested in the research, application, and teaching of sociology, and student members sponsored by an association member. It consists of seven committees with thirteen sections, and publishes eight periodicals and a monograph series. It holds an annual meeting.

ANNUAL REVIEWS (INFORMATION). 4139 El Camino Way, Palo Alto, Calif. 94306. Founded: 1932.

> This organization serves to further scientific advances by publishing annual surveys of research in a number of scientific areas, among them anthropology, psychology, and sociology.

ASSOCIATION FOR ADVANCEMENT OF PSYCHOLOGY (AAP). 1200 Seventeenth Street, N.W., Suite 400, Washington, D.C. 20036. Founded: 1974.

> This association seeks to advance psychology and to represent a variety of psychological interests and concerns in the field of public policy. Membership consists of psychological organizations and students and members of the American Psychological Association or other such national body. The AAP publishes a monthly newsletter.

ASSOCIATION FOR GROUP PSYCHOANALYSIS AND PROCESS. c/o Gerald S. Weider, 50 Kenilworth Place, Brooklyn, N.Y. 11210. Founded: 1957.

> The association has an international membership of psychiatrists, psychologists, sociologists, and psychiatric social workers. It conducts programs of research, training, and seminars and provides counsultive service. It compiled statistics and maintains a collection of books and articles on group psychoanalysis and allied areas. It publishes a monthly newsletter, and the journal GROUP PROCESS. It holds quarterly scientific meetings and semiannual clinics.

ASSOCIATION FOR HUMANISTIC PSYCHOLOGY (AHP). (Formerly, 1969, American Association for Humanistic Psychology). 325 Ninth Street, San Francisco, Calif. 94103. Founded: 1962.

> This is an international association which seeks to develop human sciences so that human qualities are recognized and fulfilled both individually and at a societal level. It comprises laymen and professionals in a variety of human and social sciences. Publications include a monthly newsletter and a quarterly journal. An annual convention is held along with special conferences and regional meetings.

ASSOCIATION FOR PSYCHOTHEATRICS (AP).  P.O. Box 160371, Sacramento, Calif. 95816.  Founded: 1976.

> This organization is composed of professionals working in the fields of mental health, psychology, education, and theater who are also qualified teachers or facilitators of psychotheatrics. It provides training courses and maintains biographical archives and a placement service. It publishes a quarterly newsletter and holds an annual meeting.

ASSOCIATION OF INTERNAL MANAGEMENT CONSULTANTS.  c/o Albert Aiello, Jr., Sperry and Hutchinson Co., 330 Madison Avenue, New York, N.Y. 10017.  Founded: 1971.

> This association seeks to maintain high standards in the practice of internal management consulting and to encourage and develop this practice. It serves as a marketplace for pooled professional resources. There are three committees: chapters, education, and ethics. It publishes the AIMC NEWSLETTER ten times a year and an annual membership roster. The association holds an annual meeting.

ASSOCIATION OF MANAGEMENT CONSULTANTS (AMC).  811 East Wisconsin Avenue, Milwaukee, Wis. 53202.  Founded: 1959.

> The AMC is an association of professional individuals and firms engaged in management consulting. It sponsors specialized education to further professional development and provides a client referral service so that firms can avail themselves of the expertise of the members. The AMC publishes a monthly newsletter and a directory of membership and services, updated three times a year. The association's convention is annual.

ASSOCIATION OF MEDICAL GROUP PSYCHOANALYSTS (AMGP).  c/o David Weisselberger, 185 East 85th Street, New York, N.Y. 10028.  Founded: 1960.

> The members of this association are all psychiatrists who practice group psychotherapy. It maintains specialized education programs, publishes a journal, and holds an annual meeting.

CENTER FOR ADVANCED STUDY IN THE BEHAVIORAL SCIENCES.  202 Junipero Serra Boulevard, Stanford, Calif. 94305.  Founded: 1954.

> The center was established by the Ford Foundation. It is not an association but rather an organization which gives fifty postdoctoral fellowships on an annual basis to scholars in the behavioral sciences.

CENTER FOR FIELD RESEARCH. 10 Juniper Road, Box 127, Belmont, Mass. 02178. Founded: 1973.

The center aims to foster cooperation in field research by organizing funding for expeditions, affording opportunities for students and scientists to exchange information, maintaining a library, and setting up an international network of research stations. It publishes the GUIDE FOR THE PREPARATION OF PROPOSALS, revised annually, and monographs of an informational nature.

COUNCIL FOR THE ADVANCEMENT OF THE PSYCHOLOGICAL PROFESSIONS AND SCIENCES (CAPPS). This is now part of AAP (see p. 172). 1200 Seventeenth Street, N.W., Washington, D.C. 20036. Founded: 1971.

The council aims to further the application of psychological expertise in a variety of areas. To this end, it attempts to educate psychologists to the legislative issues and to educate Congress to psychological expertise and to obtain governmental support for psychological training and use. It has three committees. Publications include a monthly bulletin and a newsletter, monthly. It holds an annual meeting.

HUMAN RESOURCES RESEARCH ORGANIZATION (HumRRO). 300 North Washington Street, Alexandria, Va. 22314. Founded: 1951.

This organization consists of social science and behavioral research workers who seek to increase effective human performance, especially in organizational settings. It maintains a library of 2,500 books and documents and 125 journals. It publishes an annual bibliography and an irregular report on its activities, as well as professional papers and technical reports.

INDUSTRIAL COMMUNICATION COUNCIL (ICC). P.O. Box 3970, Grand Central Post Office, New York, N.Y. 10017. Founded: 1955.

The members of the ICC work mostly in government and business organizations, directing media and establishing policy. The council seeks to assist members in communicating more effectively, both within and outside of the companies. The ICC is affiliated with the Council of Communication Societies. It publishes a monthly newsletter, the annual INFORMATION RESOURCES BANK, and some books. It meets annually and also conducts seminars and workshops.

INDUSTRIAL RELATIONS COUNSELORS (IRC). P.O. Box 228, New York, N.Y. 10036. Founded: 1926.

The IRC seeks to improve human relations in a variety of settings. It offers symposia and courses in industrial relations, carries out research, and acts as a source of information on employer-employee relations. Its publications include industrial relations memos, research reports, and monographs.

INDUSTRIAL RELATIONS RESEARCH ASSOCIATION (IRRA). 7226 Social
Science Building, University of Wisconsin, Madison, Wis. 53706. Founded:
1947.

> Members are from a variety of backgrounds with common interests
> in various aspects of labor, such as personnel administration,
> labor relations, labor legislation, and employee organizations.
> The IRRA publishes a quarterly newsletter, an annual research
> volume, annual and spring proceedings, and a membership direc-
> tory every six years. It meets semiannually.

INSTITUTE FOR DEVELOPMENT OF EDUCATION ACTIVITIES. 5335 Far
Hills Avenue, Dayton, Ohio 45429. Founded: 1965.

> This agency, affiliated with the Charles F. Kettering Foundation,
> exists to design, test, and apply new solutions to educational
> problems. It hopes to bridge the gap between research and prac-
> tice in schools. It has three divisions and publishes special
> studies and resource materials, occasional papers, monographs,
> and bibliographies. The organization sponsors seminars and sum-
> mer institutes.

INSTITUTE FOR EDUCATIONAL DEVELOPMENT (IED). c/o Fried, Frank,
Harris, Shrine, and Jackson, 120 Broadway, New York, N.Y. 10005.
Founded: 1965.

> This institute, affiliated with the Educational Testing Service, is
> presently inactive. It is engaged in encouraging changes in edu-
> cational practice through research and development. It has car-
> ried out over one hundred projects in the past five years. It
> also evaluates instructional programs and products.

INSTITUTE OF COLLECTIVE BARGAINING AND GROUP RELATIONS. 49
East 68th Street, New York, N.Y. 10021. Founded: 1968.

> The aim of the institute is to promote the concept of collective
> bargaining and to seek ways in which the collective bargaining
> process can be improved. Both management and labor are repre-
> sented on the board of directors. The institute holds seminars
> and forums and promotes research.

INSTITUTE OF MANAGEMENT CONSULTANTS (IMC). 347 Madison Avenue,
New York, N.Y. 10017. Founded: 1969.

> The IMC sponsors research, seminars, and conferences on a variety
> of topics in the field of management consulting. It also evalu-
> ates the qualifications of those who apply and presents certificates
> to those who meet the requirements of experience, education, and
> practice. The IMC publishes an irregular newsletter and holds an
> annual meeting.

INTERAMERICAN SOCIETY OF PSYCHOLOGY. (Also known as Sociedad Interamericana de Psicologia). Department of Psychology, De Paul University,
2323 North Seminary Avenue, Chicago, Ill. 60614. Founded: 1951.

> The society is composed of psychologists, psychiatrists, and other
> professionals with an interest in developing the behavioral sciences
> in the Americas. It publishes the bimonthly Spanish-English Inter-
> american Psychologist, a quarterly journal, a directory, and con-
> gress proceedings. A biennial convention is held.

INTERNATIONAL ASSOCIATION FOR ANALYTICAL PSYCHOLOGY (IAAP).
Sekretariat, Postfach 115, CH-8042 Zurich, Switzerland. Founded: 1955.

> Membership consists of individuals and groups concerned with the
> development of C.G. Jung's analytical psychology through research
> clinical work, and teaching. It maintains libraries in Zurich,
> New York, and San Francisco totaling over 8,500 volumes. It
> offers public lectures and training programs, maintains archives
> on symbolism, and compiles data for research. It holds a tri-
> ennial convention.

INTERNATIONAL ASSOCIATION OF APPLIED PSYCHOLOGY. (Formerly,
1955, International Association of Psychotechnics). 47 Rue Cesar Franck,
B-4000 Liege, Belgium. Founded: 1920.

> This association, composed of specialists in applied psychology,
> seeks to promote communication between the various applied areas
> and to further scientific and social development in these areas.
> It publishes the semiannual INTERNATIONAL REVIEW OF APPLIED
> PSYCHOLOGY and a membership directory. It holds a quadren-
> nial international congress.

INTERNATIONAL ASSOCIATION OF APPLIED SOCIAL SCIENTISTS (IAASS).
6170 East Shore Drive, Columbia, S.C. 29206. Founded: 1971.

> The aims of the association are to maintain an accreditation pro-
> cess and to inform the public as to the uses of the applied social
> sciences. There are four divisions; individuals can apply for ac-
> creditation in any or all of them: organization development,
> laboratory education, internal organization development, and
> community development. There are five committees. The assoc-
> iation publishes a quarterly newsletter and an annual membership
> directory.

INTERNATIONAL ASSOCIATION OF COUNSELING SERVICES (IACS).
(Formerly American Board on Professional Standards in Vocational Counseling;
American Board on Counseling Services). 1607 New Hampshire Avenue,
N.W., Washington, D.C. 20009.

# Organizations and Associations

This organization is affiliated with the American Personnel and Guidance Association. It evaluates, through its three accrediting boards, various centers and agencies which offer counseling services to the public. It publishes the quarterly COUNSELING SERVICE NEWS, an annual directory, and an accreditation handbook. Its convention is held annually.

INTERNATIONAL COUNCIL OF PSYCHOLOGISTS (ICP). (Formerly, 1959, International Council of Women Psychologists). 1050 Park Avenue, New York, N.Y. 10028. Founded: 1942.

Members are either psychologists or in allied fields. The council aims to promote psychology and the application of its findings. Its activities include the sponsorship of Children's International Summer Villages. It has six committees. It publishes the quarterly INTERNATIONAL PSYCHOLOGIST, the biennial INTERNATIONAL UNDERSTANDING, and a directory. The council holds regional meetings and an annual symposium.

INTERNATIONAL INDUSTRIAL RELATIONS ASSOCIATION (IIRA). c/o B.C. Roberts, London School of Economics and Political Science, Houghton Street, London, WC2A 2AE, England. Founded: 1966.

This association is made up of individuals professionally involved with industrial relations, and also of teaching and research facilities engaged in the study of industrial relations. It organizes conferences and promotes international research. Conventions are triennial.

INTERNATIONAL ORGANIZATION FOR THE STUDY OF GROUP TENSIONS. 10 West 66th Street, Suite 6D, New York, N.Y. 10023. Founded: 1970.

This society is composed of behavioral scientists and scholars from a range of areas within the social sciences. It encourages research into the causes of group tension so that it may be reduced and replaced by mutual tolerance and understanding. The organization has formed regional group centers, seminars, and study groups. It publishes the quarterly, INTERNATIONAL JOURNAL OF GROUP TENSIONS. Its convention is annual.

INTERNATIONAL SOCIETY OF SPORTS PSYCHOLOGY. Via Della Camilluccia 195, I-00135 Rome, Italy. Founded: 1965.

Membership extends through forty-seven countries and includes professionals interested in the field. The society seeks the development of research and relations between professionals, and provices information and documentation services for sports psychology. It publishes a journal three times a year, and proceedings. A quadrennial international congress is held.

INTERNATIONAL UNION OF PSYCHOLOGICAL SCIENCE (IUPS). Hogg Foundation, University of Texas, Austin, Tex. 78712. Founded: 1951.

Membership is composed of national psychological societies interested in exchanging information and ideas, organizing international congresses, and promoting student and scholar exchange. The organization carries on educational and research programs. It publishes occasional proceedings and monographs, a sextennial directory, and a quarterly journal. A quadrennial convention is held.

MENTAL RESEARCH INSTITUTE (MRI). 555 Middlefield Road, Palo Alto, Calif. 94301. Founded: 1959.

Membership consists of individuals with an interest in supporting the research of MRI, an interdisciplinary association of professionals in the behavioral sciences. Special attention is given to the family as a social unit and to the area of human communication. It maintains a variety of community-based facilities for a number of different kinds of patients. The institute publishes a quarterly newsletter and maintains a library.

NATIONAL ASSOCIATION OF SCHOOL PSYCHOLOGISTS (NASP). 1511 K Street, N.W., Suite 927, Washington, D.C. 20005. Founded: 1969.

This association seeks to provide for the health and education requirements of children and young people and to inform the public of its practices and services. It issues research reports, maintains archives, and operates a placement service. It publishes monographs and reports, a monthly newsletter, a quarterly journal digest, and an annual directory. An annual convention is held.

NATIONAL CENTER FOR THE EXPLORATION OF HUMAN POTENTIAL. 222 Westbourne Street, LaJolla, Calif. 92037. Founded: 1967.

This foundation bases its work on that of Herbert A. Otto, its chairman. It trains facilitators, carries out research, develops model programs, and spreads information in the human potential field. It has produced a series of small group programs used in a wide range of settings. It has started follow up growth support group programs to help participants make the most of their gains in the "Developing Personal Potential" workshops. It publishes a quarterly newsletter and distributes books, reprints, and a bibliography. An annual national training workshop is held in summer.

NATIONAL COUNCIL ON FAMILY RELATIONS (NCFR). (Formerly, 1948, National Conference on Family Relations). 1219 University Avenue, S.E., Minneapolis, Minn. 55414. Founded: 1938.

Members are of various disciplinary backgrounds but all are engaged in working in family life. The council evaluates existing action programs and presents awards for research and teaching. There are four sections and three committees. Publications include the quarterly JOURNAL OF MARRIAGE AND THE FAMILY. It holds an annual meeting.

NATIONAL INSTITUTES OF MARRIAGE AND FAMILY RELATIONS (NIMFR). (Formerly Institute of Marriage and Family Relations). 6116 Rolling Road, Suite 316, Springfield, Va. 22152. Founded: 1969.

These are professionally staffed centers in three locations (Springfield, Va.; Plano, Tex.; and Cheshire, Conn.) which offer diagnostic, treatment, counseling, and education services to individuals and families. They also hold seminars and workshops and operate community programs. Reports are published on seminars and workshops.

NATIONAL PSYCHOLOGICAL ASSOCIATION (NPA). P.O. Box 2436, West Palm Beach, Fla. 33402. Founded: 1946.

Membership is composed of students and professionals in psychology and the behavioral sciences. The association maintains a library and conducts seminars. Publications include a monthly bulletin, a semiannual journal, and a biennial members directory. An annual meeting is held.

NATIONAL SCIENCE FOUNDATION (NSF). 1800 G Street, N.W., Washington, D.C. 20550. Founded: 1950.

This is an independent agency in the executive branch of the federal government which deals with the support of research, basic and applied, and education in the sciences. To this end, it provides funding, educational opportunities, supports the exchange of information and the use of computers, and the development of science course materials. Through its five directorates, it administers a number of programs. Its publications include an annual guide to programs.

NTL INSTITUTE. (Formerly, 1954, National Training Laboratory in Group Development; 1969, National Training Laboratories; 1973, NTL Institute for Applied Behavioral Sciences). 1501 Wilson Boulevard, Arlington, Va. 22209. Founded: 1947.

This is a nonprofit corporation which offers training, consultation, research, and publication services. It was the creator of the laboratory method, an experience-based training process for changing behavior and outlook. Its programs are developed and conducted by a faculty of three hundred trained social scientists at

over forty colleges. The institute publishes quarterly, the JOUR-
NAL OF APPLIED BEHAVIORAL SCIENCE as well as books, monographs, and training materials.

PSYCHOLOGY SOCIETY. (Formerly, 1971, Education Society). 100 Beekman
Street, New York, N.Y. 10038. Founded: 1960.

The society promotes the use of psychology in behavior modification, treatment of prisoners and drug users, therapy, and the
solution of political and social conflicts. It recommends legis-
lation, presents awards, and operates a placement service for
members. It publishes a quarterly journal, a biennial membership list, occasional papers, and irregular proceedings. An annual
convention is held.

A.K. RICE INSTITUTE. 1610 New Hampshire Avenue, N.W., Washington,
D.C. 20009.

This institute consists of six centers in the United States, each
of which endeavors to further the principles and methods of
group relations and organizational training developed at the Centre for Applied Social Research of the Tavistock Institute of
Human Relations in London. Each center conducts its own programs. The centers are located in Cincinnati (Midwest Group
Relations Center); Los Angeles (Study Center for Organizational
Leadership and Authority-SCOLA), New York (Institute for the
Applied Study of Social Systems-IASOSS), San Francisco (GREX),
Texas (Texas Center), and Washington, D.C. (Washington-Balti-
more Center). A scientific meeting and one or more group re-
lations conferences are held yearly.

SOCIAL SCIENCE RESEARCH COUNCIL (SSRC) 605 Third Avenue, New
York, N.Y. 10016. Founded: 1923.

The members form a board of directors of this council which exists to further social science research. Of the seventeen members,
seven are designated by seven national scientific societies and the
remaining ones are elected by the board. There are a variety of
committees. The council publishes a quarterly serial (ITEMS),
an annual report, monographs, books, and a bulletin series.

SOCIETY FOR THE PSYCHOLOGICAL STUDY OF SOCIAL ISSUES--A Division
of the American Psychological Association (SPSSI). P.O. Box 1248, Ann
Arbor, Mich. 48106. Founded: 1936.

This society is composed of professionals in the social sciences
with an interest in this area. It seeks to acquire and spread
scientific knowledge on social change and other social processes
by furthering psychological research on empirical and theoretical

issues in social life. It also encourages the application of research findings. The society has eleven committees. It publishes
the quarterly JOURNAL OF SOCIAL ISSUES, and an irregular
newsletter. Its convention is annual, held with the American
Psychological Association.

SOCIETY FOR THE STUDY OF SOCIAL PROBLEMS (SSSP). 208 Rockwell Hall,
State University College at Buffalo, 1300 Elmwood Avenue, Buffalo, N.Y.
14222. Founded: 1951.

This professional society of social scientists exists for the development of research and teaching on important social issues. It presents the C. Wright Mills Award for an outstanding book on social
problems. Its fourteen divisions include community research and
development, family, intergroup relations, and sociology and
social work. Publications include SOCIAL PROBLEMS, issued
five times a year, a quarterly newsletter, and an annual directory.
It holds an annual convention.

SOCIETY OF EXPERIMENTAL SOCIAL PSYCHOLOGY (SESP). Department of
Psychology, University of Texas, Austin, Texas 78712. Founded: 1964.

Members are professionals social psychologists who have published
important work. The society presents an annual dissertation prize
of $100 for an original dissertation which constitutes a contribu-
tion to the field of social psychology. A newsletter is published
and an annual meeting is held.

WESTERN BEHAVIORAL SCIENCES INSTITUTE (WBSI). 1150 Silverado Street,
LaJolla, Calif. 92037. Founded: 1959.

This is an independent organization which conducts action-oriented,
multidisciplinary research in the behavioral sciences. Some work
concentrates on innovative strategies for dealing with problems
such as conflict resolution. Other investigations include simulation gaming and interpretation of the communication programs work
carried out here for various audiences.

WORKSHOP INSTITUTE FOR LIVING-LEARNING (WILL). 333 Central Park
West, New York, N.Y. 10025. Founded: 1966.

Members, associates, and affiliates are of social science or education background and have an interest in helping individuals
and groups with their problem solving and concept learning by
means of training groups and workshops. It provides curricula
leading to certificates of competence as affiliates and associates
of WILL. It publishes a semiannual bulletin and directory and
has published two monographs. It holds an annual exchange
workshop.

# AUTHOR INDEX

In addition to authors, this index includes all editors, compilers, contributors, and translators cited in the text.  Alphabetization is letter by letter.

## A

Abbott, Simon  163
Abelson, Philip H.  164
Abelson, Robert P.  15, 22
Abrams, Philip  167
Adams, Donald K.  21
Adorno, T.W.  59
Akey, Denise  120
Alker, Hayward R., Jr.  35
Allen, Vernon  16
Allport, Gordon W.  21, 57
Altman, Irwin  1, 29, 41, 132
Amidon, Edmund J.  105
Amitai Etzioni  22
Ammons, Carol H.  157, 160
Ammons, Robert B.  157, 160
Anastasi, Anne  11
Anderson, Norman H.  16
Antonelli, Ferruccio  149
Appley, Dee G.  79
Argyle, Michael  1, 15, 41–42, 131
Argyris, Chris  3, 64, 95, 96, 98
Aronson, Elliot  15, 21–22
Aronson, Marvin L.  92
Arrow, Kenneth J.  26
Asch, Solomon E.  48, 59
Ashmore, Richard D.  17
Atkinson, Richard C.  32
Avis, Warren E.  35

## B

Bach, George R.  79
Back, Kurt W.  79, 110
Backman, Carl W.  25
Bailey, John A.  152
Baker, Norma J.  38
Bakke, E. Wight  95–96, 98
Baler, L.A.  144
Bales, Robert F.  2, 4, 24, 27, 46, 132
Ballachey, Egerton L.  20
Bandura, Albert  15
Bany, Mary A.  105
Barnes, Douglas  75
Baron, Robert A.  14
Bartos, Otomar J.  27
Bass, Bernard M.  59, 65, 72, 131
Batchelder, Richard L.  80
Bauer, Catherine  110
Beal, George M.  65
Becker, Howard P.  14
Beech, H.R.  141
Bellows, Roger  65
Beloff, Halla  141
Bem, Daryl J.  16
Benne, Kenneth D.  2, 52, 81
Bennis, Warren G.  42, 63, 90
Ben-Zeev, Saul  27

# Author Index

Berardo, Felix M.   154
Berelson, Bernard   14, 76
Berg, Irwin A.   59
Berger, Joseph   27
Berger, M.L.   80
Berger, P.J.   80
Berger, Seymour M.   21
Berkowitz, Leonard   14-16, 22, 136
Berlyne, D.E.   22
Bernard, H. Russell   147
Berne, Eric L.   80, 109
Bernstein, Saul   107
Berscheid, Ellen   16, 42
Berzon, Betty   91
Bexton, W. Harold   109
Biddle, Bruce J.   50, 129
Bidwell, Charles E.   137
Bierer, Joshua   148
Billig, Michael   52
Bion, Wilfrid R.   1, 109
Blake, Robert   59
Blanchard, Kenneth H.   97
Blank, Leonard   80
Blau, Peter M.   53, 96
Blazer, John A.   161
Bloch, Donald A.   145
Blum, Milton L.   96
Blumberg, Arthur   81, 84
Bogardus, Emory S.   65
Bohlen, Joe M.   65
Bonner, Hubert   109
Bonoma, Thomas V.   49
Borgatta, Edgar F.   4, 132
Boskoff, Alvin   14
Bower, Eli M.   136
Braceland, Francis J.   137
Bradford, Leland P.   2, 52, 81
Brehm, Jack W.   16, 17
Breton, Raymond   28
Brewer, Garry D.   164
Brown, Charles T.   76
Browne, Clarence G.   66
Bruce, Jeanne   46
Bruce, Westley   46
Bryson, Lois   139
Buckle, Roger C.   139
Burke, W. Warner   96
Burnham, Donald L.   159
Burton, Arthur   81
Busch, Henry M.   66

Byrne, Donn   15

## C

Cabot, Hugh   2
Calhoun, Donald W.   2
Campbell, Donald T.   59, 66
Campbell, Ian   99
Cantril, Hadley   47
Carlsmith, J. Merrill   19
Carter, Robert M.   130
Cartwright, Dorwin   2, 21, 63, 98
Cassel, Russell N.   143, 145
Cathcart, Robert S.   76
Chadwick-Jones, J.K.   17
Chall, Leo P.   167
Chammah, Albert M.   30
Champion, R.A.   139
Chaplin, J.P.   119
Chase, Marian Tyler   53
Chase, Stuart   53
Chemers, Martin M.   67
Christensen, C.R.   103
Christie, Lee S.   76
Cicourel, Aaron V.   12
Cinnamon, Kenneth M.   87-88
Clarke, A.D.B.   141
Clarke, Jack A.   126
Clarke, Sylvia S.   166
Cohen, Arthur R.   17, 52
Cohen, Bernard P.   60
Cohn, Thomas S.   66
Colbert, Michael J.   100
Cole, Michael   168
Colling, Patricia   145
Collins, Barry E.   17, 22, 35
Colman, Arthur D.   109
Communications/Research/Machines,
    editors of   125
Cook, Lloyd A.   53
Cook, Stuart W.   29
Cooley, Charles H.   17-18
Coons, Alvin E.   73
Cooper, Cary L.   3, 81
Copp, James H.   164
Corsini, Raymond J.   129, 130
Coser, Lewis A.   53
Costanzo, Philip R.   25, 154
Coyle, Grace L.   63, 66
Crammer, J.L.   140-41

Crisp, Arthur H.  140
Criswell, Joan H.  28
Cronback, Lee  48
Crosbie, Paul V.  42
Crump, J. Griffin  154
Crutchfield, Richard S.  20

D

Daniels, Arlene Kaplan  166
Davidson, P.O.  142
Davis, James H.  36
Davis, Keith E.  3, 15
Davis, Murray S.  43
Dean, John P.  54
Delbecq, Andre L.  28
deMare, P.B.  146
de Rivera, Joseph  18
DeRosis, Helen A.  137
Deutsch, Karl W.  35
Deutsch, Morton  21, 29, 54
Dickson, William J.  101
Diedrich, Richard C.  3
Dion, Kenneth  15
Division Chairpersons and Editor of
  Special Publications (American
  Psychological Association)  158
Dorfman, Wilfred  162
Doob, Anthony N.  60, 153
Douglas, Tom  107
Driver, Helen I.  81
Dubin, Robert  66, 96-97
DuBois, Rachel D.  77
Duck, Steve W.  43
Duffy, John C.  143
Dunnette, Marvin D.  3
Dunphy, Dexter C.  110
Durkin, Helen E.  82
Durham, Lewis E.  117
Dye, H. Allan  3
Dyer, William G.  110

E

Educational Resources Information
  Center (ERIC)  163
Egan, Gerard  82
Ekeh, Peter P.  18
Elliott, Harrison S.  36
Elliott, Jim  146

Elwell, Elizabeth A.  28
Eron, Leonard D.  149
Ervin-Tripp, Susan M.  15
Estes, Hugh  98
Estes, W.K.  161

F

Federation Internationale de Docu-
  mentation  121
Feiner, Arthur H.  144
Feit, Marvin D.  129
Feldstein, Marc J.  113
Festinger, Leon  2, 11, 18, 110
Fiedler, Fred E.  15, 67
Fields, Sidney J.  83
Filley, Alan C.  43
Fine, Sara  9
Flament, Claude  28
Fleck, S.  166
Fleishman, Edwin A.  67, 150
Fontaine, Fernand  28
Fouraker, Lawrence E.  37
Frankenberg, Ronald  167
Freedheim, Donald K.  159
Freedman, Daniel X.  139
Freedman, Jonathan L.  15, 19, 60
Freeman, Graydon L.  67
Frenkel-Brunswik, Else  59
Freud, Sigmund  4
Frijda, Nico H.  15

G

Galinsky, M. David  90
Gamson, William A.  64
Gardner, Burleigh B.  97
Gardner, Eric F.  54
Garfinkel, Harold  12
Gazda, George M.  83
Gerard, Harold B.  20
Gerbner, George  150
Gergen, Kenneth J.  43
Gershenfeld, Matti K.  8, 88
Getzels, J.W.  22
Gibb, Cecil A.  22
Gibb, Jack R.  2, 44, 81, 117
Gibbard, Graham S.  110
Gibson, David  142
Glass, Sheldon D.  83

# Author Index

Glasser, Paul 83
Goffman, Erving 44
Goldberg, Carl 84
Goldberg, Merle C. 84
Goldman, George D. 86
Goldman, Leo 158
Golembiewski, Robert T. 3, 4, 81, 84
Goodchilds, Jacqueline D. 155
Goodstein, Leonard D. 149
Goranson, Richard E. 15
Gordon, Thomas 68
Goss, Mary E.W. 153
Gottesfeld, Mary L. 143
Gottsegen, Gloria B. 80
Gottsegen, Monroe G. 80
Gouldner, Alvin W. 68
Gouran, Dennis S. 36
Grace, Alonzo G. 68
Granick, Lois 159
Gray, Richard A. 120
Greco, Marshall C. 54
Green, Bert F., Jr. 161
Greenberg, Ira 84
Greening, Thomas C. 153
Greenwald, Anthony G. 154
Grimshaw, Allen 138
Gross, Neal 50
Guest, Robert H. 97
Guetzkow, Harold 35, 68
Gustafson, David H. 28
Guttentag, Marcia 121

## H

Haas, J. Eugene 50
Haiman, Franklin S. 69
Haire, Mason 97-98
Hakel, Milton D. 158
Haley, Frances 120
Hall, Calvin S. 21
Hall, Darl M. 36
Halpin, Andrew W. 69
Hammersley, D.W. 147
Haney, William V. 77
Harding, John 22
Hardy, James M. 80
Hare, A. Paul 4, 129, 130, 131
Harmon, Lenore W. 156
Harnqvist, Kjell 69

Harre, Rom 16
Harris, Carol 147
Harrison, Albert A. 5
Hartford, Margaret E. 108
Hartman, John J. 110
Haug, Marie 167
Hebb, D.O. 22
Heckel, Robert V. 85
Heider, Fritz 44, 48
Helsin, Richard 113
Helson, Harry 19
Hemphill, John K. 29
Henderson, George 111
Hendrick, Clyde 157
Hendry, Charles B. 72
Henry, Nelson B. 105
Hernstein, R.J. 160
Hersey, Paul 97
Hickman, C. Addison 98
Hill, William Fawcett 165
Hiller, E.T. 19
Hinkle, Roscoe C. 18
Hinton, Bernard L. 5
Hilton-Brown, W.J. 69
Hoffman, Martin L. 156
Holland, Janet 123
Hollander, Edwin P. 15, 20, 69, 132
Hollander, Sandra 90
Homans, George C. 5, 14, 16
Honey, Peter 100
Hood, Robert C. 98
Hornback, Kenneth E. 130
Hornstein, Harvey A. 96
Hough, John B. 105
Hoult, Thomas Ford 119
Hovland, Carl I. 45, 47
Huesmann, L. Rowell 16
Humovitch, Bernard 52
Humphreys, Lloyd G. 137
Hunt, James G. 67
Hunt, Raymond G. 20, 132
Hunt, William A. 6
Huszar, George B. 6

## I

Inkeles, Alex 22
Insko, Chester A. 20
Israel, Joachim 55

# J

Jackson, Ellen 127
Jacobs, Alfred 111
Jahoda, Marie 29
Janis, Irving L. 45
Jaynes, William E. 74
Jennings, Eugene E. 70
Jennings, Helen H. 70, 106
Johnson, David W. 6, 26
Johnson, Frank P. 6
Johnson, John L. 155
Johnson, Lois V. 105
Johnson, Robert B. 54
Jones, Arthur J. 70
Jones, Edward E. 15, 20
Jones, John E. 111-12, 113

# K

Kadis, Asya L. 85
Kahl, Joseph A. 2
Kahn, J.H. 91
Kahn, Robert L. 98
Kaplan, Martin F. 112
Kardiner, Abram 20
Karlin, Samuel 26
Katz, Daniel 18, 98
Katz, Elihu 77
Katz, Irwin 15
Katz, W.A. 127
Keller, Mark 163
Keller, Paul W. 76
Kelley, Harold H. 13, 20, 22,
    45, 133
Kelly, Joe 98
Kemp, C. Gratton 85
Kennedy, Robert Woods 110
Khinduka, S.K. 156
Kidder, Louise H. 45
Kiesler, Charles A. 45, 60, 138
Kiesler, Sara B. 60
Kimble, Gregory A. 152, 160
Kinkade, Robert G. 128
Kissen, Morton 86
Klein, Josephine 6-7
Klineberg, Otto 57
Knowles, Hulda F. 7
Knowles, Malcolm S. 7
Koesterich, Errol 129

Kolb, Harry D. 98
Kornhauser, Arthur W. 64
Kovacs, Arthur L. 162
Krech, David 20
Kroll, William 135
Kruglanski, Arie W. 16
Kuhn, Manford H. 98
Kujoth, Jean S. 128

# L

Laing, Ronald D. 45
Laird, Donald A. 70
Laird, Eleanor C. 70
Lakin, Martin 3, 86
Lambert, William W. 21
Lang, Gladys E. 64
Lang, Kurt 64
Lantz, Herman R. 18
Lassey, William R. 71
Lazarsfeld, Paul F. 77
Lebra, William P. 77
Lee, A. Russell 45
Lee, Hans 60
Leigh, Denis 155
Lerner, Melvin J. 16
Leroux, J. 148
Leslie, Robert C. 112
Lesse, Stanley 137
Leventhal, Gerald S. 16
Leventhal, Howard 15
Levinson, Daniel J. 59
Lewin, Kurt 18, 21, 55, 57
Li, New-Soong 77
Libo, Lester M. 55
Library of Congress 123
Library of Congress and the National
    Union Catalog Subcommittee, Re-
    sources Committee, Resources and
    Technical Services Division, Ameri-
    can Library Association 124
Lieberman, Morton A. 86, 92
Liebert, Robert M. 14
Liff, Zanvel 71
Lifton, Walter M. 7, 112
Likert, Rensis 99
Lindskold, Svenn 13
Lindzey, Gardner 21-22
Lippitt, G. 2
Lippitt, Ronald 2, 46, 52, 57,
    61, 112

# Author Index

Lonner, Walter J. 151
Louttit, Chauncey M. 118
Loveday, Peter 99
Lubin, A.W. 130
Lubin, Bernard 130
Luce, R. Duncan 76
Luft, Joseph 7
Lumpkin, Katherine D. 50

## M

McClelland, David C. 71
Maccoby, Michael 71
McConkie, Mark 3
McCormick, Regina 120
McEachern, Alexander W. 50
McGinnies, Elliott 7
McGrath, Joseph E. 22, 29, 132
McGuire, William J. 15, 22
Machover, Solomon 86
McInnis, Raymond G. 126
MacKenzie, Kenneth D. 29
Macy, Josiah, Jr. 76
Mahar, Linda 67
Maher, Brendan A. 151
Maier, Norman R.F. 36-37, 99
Malamud, Daniel I. 86
Malik, Leela G. 28
Mangham, I.L. 81
Mangold, Margaret M. 165
Mann, Richard D. 110
Mark, Charles 127
Martin, Charles A. 154
Mason, Ward S. 50
Massarik, Fred 102, 149
Mayer, Thomas F. 30
Mead, George Herbert 17, 23
Meadow, Herman 49
Mehrabian, Albert 60
Melman, Seymour 99
Merton, Robert K. 14, 23
Messick, Samuel 164
Meyers, Donald I. 162
Mikalachki, Alexander 55
Miles, Matthew B. 86, 106
Milgram, Stanley 22
Miller, Eric J. 100
Miller, Ernest C. 158
Miller, James G. 30, 109, 140
Miller, Lorraine F. 44

Miller, Roger R. 165
Mills, Judson 23
Mills, Theodore M. 8, 46
Milman, Donald S. 86
Miner, John B. 135
Mintz, Elizabeth E. 87
Mischel, Walter 16
Mitchell, Geoffrey D. 120
Moment, David 49, 51
Moore, David G. 97
Moore, John W. 163
Moreno, Jacob L. 23, 85, 87, 92
Moreno, Zerka T. 146
Morris, Kenneth T. 87
Morrison, Denton E. 130
Moscovici, Serge 15
Mosteller, Frederick 22
Mouton, Jane 59
Mowrer, O. Hobart 88
Murchison, Powell 153, 155, 156
Murphy, Gardner 11, 57

## N

Napier, Rodney W. 8, 88
Naylor, James C. 157
Nemeth, Charlan 16
Nemhauser, George L. 157
Nessel, Jack 161
Neumeyer, Martin H. 167
Nevison, Myrne B. 142
Newbrough, J.R. 150
Newcomb, Theodore 48, 57, 113
Newman, Ruth G. 106
Newstetter, Wilber I. 113
Niemi, Richard G. 37
Northen, Helen 108
Northway, Mary L. 8
Nye, Robert D. 56

## O

O'Connor, John 38
Ofshe, Richard 30
Ofshe, S. Lynne 30
Ohlsen, Merle M. 89
Olds, James 46
Oliner, Samuel P. 147
Olmsted, Donald W. 9
Olmsted, Michael S. 9

Orwant, Carol J. 30
Osaka, Ryoji 159
Osipow, Samuel H. 151

## P

Parsons, Talcott 24, 46
Penland, Patrick 9
Perlman, Helen Harris 37, 51
Petrullo, Luigi 48, 72
Pfeiffer, J. William 111-12, 113
Phillipson, Herbert 45
Pigors, Paul J.W. 72
Pinard, Maurice 28
Platts, Grace N. 44
Pollack, Gertrude K. 114
Porter, Lyman W. 138
Preiss, Jack J. 51
Prokasy, William F. 162
Proshansky, Harold 22, 24
Putzey, Lloyd J. 129, 130

## R

Rackham, Neil 100
Rankin, Earl F., Jr. 50
Rapoport, Anatol 30, 98
Rashevsky, N. 31
Raven, Bertram H. 9, 22, 132
Raudabaugh, J. Neil 65
Reed, Judith 143
Reeves, Elton T. 10
Reitz, H. Joseph 5
Rice, A. Kenneth 72, 100, 109
Rice, Charles E. 160
Riedl, Otto 52
Rieff, Philip 17
Riesel, J. 92
Riley, Matilda W. 31
Rissman, Francine 151
Roethlisberger, Fritz J. 101, 103
Rogers, Carl R. 3, 89
Rohrer, John H. 24
Rokeach, Milton 59
Rokkan, Elizabeth 52
Rommetveit, Ragnar 52
Rose, Arnold M. 24
Rosen, Alex 54 ;
Rosenbaum, Max 3, 89, 146
Rosenberg, Seymour 21

Rosenberg, Stan 8
Rosenzweig, Mark R. 138
Ross, Lee 16
Ross, Murray G. 72
Rossi, Peter H. 166
Rothman, Jack 114
Rubin, Jeffrey Z. 9
Ruitenbeek, Hendrik M. 89
Russett, Bruce M. 150

## S

Sacks, Harvey 12
Sahakian, William S. 24
Salzberg, H.C. 85
Samovar, Larry A. 76
Sanford, R. Nevitt 59
Saretsky, Lorelle 87
Sarri, Rosemary 83
Saunders, Beatrice N. 166
Sax, Saville 90
Sayles, Leonard R. 101
Scarpitti, Frank R. 91
Schacter, Stanley 15, 46, 110
Scheidlinger, Saul 47, 148
Schein, Edgar H. 90
Schlenker, Barry R. 49
Schlesinger, Herbert J. 160
Schmitt, Raymond L. 47
Schopler, John 15, 20
Schorr, Thelma M. 136
Schuman, Howard 168
Schutz, William C. 31
Schwartz, Shalom H. 16
Schwartz, Steven 112
Scott, Ellis L. 74, 101
Scott, James W. 126
Scott, W. Richard 96
Scott, William G. 3
Sears, David O. 15, 19, 22
Seashore, Charles 3
Seashore, Stanley E. 56
Secord, Paul F. 25, 149
Seeman, Melvin 72
Seidenberg, Bernard 24
Selekman, Benjamin M. 101
Senn, Peter R. 132
Shaffer, John B. 90
Shartle, Carroll L. 73, 74

# Author Index

Shaw, Marvin E. 10, 15, 25
Sheperd, Clovis R. 10
Sherif, Carolyn 11, 25, 47, 56
Sherif, Muzafer 10-11, 24, 25, 47, 56, 59
Sherman, Barry 87
Shibutani, Tamotsu 11
Shils, Edward A. 24
Shirley, Norma 126
Short, James F., Jr. 114
Shubik, Martin 31
Sidowski, Joseph B. 140
Siegel, Sidney 37
Sills, David L. 122
Simon, Herbert A. 102
Slater, Philip E. 11
Slavson, Samuel R. 90-91
Slip, Samuel 155
Sloan, Douglas 168
Smelser, Neil J. 12
Smith, Peter B. 12
Smith, Robert 141
Smith, William S. 38
Snadowsky, Alvin 89
Solomon, Herbert 28, 32
Solomon, Lawrence N. 91
Speier, Matthew 12
Spence, Janet T. 142, 144
Spradlin, Wilford 111
Sprott, Walter J. 12
Steiner, Ivan D. 15, 38
Steiner, Jerome 155
Stephenson, Richard M. 91
Steuer, M.D. 123
Stewart, Angus 141
Stewart, Robert A.C. 165
Stewart, V. Mary 45
Stock, Dorothy 48
Stoetzel, Antoine H. 35
Stogdill, Ralph M. 48, 57, 73, 74, 102, 131, 133
Stouffer, Samuel A. 14, 25
Stotland, Ezra 15, 52
Strachey, James 4
Strodtbeck, Fred L. 114, 129
Struefert, Siegfried 150
Struening, Elmer L. 121
Sudnow, David 12
Suefeld, Peter 150

Sullivan, Dorothea F. 108
Suppes, Patrick 26, 28, 32

## T

Taguiri, Renato 22, 48
Tajfel, Henri 22
Tannenbaum, Percy H. 15
Tannenbaum, Robert 102
Taylor, Dalmas 41
Taylor, E. 67
Tead, Ordway 74
Tedeschi, James R. 13, 48-49
Terauds, Anita 1
Thelen, Herbert A. 2, 3, 48, 103
Theodorson, Achilles G. 124
Theodorson, George A. 124
Thibaut, John W. 13, 20, 22, 133
Thomas, Dorothy S. 32
Thompson, George G. 54
Thompson, Sheila 91
Tichy, Monique K. 118
Tiger, Lionel 13
Todd, Frankie 75
Tompkins, Margaret 126
Triandis, Harry C. 15, 49, 133
Trist, E.L. 147
Twyman, J. Paschal 50
Tyler, Ralph W. 14

## U

Upshaw, Harry S. 15
U.S. Research and Development Board, Committee on Human Resources. Panel on Human Relations and Morale 103

## V

Van De Ven, Andrew H. 28
Van Kaam, Adrian 147
Verba, Sidney 74
Vinter, Robert 83
Viseltear, Elaine 136
Viteles, Morris S. 103
Voos, Henry 131
Vroom, Victor H. 22, 38, 75

190

# Author Index

## W

Walford, Albert J.   121
Walker, Nancy   15
Walster, Elaine H.   16, 42
Wassell, B. Bohdan   92
Watson, Goodwin   26, 57
Watson, J.P.   140
Watson, Jeanne   46
Wechsler, David   59
Weick, Karl E.   22, 135
Weiner, Herbert   162
Weisberg, Herbert F.   37
Weiss, Robert S.   103
Weschler, Irving R.   92, 102
Wetzel, Christopher G.   163
Whitaker, Dorothy S.   92
White, Carl M.   127
White, Ralph K.   61
Whiteley, John M.   144
Whiting, John W.M.   22
Wicklund, Robert A.   16
Williams, Clive   139
Williams, Joanna   152
Williams, Robin M., Jr.   57
Willner, Dorothy   32
Wilmot, William W.   78
Wilson, Everett K.   165
Wilson, M.O.   11

Winder, Alvin E.   79
Winkel, Gary H.   145
Witt, Robert E.   61
Wittenberg, Rudolph M.   75
Wolberg, Arlene R.   92
Wolberg, Lewis R.   92
Wolf, Alexander   71, 93
Wolman, Benjamin B.   122, 148
Wrightsman, Lawrence S., Jr.   26, 38
Wynar, Bohdan S.   125
Wyncoop, Sally   120

## Y

Yalom, Irvin D.   86, 93
Yakes, Nancy   120
Yetton, Philip W.   38, 75

## Z

Zajonc, Robert B.   21, 26
Zaleznik, Abraham   49, 51, 75, 103
Zander, Alvin   2, 49, 52, 61
Zelditch, Morris, Jr.   138
Zener, Karl E.   21
Zimpfer, David G.   130
Znaniecki, Florian   13

# TITLE INDEX

This index includes the titles of all books cited in the text. In some cases titles have been shortened. Alphabetization is letter by letter.

## A

Achieving Society, The 71
Adaption-Level Theory 19
Additions to a Bibliography on the Present Status of Role Theory 129
Adjustment 69
Administrative Behavior 102
Advances in Experimental Social Psychology (Vol. 1) 14
Advances in Experimental Social Psychology (Vol. 2) 15
Advances in Experimental Social Psychology (Vol. 3) 15
Advances in Experimental Social Psychology (Vol. 4) 15
Advances in Experimental Social Psychology (Vol. 5) 15
Advances in Experimental Social Psychology (Vol. 6) 15
Advances in Experimental Social Psychology (Vol. 7) 16
Advances in Experimental Social Psychology (Vol. 8) 16
Advances in Experimental Social Psychology (Vol. 10) 16
American Behavioral Scientist 117
American Behavioral Scientist Guide to Recent Publications in the Social and Behavioral Sciences 117
American Doctoral Dissertations 117

American Library Resources 117
American Reference Books Annual 117
Analysis of Groups 110
Anatomy of Leadership, An 70
Annotated Bibliography of Research, 1947-60, An 117
Annual Handbook for Group Facilitators 111
Annual Review of Psychology 118
Applications of Graph Theory to Group Structure 28
Art of Group Conversation, The 77
Art of Group Discipline, The 75
Art of Leadership, The 74
Authoritarian Personality, The 59
Autocracy and Democracy 61

## B

Bargaining and Group Decision Making 37
Basic Approaches to Group Psychotherapy and Group Counseling 83
Basic Studies in Social Psychology 24
Behavioral Sciences Today, The 14
Behavioral Science Techniques 118
Behavior of Industrial Work Groups 101
Beyond the Couch 93
Beyond Words 79
Bibliographic Guide to Psychology: 1975 118

# Title Index

Bibliographic Index  117
Bibliography of Bibliographies in Psychology, 1900-27  118
Bibliography of Group Psychotherapy, 1906-56  129
Bibliography of Publications Relating to the Small Group, A  132
Book Review Digest  117
Book Review Index  117

## C

Carl Rogers on Encounter Groups  89
Choice  119
Civilian Morale  57
Classroom Group Behavior  105
Collective Dynamics  64
Communication: Patterns and Incidents  77
Communication and Learning in Small Groups  75
Communication and Learning in Task-Oriented Groups  76
Communication and Persuasion  45
Communication in Organizations  130
Comprehensive Dissertation Index  117
Concept of Role Conflict, The  50
Conflict, Conformity, and Social Status  60
Conflict, Power and Games  49
Conflict among Humans  56
Conformity  60
Conformity and Deviation  59
Confrontation  80
Content Analysis in Communication Research  76
Controversial Issues in Human Relations Training Groups  88
Cooperation and Competition  38
Counseling and Learning through Small-Group Discussion  81
Creative Leadership  65
Current Contents  119
Current Developments in the Study of Leadership  67
Current National Bibliographies  117
Current Perspectives in Social Psychology (3d ed.)  132
Current Perspectives in Social Psychology (4th ed.)  20

## D

Decisions, Values, and Groups  32
Developing Interactive Skills  100
Deviancy: The Psychology of Being Different  60
Dictionary of Modern Sociology  119
Dictionary of Psychology  119
Dictionary of Sociology, A  120
Directory of Social Studies/Social Science Organizations  120
Discussion: The Process of Group Decision-Making  36
Dissertation Abstracts International  117
Dissertation Abstracts International: Retrospective Index  117
Dyadic Communication  78
Dynamic Factors in Industrial Productivity  99
Dynamics of Group Action  36
Dynamics of Group Behavior, The  10
Dynamics of Groups at Work  103
Dynamics of Instructional Groups, The  105
Dynamics of Interpersonal Behavior, The  49
Dynamics of Participative Groups  44
Dynamics of Planned Change, The  46
Dynamic Theory of Personality, A  21

## E

Educational Resources Information Center  128
Education of Youth for Leadership, The  70
Emotional Dynamics and Group Culture  48
Encounter: Group Processes for Interpersonal Growth  82
Encounter: Group Sensitivity Training Experience  84
Encounter: The Theory and Practice of Encounter Groups  81
Encounter Groups: Basic Readings  82
Encounter Groups: First Facts  86
Encyclopedia of Associations  120

Enterprise and Its Environment  100
Equity Theory  16
Examination of Role Theory, An  51
Exchange and Power in Social Life  53
Executive Performance and Leadership  73
Experiences in Groups and Other Papers  1
Experimental Social Psychology  23
Experimental Social Psychology: Text with Illustrative Readings  20
Experiments in Social Process  30
Explorations in Cognitive Dissonance  17
Explorations in Group Work  107
Explorations in Role Analysis  50

F

Face to Face  82
Facilitating Individual Growth and Societal Change  7
Family, The  50
Family, Socialization, and Interaction Process  46
Field Theory as Human Science  18
Field Theory in Social Science  21
Formal Organizations  96
Foundations of Group Counseling  85
Foundations of Social Psychology  20
From Group Dynamics to Group Psychoanalysis  86
Functions of Social Conflict, The  53
Further Explorations in Group Work  107
Fusion Process, The  95

G

Games-Man, The  71
Game Theory and Related Approaches to Social Behavior  31
Gang Delinquency and Delinquent Subcultures  114
Government Publications and Their Use  117
Government Reference Books, a Biennial Guide to U.S. Government Publications  120
Group Adjustment  113

Group Analysis  92
Group as Agent of Change, The  111
Group Aspirations and Group Coping Behavior  49
Group-Centered Leadership  68
Group Cohesion Reconsidered  55
Group Cohesiveness in the Industrial Work Group  56
Group Counseling  89
Group Development  2
Group Dynamics  2
Group Dynamics: Principles and Applications  109
Group Dynamics: The Psychology of Small Group Behavior  10
Group Dynamics and Individual Development  9
Group Dynamics and Social Action  52
Group in Depth, The  82
Group Influence on Consumer Brand Choice  61
Group Interaction as Therapy  91
Group Leadership and Democratic Action  69
Group Life: The Nature and Treatment of Its Specific Conflicts  54
Group Performance  36
Group Problem-Solving through Discussion  38
Group Procedures  3
Group Process and Productivity  38
Group Process and Gang Delinquency  114
Group Process as a Helping Technique, The  91
Group Processes: An Introduction to Group Dynamics  7
Group Processes: Selected Readings  12
Group Processes Today  86
Group Psychoanalysis  92
Group Psychology and the Analysis of the Ego  4
Group Psychotherapy: A Behavioral Approach  85
Group Psychotherapy: A Bibliography of the Literature from 1956 through 1964  130
Group Relations at the Crossroads  11

Group Relations Reader 109
Groups, Leadership and Men 68
Groups: Theory and Experience 8
Groups and Organizations 5
Groups in Harmony and Tension 56
Groups in Schools 106
Groups in Social Work 108
Groups in Theory and Practice 99
Group Structure and the Newcomer 46
Group Techniques for Program Planning 28
Group Therapy 1976 92
Group Training Techniques 80
Group Work in the Helping Professions 130
Groupwork Practice 107
Guide to Book Review Citations, A 120
Guide to Reference Books 117
Guide to Reference Materials 121

## H

Handbook of Evaluation Research 121
Handbook of Industrial and Organizational Psychology 3
Handbook of Leadership 73, 133
Handbook of Non-Verbal Group Exercises, A 87
Handbook of Small Group Research 4, 131
Handbook of Social Psychology, The (Vol. 1) 21
Handbook of Social Psychology, The (Vol. 2) 22
Handbook of Social Psychology, The (Vol. 3) 22
Handbook of Social Psychology, The (Vol. 4) 22
Handbook of Social Psychology, The (Vol. 5) 22
Handbook of Structured Experiences for Human Relations Training, A 113
Handbook of Verbal Group Exercises, A 88
Harvard List of Books in Psychology, The 121
How to Pick Leaders 67

Human Relations 2
Human Behavior and Social Processes 24
Human Behavior and Its Control 6
Human Group, The 5
Human Nature and the Social Order 17
Human Social Behavior 14
Human Groups 12
Human Dilemmas of Leadership 75
Human Circle, The 84
Human Relations in Administration with Readings and Cases 97
Human Relations in Industry 97
Human Organization, The 99
Human Relations 111
Human Judgement and Decision Processes in Applied Settings 112
Humanities Index 121

## I

Improving Leadership Effectiveness 67
In Common Predicament 56
Increasing Leadership Effectiveness 64
Index Bibliographicus 121
Index to American Author Bibliographies 117
Index to Psychology, Multimedia 122
Individual and His Society, The 20
Individual Behavior and Group Achievement 48, 133
Individual Change through Small Groups 83
Individual Behavior and Group Achievement 102
Individual in Society 20
Individuals, Groups, and Economic Behavior 98
Individuals and Groups 5
Industrial Psychology and Its Social Foundations 96
Inside a Sensitivity Training Group 92
Instructor's Manual 88
Instrumentation in Human Relations Training 113
Intensive Group Experience, The 89

Intensive Group Psychotherapy 79
Interaction Analysis 105
Interaction in Small Groups 42
Interaction Process Analysis 27
International Bibliography of
  Sociology 122
International Encyclopedia of Psy-
  chiatry, Psychology, Psychoanalysis
  and Neurology 122
International Encyclopedia of the
  Social Sciences 122
International Index 123
Interpersonal Attraction 42
Interpersonal Behavior 49, 133
Interpersonal Conflict Resolution 43
Interpersonal Dynamics 42
Interpersonal Encounter 86
Interpersonal Perception 45
Interpersonal Underworld, The 31
Intimate Relations 43
Introduction to Group Dynamics 7
Introduction to Group Therapy, An
  90
Irregular Serials and Annuals 117

J

Joining Together 6

L

Labor Relations and Human Relations
  101
Leader Behavior 73
Leader in the Group 71
Leaders, Groups, and Influence 69
Leaders and Leadership 65
Leadership: Abstracts and Bibliog-
  raphy, 1904-74 131
Leadership: A Study of Role Expecta-
  tions and Performance 74
Leadership, Psychology, and Or-
  ganizational Behavior 65, 131
Leadership and Decision-Making 38,
  75
Leadership and Dynamic Group Action
  65
Leadership and Effective Management
  67
Leadership and Interpersonal Behavior
  72

Leadership and Isolation 70
Leadership and Its Effects upon the
  Group 66
Leadership and Organization 102
Leadership and Perceptions of Or-
  ganization 101
Leadership and Productivity 66
Leadership and Role Expectations 74
Leadership and Social Change 71
Leadership and Structures of Personal
  Interaction 73
Leadership Behavior of School Super-
  intendents 69
Leadership in American Education 68
Leadership in Group Work 66
Leadership of Discussion Groups 114
Leadership or Domination 72
Learning and Change in Groups 81
Learning for Leadership 72
Learning to Work in Groups 106

M

Major Variables of the Small Group
  Field 1
Management and the Worker 101
Manual for Their Measurement, A 29
Manual of Intergroup Relations, A 54
Marathon Groups 87
Markov Learning Models for Multi-
  person Interactions 32
Mathematical Approaches to Politics
  35
Mathematical Methods in Small Group
  Processes 28
Mathematical Methods in the Social
  Sciences, 1959 26-27
Mathematical Models of Group
  Structure 30
Mathematical Sociology 123
Mathematical Theory of Human
  Relations 31
Mathematical Thinking in the Measure-
  ment of Behavior 32
Measuring Group Cohesiveness 55
Men in Groups 13
Methods for Studying Work and
  Emotionality in Group Operation
  27

# Title Index

Methods in the Study of Administrative Leadership 74

Microcosm 11

Mind, Self, and Society from the Standpoint of a Social Behaviorist 23

Models of Group Therapy and Sensitivity Training 90

Modern Dictionary of Sociology, A 124

Modern Organization Theory 97

Modern Sociological Theory in Continuity and Change 14

Modern Theory and Method in Group Training 110

Monologue to Dialogue 76

Monthly Catalog of United States Government Publications 117

Motivation, Productivity, and Satisfaction of Workers, The 103

Motivation and Morale in Industry 103

Motives and Goals in Groups 61

## N

National Union Catalog: A Cumulative Author List, The 124

National Union Catalog, 1956/through 1967, The 124

National Union Catalog: Pre-1956 Imprints, The 124

New Group Therapies, The 89

New Group Therapy, The 88

New Perspective, A 28

New Perspectives on Encounter Groups 91

New Psychology of Leadership, The 70

New Studies in the Social and Behavioral Sciences 117

New Understanding of Leadership 72

New York Times Book Review Index, 1896-1970 124

1957 Bibliography of Group Psychotherapy 130

1972 Annual Handbook for Group Facilitators, The 113

1977 Annual Handbook for Group Facilitators 111

1978 Annual Handbook for Group Facilitators, The 112

## O

Organizational Behaviour 98

Organizational Change through Effective Leadership 97

Organizational Communication 131

Organizational Structure and Dynamics 96

Organizational Theory in Industrial Practice 98

Outline of Social Psychology, An 11

## P

Personal and Organizational Change through Group Methods 90

Personal Influence 77

Personality and Organization 95

Persona Social Role and Personality 51

Person Circle, The 83

Person Perception and Interpersonal Behavior 48

Persons-in-Groups 2

Planning of Change, The 63

Popular Guide to Government Publications, A 117

Power and Discontent 64

Practical Application of Democracy 6

Practical Handbook of Group Counseling, The 83

Practice of Group Therapy, The 91

Practice of Group Work, The 108

Practicum of Group Psychotherapy 85

Presentation of Self in Everyday Life, The 44

Primary Group, The 110

Primer of Sociometry, A 8

Principles of Group Treatment 80

Principles of Human Relations 99

Prisoner's Dilemma 30

Probability Models of Collective Decision Making 37

Problems of Power in American Democracy 64

Problem Solving and Creativity in Individuals and Groups 36

Problem-Solving Discussions and Conferences 37

# Title Index


Process of Group Thinking, The  36
Process of Organization  103
Promoting Social Justice in the Multi-group Society  114
Psychoanalysis and Group Behavior  47
Psychodrama  84
Psychological Abstracts  125
Psychology of Affiliation, The  46
Psychology of Behavior Exchange, The  43
Psychology of Commitment, The  45
Psychology of Ego-Involvements, The  47
Psychology of Inter-Group Relations  45
Psychology of Interpersonal Behavior, The  41
Psychology of Interpersonal Relations, The  44
Psychology of Organizations, The  98
Psychology of Social Norms, The  10
Psychosources  125
Psychotherapy through the Group Process  92

R

Reader's Guide to Periodical Literature  125
Readings in Group Work  108
Readings in Human Relations  3
Readings in Social Psychology  19
Readings on the Sociology of Small Groups  8
Reality Games  90
Reduction of Intergroup Tensions, The  57
Reference Books in Paperback  125
Reference Groups  47
Reference Other Orientation, The  47
Research Materials in the Social Sciences  126
Research Methods in Social Relations with Especial Reference to Prejudice  29
Research Methods in the Behavioral Sciences  18
Resolution of Conflict, The  54

Resolving Social Conflicts  55
Roads to Agreement  53
Role Conception and Group Consensus  50
Role Development and Interpersonal Competence  51
Role Relations in the Mental Health Professions  52

S

Scientific Study of Social Behaviour, The  1, 131
Self-Evaluation and Rejection in Groups  55
Sensitivity Training and the Laboratory Approach  84
Serials in Psychology and Allied Fields  126
Sharing Groups in the Church  112
Shared Participation  35
Simple Models of Group Behavior  27
Small Group, The  9
Small Group.  An Analysis of Research Concepts and Operations, The  4
Small Group Research: A Synthesis and Critique of the Field  29, 132
Small Group Communication  76
Small Groups  4
Small Groups: Some Sociological Perspectives  10
Small Groups: Studies in Social Interaction  132
Small Groups and Political Behavior  74
Social Actions  13
Social Behavior: A Functional Analysis  7
Social Behavior: Its Elementary Forms  5
Social Casework  37
Social Encounters  42
Social Exchange Theory: Its Structure and Influence in Social Psychology  17
Social Exchange Theory.  The Two Traditions  18
Social Groups, Roles and Leadership  9
Social Influence Processes, The  48

# Title Index

Social Interaction 41
Social Judgement 47
Social Norms and Roles 52
Social Organization 18
Social Penetration 41
Social Pressures in Informal Groups 110
Social Process 18
Social Process in Organized Groups 63
Social Psychology (Asch) 59
Social Psychology (Secord and Backman) 25
Social Psychology (Sherif and Sherif) 25
Social Psychology: A Brief Introduction 22
Social Psychology: An Experimental Approach 26
Social Psychology: Experimentation, Theory, Research 24
Social Psychology: Interdependence, Interaction, and Influence
Social Psychology: Issues and Insights 26
Social Psychology: People in Groups 9
Social Psychology: Social Influence, Attitude Change, Group Processes, and Prejudice 17
Social Psychology and Intergroup Relations 52
Social Psychology at the Crossroads 24
Social Psychology in the Seventies 26
Social Psychology of Group Processes for Decision-Making, A 35
Social Psychology of Groups, The 133
Social Relations and Morale in Small Groups 54
Social Relations and Structures 19
Social Research to Test Ideas 25
Social Science and Its Methods 132
Social Science Research Handbook 126
Social Sciences and Humanities Index 126
Social Sciences Index 126

Social Status and Leadership 72
Social Technology of Organization Development, The 96
Social Theory and Social Structure 23
Social Work with Groups 108
Society and Personality 11
Sociological Abstracts 127
Sociological Studies in Scale Analysis 31
Sociology of America 127
Sociology of Small Groups, The 8
Sociometry in Group Relations 106
Sociometry Reader, The 23
Some New Techniques for Studying Social Behavior 32
Sources of Information in the Social Sciences 127
Standard Periodical Direction, The 117
Strategic Interaction 44
Structure and Dynamics of Organizations and Groups, The 109
Studies in Group Behavior 66
Studies in Leadership 68
Studies in Social Interaction 12
Studies in Social Power 63
Study of Groups, The 6
Study of Leadership 66
Subject Guide to Major United States Government Publications 127
Subject Guide to Periodical Indexes and Review Indexes 128
Symposium on Research in Group Behavior 103
Systems of Organization 100

## T

Tactics of Social Influence 60
Task and Organization 100
Team Achievement under High Motivation 57
Theories of Group Processes 3
Theories of Social Psychology 25
Theory and Practice in Interpersonal Attraction 43
Theory and Practice of Group Psychotherapy, The 93
Theory of Collective Behavior 12

Theory of Group Structures, A  29
Theory of Leadership Effectiveness,
   A  67
Thesaurus of Psychological Index
   Terms  128
T-Groups: A Survey of Research  81
T-Groups and Therapy Groups in a
   Changing Society  79
T-Group Theory and Laboratory
   Method  81
Toward Better Human Relations  53
Toward Self-Understanding  86
Training in Community Relations  112
Transcultural Research in Mental
   Health  77
Types of Formalization in Small-Group
   Research  27

U

Ulrich's International Periodicals

Directory  128
Understanding Organizational Be-
   havior  95
Using Sensitivity Training and the
   Laboratory Method  80
Utility and Choice in Social Inter-
   action  30

W

Who Shall Survive?  87
Working Papers in the Theory of
   Action  24
Working with Groups: Group Process
   and Individual Growth  112
Working with Groups. The Social
   Psychology of Discussion and
   Decision  7
World Bibliography of Bibliographies,
   A  117

# SUBJECT INDEX

References are to page numbers and underlined numbers refer to major areas of emphasis on that subject. Alphabetization is letter by letter.

## A

Absenteeism (labor), effect of work groups on 56
Academy of Psychologists in Marital and Family Therapy 169
Achievement
  in producing entrepreneural behavior 71
  relationship to team motivation 71
Adaptation, concept of 19
Adolescents. See Youth
Adult education, group behavior in 2
Aesthetics, social psychology of 22
Affectivity 19
Affiliation, psychology of 46
Aggression 9, 13
  cathartic effect of 16
  deviancy and 60
  roots of 56
Aggressiveness
  concept of 15
  conflict and 56
  media violence and 15
Alcoholism
  periodicals concerned with 147, 161, 163
  treatment of 85, 89, 114
Altruism
  factors affecting 16
  social psychology of 13

American Academy of Psychotherapists (AAP) 169
American Association for Humanistic Psychology (AHP)
American Association for the Advancement of Science 6
American Association of Marriage and Family Counselors (AAMFC) 169
American Board of Professional Psychology (ABPP) 170
American Board on Professional Standards in Vocational Counseling. See International Association of Counseling Services (IACS)
American Educational Research Association (AERA) 170
American Foundation for Psychoanalysis and Psychoanalysis in Groups 170
American Group Psychotherapy Association (AGPA) 170
American Institutes for Research in the Behavioral Sciences (AIR) 170-71
American Management Associations (AMA) 171
American Personnel and Guidance Association (APGA) 171, 177

# Subject Index

American Psychological Association
(APA) 171. See also Society for the Psychological
Study of Social Issues
American Society of Group Psychotherapy and Psychodrama
(ASGPP) 171
American Sociological Association
(ASA) 172
Annual Conference on the Use of
On-Line Computers in Psychology, Proceedings 140
Annual Reviews (Information) 172
Anomie 23
Antidemocratism 59
Anti-Semitism 59
Anxiety
effect on affiliation 46
interpersonal attraction and 42
in work groups 56
See also Emotion
Aptitude tests, in executive screening
68
Armed forces. See Military
Art, sociology of 14
Association for Advancement of Psychology (AAP) 172
Association for Group Psychoanalysis
and Process 172
Association for Humanistic Psychology
(AHP) 172
Association for Psychotheatrics (AP)
173
Association of Internal Management
Consultants 173
Association of Management Consultants 173
Association of Medical Group Psychoanalysts (AMGP) 173
Attitudes 15, 21, 45
of adolescents toward religion 52
bibliography of research on 123
changing of 17, 20, 22, 23,
60, 70
effects of communication on 15
group 20, 23
group influences on 59
influence on problem solving 39
interpersonal 16
leadership and 70

measurement of 22
among mental health professionals
52
nature of 22
periodicals concerned with 140,
143, 155
relationship to behavior 26, 73
social judgment and 47
surveys of in industry 103
see also Belief systems; Opinions;
Values and norms
Attraction, interpersonal 14, 15,
16, 19, 23, 42, 43
leadership and 69-70
in the social influence process 49
Authoritarianism 59
of leaders 68
Authority
the leader and 66, 74
organizational 97, 98, 102
self-esteem and 75
between superiors and subordinates
73
Autocracy 61

## B

Balance theory 42
Bargaining
conflict and 16
interpersonal 43
models of 37-38
Behavior. See Group behavior;
Human behavior
Behavioral sciences. See Social
sciences
Behaviorism, functional 7
Behavior modification 12, 60
in encounter groups 6
of juvenile delinquents 91
Belief systems
as a basis for a typology of collective behavior 12
changing of 20
member-leader phenomena of 11
see also Attitudes; Opinions; Values
and norms
Biology
relationship to sociology of groups
13

of social interaction 42
of survival 18
Bion, Wilfred R. 48, 84
Birth order, effect on affiliation 46
Blau, Peter M. 17
Boards of education, role of 68
Body movement, analysis of social
  behavior in terms of 41–42
Bureaucracy 97
  sociology of 23

C

Center for Advanced Study in the
  Behavioral Sciences 173
Center for Field Research 174
Children
  analysis of social and emotional
    responses of 32
  group therapy and counseling with
    83, 89, 90, 91
  periodicals concerned with 136,
    143, 159, 162
  in social work group settings 107
  sociometric explorations of 23
  see also Education; Parents; Siblings;
    Youth
Church groups. See Religion, group
  work in
Clinical psychologists, attitudes and
  behavior among 52
Clinical psychology, group processes
  in 7
Coalitions, formation of 14, 37
Coercion, by leaders 65
Cognitive dissonance theory 15, 17
  25
Cognitive processes 19, 21, 76
  in conformity 60
  in group decision making 36
  influence of culture on 14
  in the social influence process 49
Cohesion, group 6, 52–57, 109
  of gangs 114
  productivity and 38
  social psychology of 10
  as a variable of performance 36
  see also Conflict
Collective bargaining. See Labor-
  management relations

Collective behavior. See Group behavior; Interpersonal relations
College students. See Students
Committees, methodology of operation
  of 30
Communes 89
Communication 36, 43, 63, 75–78,
  112, 113
  associations concerned with 178,
    181
  bibliography of 123, 130, 131
  effect on attitude change 15
  in encounter and marathon groups
    83, 87
  fear and 15
  in game theory 90
  individual self-development through
    involvement in 9
  in industry 96
  in intergroup relations 54
  leadership and 71
  models of 28–29, 32
  networks of 14, 28–29
  in opinion change 45
  organizational 96, 97, 102, 130,
    131
  periodicals concerned with 150,
    155, 161
  in problem solving 39
  significance of in strategic inter-
    action 44
  social 17
  social judgment and 47
  textbooks on 3, 6, 8, 9, 11,
    14, 15, 18
  training for group 8
  see also Mass media
Community
  associations concerned with the
    176, 178
  change in the 46, 111
  discipline in the 75
  group dynamics of the 109
  influence on leadership style 73
  intergroup relations in the 54
  leadership and changes in the 71
  periodicals concerned with the
    147, 150, 159
  problem-solving techniques in the
    35

# Subject Index

sociometric explorations of the 24, 87
see also Neighborhoods
Competition and cooperation 54
  game theory in 38–39
  models of 37
  see also Conflict
Conditions of labor. See Work, conditions of and efficiency in
Conference in Social Psychology, second (1952) 11
Conferences, conducting of 36
Conflict 2, 10, 18, <u>52–57</u>, 64, 112, 114
  bargaining and 16
  in communes 89
  due to roles assumed by participants 10
  game theory in 84
  intergroup 26, 31, 47, 54, 56, 57, 109
  leadership and 65
  models of 27, 60
  in organizations 96
  periodicals concerned with 148, 150–51
  resolution of 27, 43
    associations concerned with 181
  in roles 10, 26, 50, 51, 73
  in social penetration 41
  in social work group settings 107
  in work situations 75
  see also Competition and cooperation
Conformity 14, 19, 23, 43, 59, 60, 64
  of adolescents 47–48
  conflict and 56
  deviancy and 60
  leadership and 70
  models of 60
  situational factors in 15
  social influence and 8
  see also Social pressure
Consumers, influence of groups on brand choices by 61
Content analysis 22, 76
Conversation
  attributing meaning to 76
  group 77

see also Discussion; Speech
Conversion, mass 64
Cooperation. See Competition and cooperation
Cooperative Conference for Administrative Officers of Public and Private Schools (1950) 68
Council for the Advancement of the Psychological Professions and Sciences (CAPPS) 174
Counseling
  associations concerned with 169, 176–77
  educational 13
  employment 151
  nondirective 99
  periodicals concerned with 142, 144, 151
  see also Group counseling
Creativity
  in leadership 65, 68
  in problem solving 36
Criminal justice system
  decision–making theory in 112
  periodicals concerned with 151
  see also Gangs; Juvenile delinquents; Police
Crowds, behavior of 64. See also Riot control
Culture
  in communication 78
  as an expression of biological tendencies 13
  in group structure 8
  influence on cognitive processes 14
  influence on leadership style 73
  intergroup relations and 57
  periodicals concerned with 156
  relationship to group and interpersonal behavior 41
  relationship to social interaction 42
  as a variable in group interaction 8

## D

Data analysis 22
Decision making. See Problem solving

Democracy 61
  group dynamics and 55, 65
  in industry 96, 99
  of leaders 68, 69, 71, 75
  problems of power in 64
  in problem solving 36, 38, 52, 53
  see also Antidemocratism
Deprivation, identification with gangs
      and 47. See also Relative
      deprivation
Deviance 43, 59, 60
  rejection of by groups 55
Discipline, group 75
Discussion, group
  contrasted with group conversation
      77
  leadership of 114
  as a means of problem solving 38
  small-group 81-82
Dissonance (psychology) 45
Drug abuse treatment, periodicals con-
      cerned with 147
Dyads 1, 5, 13, 26, 31, 42, 43, 45
  communication in 78
  see also Husband and wife; Siblings

E

Economics
  periodicals concerned with 167
  pressure groups in 99
  social psychology of 22
Education
  associations concerned with 170,
      171, 175, 176, 178
  group processes in 61, 103,
      105-6, 109, 110, 111,
      112, 114
    bibliography of 130
    leadership in 47, 66, 68, 70,
        72-73, 74
    textbooks on 7
    therapy 90
  guidance in 13
  for organizational change 100
  periodicals concerned with 138,
      140, 141, 143, 145, 152,
      154, 157, 163-64, 167,
      168

social psychology of 22
  see also Adult education; Boards
      of education; School super-
      intendents; Teachers
Educational Testing Service 175
Education Society. See Psychology
      Society
Ego 47, 72. See also Superego
Emotion 42, 48, 70
  effect on affiliation 46
  in group problem solving 36
  models for the study of in groups
      27
  role of in communication 79
  see also Anxiety
Emotionally disturbed, group therapy
      with 91
Empathy, social psychology of 15
Employment
  counseling for 151
  periodicals concerned with 140,
      152, 156
  see also Executives; Labor-manage-
      ment relations; Job satisfac-
      tion; Job training; Work
Encounter groups 80-81, 82-83, 84,
      86, 89, 90, 91, 111
  behavior modification in 6
  nonverbal exercises in 87
  origins and history of 79
  simulations of 9
Entropy 98
Environment
  of the home 161
  individual behavior and 6, 11,
      145
  interaction with personality in
      organizations 6
  leadership and 73
  relationship to psychiatric disorders
      166
  response of small groups to 5
Equity theory 14, 16
Ethics
  of leadership 68
  in sensitivity training 86
Ethnic groups 114
Ethnocentricism 59
Evaluation. See Self-evaluation
Exchange theory 42

# Subject Index

Executives
developmental theory in education
of 51
leadership of 70, 71, 72–73,
74, 75
organizational behavior of 99
recruitment and selection of 67–68
see also Management; Organizational behavior
Expectancy theory 112
Expectation, influence on listening
76

## F

Factor analysis 32
Family 12, 72, 111
associations concerned with 169,
178–79
dynamics of 78
experimental findings on 15
life-style and residential location
of 110
as part of society 46
periodicals concerned with 138,
145–46, 154, 167
roles in the 50–51
Fear, communication of 15
Field theory 18, 21, 25
Film. See Movies
Ford Foundation 173
France, sociological research and
theory in 14
Franklin (Leo M.) lectures in Human
Relations 53
Freedom 17
social psychology of perceived 15
Freud, Sigmund 4, 21, 47, 53, 88,
144
Friendship
determinants of 41
interpersonal relations in 43
social psychology of 9
Fromm, Erich 144
Fundamental Interpersonal Relations
Orientation (FIRO) 31

## G

Game theory 27, 30, 31–32, 38–39,
49, 53, 111

associations concerned with 181
in group treatment 80, 90
periodicals concerned with 164
in sensitivity training 84
Gangs 114–15
deprivation and membership in 47
preschool 32
see also Juvenile delinquents
Gestalt psychology, in group therapy
90
Goals, group 8, 49–50, 61, 65,
82, 83, 84, 88
in planned change 63
in social work group settings 107,
108
Government, responsibility for educational leadership 68
Great Britain, sociological research
and theory in 14
Group behavior
bibliography of reference works
on 117–33
influences on 59–61
organizations and associations concerned with 114, 120,
169–81
periodicals concerned with 135–68
textbooks 1–33
of models and methodologies in
26–33
see also Dyads; Encounter groups;
Ethnic groups; Family; Human
behavior; Informal groups;
Intergroup relations; Interpersonal relations; Marathon
groups; Peer groups; Primary
groups; Reference groups;
Sensitivity training; Social
groups; Social work, group
settings in; T-groups; Task-
oriented groups; characteristics
and activities of groups (e.g.
Coalitions; Coersion; Communication; Competition and cooperation; Leadership; Power
[social science]; Problem
solving)
Group cohesion. See Cohesion, group
Group counseling 3, 7, 81–82, 83,
85, 89, 91

bibliography 130
see also Counseling
Group discipline. See Discipline,
group
Group discussion. See Discussion,
group
Group dynamics 36, 44, 48, 49,
53, 55, 65, 103, 109
application of to leadership improvement 70
in church work 112
in education 105, 106
of group psychotherapy 79, 82,
85, 86
instructor's manual for 88-89
periodicals concerned with 138
of social action 52
textbooks on 1, 2, 3, 5, 7, 8,
9, 10, 19, 21
Group goals. See Goals, group
Group membership. See Membership,
group
Group pressure. See Social pressure
Group records, forms and uses of 66
Group therapists and facilitators 92
handbooks for 111-12, 113-14
issues and concerns of importance
to 88
periodicals concerned with 146
roles and problems of 86, 89
training of 8, 85, 93
Group therapy 79, 82, 83, 85,
86-87, 88, 89, 90-91,
92-93, 109, 110, 111
associations concerned with 169,
170, 171, 172
bibliography 129, 130
leadership in 47, 114
periodicals concerned with 137,
144, 146, 147-48, 155,
162-63, 165
textbooks on 3
transactional analysis in 80
see also Encounter groups
Group topography 9

## H

Harvard Symposium on Person Perception (1957) 48

Hawaii, University of. East-West
Center 78
Heredity, leadership and 65
Homans, George C. 17, 18
Horney, Karen 92
Hospitals
groups as agents of change in 111
role conception in 50
Hostility, social psychology of 13,
23
Housing, life-style and location of
110
H-Scale 26
Human behavior 26, 48, 69
adaption-level theory in 19
associations concerned with 171
commitment to 45
complexity of 26
influence of social pressure on 5
interpretation of 44
models and methods in the investigation of 30-31
periodicals concerned with 136,
138, 140, 149, 165
psychology of 41-42, 43
relationship to attitudes 26
in relation to setting 6, 11, 145
see also Behavior modification;
Interpersonal behavior;
Organizational behavior
Human nature 26
Human relations. See Group behavior;
Interpersonal relations
Human Relations Research Group,
bibliography of publications
102
Human Resources Research Organization
(HumRRO) 174
Husband and wife, interpersonal relations between 43, 45.
See also Marriage; Parents

## I

Identity, as a role problem 51
Individuals 20-21, 42
behavior of in relation to setting
6, 11, 145
discipline in 75
formulation of norms by 10

in groups 5, 6, 7, 9, 10, 23, 48, 51, 109, 110
interdependence of 9, 13, 23
in organizations 95, 100-101, 102
planned change and 46
problem solving by 36
producing change in 111
psychology of groups explained in terms of 4
small groups as an interface between society and 8
in the social system 25
see also Self
Industrial Communication Council (ICC) 174
Industrial psychology 3, 22, 96, 98, 101, 158
Industrial Relations Counselors (IRC) 174
Industrial Relations Research Association (IRRA) 175
Industry
  associations concerned with 174-75
  communications in 96
  group dynamics of 109
  group formation in 75
  human relations in 1, 97, 99, 103, 104
  leadership in 66, 67, 70, 96, 101
  morale in during World War II 57
  periodicals concerned with 167
  problem-solving technology in 35
  sociometric explorations of 24
  see also Executives; labor-management relations; Management; Work groups
Informal groups 96
Information sciences, group processes in 9
Initiation rites, as an expression of the male bond 13
Innovation, leadership influence on 15
Insecurity, interpersonal attraction and 42. See also Security
Institute for Development of Education Activities 175
Institute for Educational Development (IED) 175
Institute for Social Research. Research Center for Group Dynamics 52
Institute of Collective Bargaining and Group Relations 175
Institute of Management Consultants (IMC) 175
Institute of Marriage and Family Relations. See National Institute of Marriage and Family Relations
Institutions 18, 101
  dynamic aspects of change in 64
  organization of for task performance 100
  in the organization of social relationships 19
  social psychology of 98
  see also Organizational behavior
Integration theory 23, 46, 112
  as applied to social attribution 16
Interaction analysis 105
Interamerican Society of Psychology 176
Intergroup relations 52-53, 54, 72, 77, 112-13, 114
  conflict in 26, 31, 48, 54, 56, 57, 109
  periodicals concerned with 154
  textbooks on 5, 12, 20, 24, 26
International Association for Analytical Psychology (IAAP) 176
International Association of Applied Psychology 176
International Association of Applied Social Scientists (IAASS) 176
International Association of Counseling Services (IACS) 176-77
International Council of Psychologists (ICP) 177
International Industrial Relations Association (IIRA) 177
International Organization for the Study of Group Tensions 177
International relations, social psychology of 22, 56
International Society of Sports Psychology 177
International Union of Psychological Science (IUPS) 178

Interpersonal attraction. See Attraction, interpersonal
Interpersonal Perception Method (IPM) 45
Interpersonal relations 41-50, 53, 103
    applications of to industry and organizations 1
    bibliography of research on 133
    conflict resolution in 43
    in facilitating group cohesion 56
    in industry 1, 97, 99, 103, 104
    as an influence in groups 24, 102
    management of power in 75
    measurement techniques in 113
    models of 12, 31, 49
    periodicals concerned with 136, 147, 155
    philosophy of 3
    psychology of 44, 45
    role stress and 98
    sociometric measures of 66, 73
    textbooks on 1, 2, 3, 12-13, 19, 20, 22, 23, 26
    training and development in 3, 72
    see also Attraction, interpersonal
Interviewing 22
    in group therapy 91
Italy, sociological research and theory in 14

**J**

Japan, sociological research and theory in 14
Job satisfaction 96, 103, 104
Job training, periodicals concerned with 140
Johari Window model 7
Judgment 47, 56
    in communicative processes 76
    group influences on 59
    social influences on group 8
    theory of 112
Juvenile delinquents 114
    effect of movie violence on 16
    group therapy for 91
    see also Gangs

**K**

Kelley, Harold 17, 20
Knowledge, sociology of 14, 23. See also Learning

**L**

Labor-management relations 101
    associations concerned with 174-75, 177
    periodicals concerned with 138
Language. See Semantics; Speech
Law, sociology of 14
Leadership 14, 43, 54, 61, 63, 64-75, 76, 89, 109, 110, 111
    bibliography of 131, 133
    democratic 68, 69, 71, 75
    of discussion groups 114
    of encounter and T-groups 81, 82, 83
    of experiential groups 3
    gang 114
    of group conversation 77
    group influences on 72
    importance to the functioning of democracy 55, 65
    in industry 66, 67, 70, 96, 101
    influence of on innovation 15
    in interpersonal conflict resolution 43
    Leader Match concept of 67
    models and methodologies of 30, 67, 71, 75
    organizational 66, 70, 71, 72, 73, 74, 75, 97, 101-2, 103
    orientation of the group to 11-12
    psychoanalytic views of 47
    role of in problem solving 37, 38
    in social work group settings 107
    textbooks on 2, 3, 6, 8, 9, 10, 11, 17, 19, 20, 21, 22, 24
    training for 8, 66, 67, 69, 70, 72, 103
    women and 74
Learned helplessness model 16
Learning 19, 56, 75-76
    double loop 64

# Subject Index

in encounter groups 86
in group situations 80, 84, 106, 109
influence of self-esteem on 106
models of 27, 64
periodicals concerned with 143, 161
social 20
see also Knowledge
Legislative bodies, problem solving in 36
Levi-Strauss, Claude 18
Lewin, Kurt 18
Libraries, group processes in 9
Life-styles, group formation and residential location according to 110
Listening 76
Logic, philosophy of applied to the behavioral sciences 31
Loneliness, interpersonal attraction and 42
Loyalty, group 102

# M

Management
associations concerned with 171, 173, 175
periodicals concerned with 135, 158, 163
see also Executives; Organizational behavior
Marathon groups 85, 87, 89
Marques culture (Polynesia), psychoanalytic concepts applied to 20
Marriage
associations concerned with 169
importance of roles in 51
periodicals concerned with 138, 154
see also Husband and wife
Mass media
role of people in the flow of 77
social psychology of 22
violence in 15
see also Communication; Movies
Membership, group 2, 11, 26, 54
effect on emotional states 46

ego-involvement and 47
in facilitation of cohesiveness 56
group character dependency on 48
multiple 24
perception and 11
relationship to the leader 11-12
in social work settings 107
at work 101
Men, behavior of in groups 13
Mental health
associations concerned with 178
periodicals concerned with 140, 141, 144, 146, 162
religious factors in 78
social psychology of 22
Mental health professions, intergroup attitudes and behavior in 52
Mental Health Research Institute (MRI) 178
Mentally handicapped, periodicals concerned with 147
Mentally ill 41
group therapy with 91
periodicals concerned with 147
in social work group settings 107
Military
group behavior research in 103
interdisciplinary research in solving problems of 33
leadership and group relations in 69
sociometric explorations of 24
Models and modeling 12, 20, 21, 23, 26-33, 49, 109
of conformity situations 60
of double loop learning 64
of group counseling 83
of leadership 67, 71, 75
of organizational behavior 95
periodicals concerned with 164
of primary groups 110
of problem solving and decision making 30, 33, 35, 37-38
of social influence 49
see also Game theory
Morale 57, 63
effect of leaders on 66
group-effectiveness component of 54
in industry 97, 103

relationship to motivation 57
Morality, group 3
Moreno, Jacob L. 85, 92
Motion pictures. See Movies
Motivation 2, 3, 11, 38, 42-43,
    56, 61
  in game theory 39
  individual differences in 51
  in industry 95, 96, 103-4
  organizational 96, 99
  periodicals concerned with 140,
      155
  phase movement in relation to 24
  relationship to team achievement
      57
  social 22
  see also Morale
Movies, effect of violence of on
    delinquents 16

N

National Association of Directors of
    Educational Research. See
    American Educational Research
    Association (AERA)
National Association of School Psy-
    chologists (NASP) 178
National Center for the Exploration of
    Human Potential 178
National Council on Family Relations
    (NCFR) 178-79
National Institutes of Marriage and
    Family Relations 179
National Psychological Association
    (NPA) 179
National Science Foundation (NSF)
    179
National Training Laboratory in Group
    Development. See NTL
    Institute
Needs, interaction of social values
    with 10
Neighborhoods 12
  periodicals concerned with 147
  see also Community
New Mexico, University of. Be-
    havioral Science Division.
    First Interdisciplinary Con-
    ference 32

Nonverbal group exercises. 87. See
    also Verbal group exercises
Norms. See Values and norms
NTL Institute 179-80
Nursing, periodicals concerned with
    136

O

Obedience, as a producer of conflict
    56
Occupational status, in facilitation of
    work group cohesiveness 56
Occupational therapy, periodicals con-
    cerned with 136
Ohio State Leadership Studies 29, 73
Operations research
  decision making in 102
  periodicals concerned with 157
Opinions
  changing of 45
  leaders of 77
  periodicals concerned with 143
  see also Attitudes; Belief systems;
      Values and norms
Organizational behavior 1, 5, 7,
    42, 95-104, 109, 110
  associations concerned with 176
  bibliography 130, 131, 133
  communications and 96, 97, 102,
      130, 131
  effect of encounter groups on 89
  individuals in 95, 100-101, 102
  interaction with personality 6, 95,
      98
  intergroup relations in 54
  leadership and 66, 70, 71, 72,
      73, 74, 75, 97, 101-2,
      103
  managing conflict of 96
  models of 95
  periodicals concerned with 157
  problem solving and 52
  producing change in 111
  psychology of 3, 99, 157
  see also Human behavior; Industry,
      human relations in; Institu-
      tions
Otto, Herbert A. 178

# Subject Index

## P

Parents
  group counseling of 83
  importance of roles of 51
Participative management. See
      Leadership, democratic
Peace, periodicals, concerned with
     151
Peer groups, in organizations 96
Peer pressure. See Social pressure
Perception 19, 23, 56
  as a function of group membership
     11
  leadership and 66
  periodicals concerned with 138,
     157, 161
  person 19, 22, 48
  social 11
  in the social influence process 8,
     49
  in understanding group processes 8
  see also Interpersonal Perception
     Method (IPM); Self-perception
Personality 22, 23
  development of in church group
     settings 112
  development of in social group
     work settings 108
  in executive selection 68
  importance of roles to 51
  influence of on problem solving 39
  leadership and 65, 66, 68, 70
  models for measuring aspects of in
     groups 27
  organizational behavior and 6,
     95, 99
  periodicals concerned with 136,
     141, 144, 154-55, 156,
     157, 165
  prejudice and 59
  role stress and 98
  in the social influence process 49
  theory of 16, 21, 31
  treatment of disorders of 92
  variables of in the promotion of
     democracy 61
Personnel management. See Execu-
     tives; Industry, leadership in;
     Management; Organizational
     behavior

Personnel screening, executive 68
Persuasion 15, 19
  in groups 8, 77
  in opinion change 45
Physical contact, in human relations
     training groups 88 ·
Play, as an expression of the male
     bond 13
Police, role analysis of 51
Politics 74-75
  as an expression of the male bond
     13
  game theory in 32
  group theory of 99, 109
  of intergroup behavior 53
  models of 35
  periodicals concerned with 167
  social psychology of 22
  see also Voting behavior
Power (social science) 2, 6, 9, 15,
     53, 114
  bibliography of 130
  in communicative processes 76
  conflict in claims to 53
  dynamics of 63-64
  game theory in 32
  in interpersonal relations 43, 75
  organizational 97
  the tactical use of 49
  see also Leadership
Pragmatism, in the study of groups 11
Prejudice 17, 22
  conflict and 56
  group 11, 55
  models of 29
  personality correlates of 59
  psychology of 45
Pressure groups, in politics and
     economics 99. See also
     Social pressure
Primary groups 110. See also
     Family; Informal groups; Peer
     groups
Prisoner's Dilemma Paradigm 16
Problem solving 15, 35-39, 72,
     109, 112
  bibliography of 123
  democratic 36, 38, 52, 53
  in industry 99-100
  in interpersonal relations 43

models of 28, 30, 33, 35, 37
organizational 97, 102
periodicals concerned with 157
role performance in 51
in social work group settings 107
textbooks on 2, 6, 8, 14, 15, 22
training for 8
Productivity 99–100, 103–4
    effect of work groups on industrial 56
    influence of leaders on 65, 66
    relationship to motivation 57
Promotions, of executives and leaders 67
Psychiatric social workers, attitudes and behavior among 52
Psychiatrists, attitudes and behavior among 52. See also Group therapists and facilitators
Psychiatry, periodicals concerned with 136–37, 138–39, 140–41, 143, 146–47, 148, 159, 166
Psychoanalysis 25
    applied to leadership strategies 71, 75
    applied to the study of primitive cultures 20
    associations concerned with 170, 172, 173
    periodicals concerned with 137, 144
    in the study of groups 1, 11, 47
Psychodrama 84–85, 90
    associations concerned with 171, 173
    periodicals concerned with 146
    see also Sociodrama
Psycholinguistics 22. See also Sociolinguistics
Psychologists. See Clinical psychologists; Group therapists and facilitators
Psychology
    associations concerned with 170, 171, 172, 174, 176, 177–78, 179, 180–81
    dictionaries and encyclopedias 119, 122
    of groups 4, 10, 53

of industry and organizations 3, 22, 96, 99, 101, 157, 158,
    periodicals concerned with 135, 137, 138, 139, 140, 141, 142, 144, 148, 149, 150, 151–52, 153, 155, 157, 158–62, 168
    see also Clinical psychology; Gestalt psychology; Social psychology
Psychology Society 180
Psychopathology 54–55
    group therapy in the treatment of 91
Psychoses, group therapy in the treatment of 91
Psychotherapy. See Group therapy
Public meetings, group dynamics of 103
Public will 18
Punishment, psychology of 21

R

Race realtions
    conflict resolution in 54, 57
    periodicals concerned with 138, 161, 163, 167
    psychology of 15, 45
    see also Anti-Semitism; Prejudice
Reactance theory 16
Recruitment, of executives and leaders 67–68
Reference groups 11, 47–48
Reference theory, relationship to the consumer-purchase process 61
Reinforcement theory of social psychology 25
Rejection, within groups 55
Relative deprivation 26
Religion
    attitudes of adolescents toward 52
    group work in 112, 114
    intergroup relations in 57
    member-leader phenomena of 11
    in mental health 78
    social psychology of 22
    sociology of 14
    therapeutic potential of 88

# Subject Index

Resources, conflict in claims on scarce 53
Responsibility
  of education for leadership training 70
  of government for educational leadership 68
  of industry in social action 81
  of the leader 66, 74
  of superiors and subordinates 73
Rewards, psychology of 21
Rice (A.K.) Institute 180
Riot control 114
Role Conception Inventory 50
Role Performance Rating Chart 50
Role playing 11, 23, 99, 113
  in promoting agreement 53
  in training to improve group interaction 7
Roles 2, 9, 12, 20, 23, 24, <u>50-52</u>, 181
  bibliography of 129
  conflicts of 10, 26, 50, 51, 73
  in human interaction 43
  implications of 21
  of leaders 73, 74
  in organizations 98
  of school superintendents 50, 69
  structure of 24, 31
  theories of 21
  variety of in every day life 44
  see also Sex roles

## S

Sampling 76
Scapegoating, applied to social work group settings 107
School superintendents, role of 50, 69
Schwartz, Emanuel K. 71
Science
  associations concerned with 179
  periodicals concerned with 164
  philosophy of 21, 31
  sociology of 23
Secret societies, as an expression of the male bond 13
Security, gangs as providers of 47. See also Insecurity

Self 44
  social communication and 17
Self-awareness, objective 16
Self-awareness groups 89
Self-esteem
  in the classroom 106
  in the face of authority 75
  growth of in marathon groups 87
Self-evaluation 2, 55
Self-perception 78
  theory of 16
  see also Perception
Semantics, place of in promoting agreement 53
Sensitivity training 79-80, 84, 86, 92, 110
  for leadership development 103
  periodicals concerned with 146
Sex roles 52
  in human relations training groups 88
"Shared participation" (problem-solving technique) 35
Siblings, interpersonal relations between 43. See also Children
Simulation methods. See Game theory; Models and modeling
Size
  effect of in group productivity 38
  as a variable of group performance 36
Social action
  group dynamics of 52, 103
  individual responsibility for 81
Social attribution, integration theory applied to 5
Social behavior. See Group behavior; Human behavior; Interpersonal relations
Social change 18
  leadership and 71
  overcoming resistance to 69
  periodicals concerned with 150
  planning of 46, 63
  power and 64
  social work groups and 108
Social class 18
  application of Markov chain models to 27

in human relations training groups
88
see also Status
Social control, power and 64
Social deviance. See Deviance
Social exchange 115
inequity in 15
theory of 17, 18
Social groups 114
influence on consumer brand choices
61
leadership in 47
Social influence. See Social pressure
Social interaction. See Group behavior; Interpersonal relations
Socialization 22, 25, 46, 84
periodicals concerned with 155
in the study of group behavior 11
training in 41, 42
Social movements 64
Social organization 18
of employees 101
Social performance 15
Social pressure 2, 8, 9, 13, 23,
25, 48-49, 50, 52, 60
community flow of 77
on individual behavior 5
influence of on cognitive processes
14
periodicals concerned with 155
see also Conformity; Power (social
science)
Social problems
applications of social psychology
to 26
associations concerned with 181
periodicals concerned with 136,
141, 166
Social psychology 59
associations concerned with 181
of organizations 98
periodicals concerned with 136,
138, 145, 148, 150, 153,
154-55, 156, 163, 167
in problem solving 35
research methods in 22
textbooks on 2, 5, 7, 9, 10,
11, 13, 14-26, 41, 65,
132, 133
Social roles. See Roles

Social Science Research Council
(SSRC) 180
Social sciences
associations concerned with 169-81
bibliography of 117-28
classification of knowledge of 29,
132
graduate programs in applied 112
periodicals 135-68
techniques of science and logic
applied to 31
Social status. See Status
Social stratification. See Social class
Social welfare, periodicals concerned
with 156
Social work
group settings in 90, 107-8
periodicals concerned with 143,
156, 165, 166-67
problem solving in 37
see also Psychiatric social workers
Sociedad Interamericana de Psicologia.
See Interamerican Society of
Psychology
Society
effect of organizations on 96
the family in 46
the individual in 25
influence on group behavior 8
models of 31
nature of 18
organization of social relationships
and 19
small groups as an interface between
individuals and 8
small groups as the basis for 5
sociometric planning of 87
theory of 24
Society for the Psychological Study of
Social Issues (SPSSI) 180-81
Society for the Study of Social Problems (SSSP) 181
Society of Experimental Social Psychology (SESP) 181
Sociodrama 87. See also Psychodrama
Sociolinguistics 15. See also Psycholinguistics
Sociology
associations concerned with 172
bibliography of 122, 123, 127,
167

# Subject Index

dictionaries 119, 120, 124
of men in groups 13
periodicals 137, 138, 139, 141,
    153, 164, 165, 167
textbooks on 8, 9, 10, 14-26
Sociometry 8-9, 23-24, 87
applied to the classroom 106
bibliography on 123
in leadership studies 70, 72
periodicals concerned with 146,
    168
in personal interaction studies 66,
    73
Speech 76
analysis of social behavior in terms
    of 41
see also Conversation; Semantics
Spouses. See Husband and wife
Status
conflict and conformity situations
    and 60
conflict over claims to 53
gangs and 47, 114
leadership and 65, 68, 70, 73,
    74
in the study of group behavior 11,
    114
see also Occupational status; Social
    class
Status congruence 15
Stimulus-response theory 21
Stress (physiology), interpersonal
    attraction and 42
Students, periodicals concerned with
    143, 161
Subjective Expected Utility (SEU)
    theory 49
Submission, social psychology of 13
Sullivan, Harry Stack 144
Superego 24
Survival, social factors in the biology
    of 18
Sweden, leadership and group relations
    in the Navy of 69
Symbols, formation of social 24
Symposium on Mathematical Methods
    in Small Group Processes
    (1961) 28
Systems theory, in group therapy 92

## T

Tanalas (Madagascar), psychoanalytic
    concepts applied to the study
    of 20
Task-oriented groups, communication
    and learning in 76-77
Teachers, interaction analysis in the
    education of 105
Technology, humanizing of 71
Teenagers. See Youth
T-groups 80, 81, 90, 111
historical overview of 79
see also Encounter groups; Marathon
    groups; Sensitivity training
Thibaut, John 17, 20
Threats
effects of in conflict resolution 54
the potential of power in 63
rejection of deviants by means of
    55
Trade unions. See Labor-management
    relations
Transactional analysis 80, 109, 111,
    114
Transference (psychology) 89, 93
Transorientational theories in social
    psychology 25
Transportation, decision-making theory
    in 112
Trust 54, 64
concept of in groups 3, 111, 112

## U

Unions. See Labor-management
    relations
U.S. Office of Naval Research.
    Human Relations and Morale
    Branch 69
Utility theory 27
Bernoullian 32
Utopian communities, social psychology
    of 2

## V

Values and norms 8, 11, 12, 20,
    24, 77
in the classroom 106

conceptualization and research designs for 33
conflict between 2, 53
formulation of individual 10
of gang members 47, 115
in human interaction 43
importance of to democracy 55
interaction with basic needs 10
learning to change 64
periodicals concerned with 143, 153
in planned change 63
roles and 52
in social work group settings 107
see also Attitudes; Belief systems; Opinions
Verbal group exercises 88. See also Nonverbal group dexercises
Villages, as a group 12
Violence
aggressive behavior and 15
effect on delinquents of movie 16
periodicals concerned with 148
Voting behavior
game theory in 32
models of 37

**W**

War
as an expression of the male bond 13
periodicals concerned with 151
see also World War II
Wawokiye Camp Research Project 113
Western Behavioral Sciences Institute (WBSI) 181
Western Electric Co., Hawthorne Plant 101
Will. See Public will

Wolff, Alexander 71
Women, as leaders 74
Work
conditions of and efficiency in 101
conflicts at 75
effect of leadership style on 71
as an expression of the male bond 13
importance of roles in 51
influence of self-esteem in 106
models for the study of in groups 27
periodicals concerned with 167-68
see also Absenteeism (labor); Labor-management relations
Work groups 55-56, 72, 101
social structure of 96
Workshop Institute for Living-learning (WILL) 181
World War II, civilian morale during 57

**Y**

Yale University. Labor and Management Center 95
Young Men's Christian Association (YMCA), sensitivity training in 80
Youth
ego in 47
group counseling of 83, 89
in groups 47-48, 75
leadership training for 70
periodicals concerned with 135, 143
sex roles of 52
sociometric explorations of 23